Are You Thinking Clearly?

Miriam Frankel is an experienced freelance science journalist and science editor for The Conversation, a media organisation that delivers research-based news and analysis articles to a global audience of tens of millions. She has written for publications including *New Scientist, Nature, FQXi, Physics World* and several Swedish magazines.

Matt Warren has worked as a journalist for over twenty years. He has been an award-winning magazine editor, written for numerous newspapers, worked as a features editor for the *Daily Mail*, and authored books for Lonely Planet. He now works on special projects for The Conversation.

Are You Thinking Clearly?

*Why you aren't, and what
you can do about it*

MIRIAM FRANKEL &
MATT WARREN

HODDER

First published in Great Britain in 2022 by Hodder Studio
An imprint of Hodder & Stoughton
An Hachette UK company

This paperback edition published in 2023

1

A CIP catalogue record for this title is available from the British Library

Paperback ISBN 9781529388718
ebook ISBN 9781529388695

Typeset in Minion Pro by Manipal Technologies Limited

Printed and bound in Great Britain by Clays Ltd, Elcograf S.p.A.

Hodder & Stoughton policy is to use papers that are natural, renewable
and recyclable products and made from wood grown in sustainable forests.
The logging and manufacturing processes are expected to conform to the
environmental regulations of the country of origin.

Hodder & Stoughton Ltd
Carmelite House
50 Victoria Embankment
London EC4Y 0DZ

www.hodder.co.uk

For Torben and Miles, who give our thoughts fresh purpose

Contents

Introduction

Which song would you choose for your funeral? If you live in the Western world, a likely candidate is Frank Sinatra's 'My Way', which has topped the UK funeral music charts for several years on the trot. It's a revealing choice, because 'My Way' isn't just a catchy croon about love, laughter, regret and loss – it also tells us something about how people think and want to be perceived: as individual, free spirits who did it 'their way'. We hope that we can leave a unique mark on the world, chart our own course – and think for ourselves. And we often imagine that this is the best way to think, sticking with our own reason while minimising outside influence. 'My Way' affirms that widespread, individualistic human desire. But what does it even mean to 'think for yourself', and to what extent is it possible – or helpful? After all, if each of us thinks so independently, why do so many of us opt to shuffle off to the exact same Sinatra song?

The truth is that we are all less able to think freely and clearly than we imagine. The human brain is highly biased and gullible, our memories malleable and unreliable. From the moment we are conceived to the day we die, our thoughts and actions are shaped by a noisy clamour of conflicting factors. From our genetic coding and the bacteria living inside of us, to the language we speak and the apps on our phone, a host of factors are pulling our strings, often without us even realising it.

Every thought, emotion and action is also shaped by the particular circumstances of your existence. Your age, your parents, friends and neighbours, your childhood experiences, the news you consume and the food you eat – all these play a part. You may want to do things 'your way', but how much control do you really have over your thinking? And when is it better to listen to others, to admit you're wrong and change your mind? Researchers have spent decades uncovering and exploring the cacophony of things that shape our thinking. Many of the answers are out there – and now they're all (or mostly) here, in this book.

We specialise in translating academic research into articles and books the public can enjoy, understand and, crucially, learn from. We've worked with hundreds of neuroscientists and geneticists, linguists, psychologists, philosophers, sociologists, anthropologists and behavioural economists. It's like working in a sweetshop, but instead of jars of humbugs, cola cubes and gobstoppers, we get to sample a dazzling smorgasbord of knowledge, research and ideas. Through this work, we've seen the myriad ways in which the human mind can be manipulated. And when you delve deeper and stop to consider the conflicting nature of scientific studies, as we have, the picture becomes even more complex. When a geneticist tells us one thing and a psychologist tells us another, who's right? Which study gets closest to unveiling the secrets of the human mind? Which area offers the best solutions? The honest answer is all of them, and none of them. That's simply because, if you want the answers to life's biggest questions, and if you want to apply them to your own life, you need to opt for a pick-and-mix, rather than just one flavour.

And that's exactly what we're going to do in this book. We aim to explain your thinking – whether that's thinking about yourself or others, how you make decisions, solve problems, remember or imagine – based on many different areas of research across twenty-nine short chapters. By doing so, we'll help you better understand your own brain, challenge your thought processes and learn how to make better decisions. We'll explore genetics, biology and personality; cognition, emotions and experiences; beliefs, stereotypes, culture, language and technology. We'll ask how routines and habits, being in love or believing in evil warp our thinking, and how subtle signals from our bodies can drive our intuitions and emotions. We'll probe how we can be misled by statistics, duped into adopting false memories or someone else's opinion, ensnared by advertisers or trapped in the past. We'll get to the bottom of why so many of us can't help but keep up with the Joneses. And we'll dip into psychedelics, too. We'll reveal the studies and stories that have progressed our understanding, and the science underpinning what's happening in your brain. We want to open your eyes to the inner workings of your mind. And maybe – just maybe – we'll be able to help you think more clearly in the future.

But this book isn't going to dictate to you how you should think – we'll leave that to the despots and pub bores. Nor will it offer one key ingredient, such as mindfulness or positive thinking, to make good decisions. While a boost in optimism can help unlock minds that are stuck in negative thinking patterns, for example, it might make others more gullible, blinkered, even dangerously overconfident. And while habits can reduce the stresses of everyday life and free up mental bandwidth, they can also make us rigid, compulsive and close-minded. Everyone is different, after all – and each of us is disproportionately affected by different factors.

Luckily, then, this book isn't written by one biased author – it is written by two biased authors constantly spotting faults in each other's thinking. And we've learned that there isn't just one way to think more clearly, just as there isn't only one approach to achieving happiness. To claim that there is would be to suggest that we're all the same; robots who can be reprogrammed at will. Instead, by drawing on the latest and most rigorous interdisciplinary research, and the extraordinary and surprising true stories that bring it to life, this book will investigate and map the daunting terrain of the human mind, and set out ways to navigate its obstacles.

Not everyone has the same starting or end point. Some of us have strong legs and are happy to climb the tallest mountains and take the road less travelled. Others may, understandably, look for shortcuts. And so it is with our minds. While this book will describe the landscape and clearly red-flag the dangers, we can't draw you the perfect route – you will have to find Your Way. It won't be easy, but it will set you on a better path. You'll have to look deep inside yourself and come face to face with some of the biggest obstacles your mind must overcome. You will need to break out of your comforting echo chambers and question the time-saving habits you rely on. But if you're ready to do all that, then this book will help you to think more freely – and see your mind, and the world around you, in a truly liberating new light.

1

Do you wear a watch?

Explorer and scientist Christian Clot put on a pair of dark glasses and stepped out of the shadows into the bright spring sunshine.[1] It was April 2021 and it had been forty days since Clot and his team had gone underground in the Grotte de Lombrives cave in south-west France with the intention of isolating not just from normal life, but from time itself. The group of eight men and seven women – among them a jeweller, a nurse, a maths teacher – had locked themselves in the sprawling cavern on 14 March as part of the Deep Time research project.[2] Led by Clot, their goal was to live without clocks, daylight and outside contact to better understand how the human mind adapts to a timeless world – and, ultimately, learn more about its impact on our thoughts, feelings and ability to function.

What the participants experienced was deeply strange – and still haunted some of them months later. The artificially illuminated cave system, which stretched for over a kilometre, contained separate, well-equipped areas for sleeping, cooking, socialising, scientific work and toilet breaks. There was space for exploration and plenty of research work to be done. But while the clocks outside counted down the minutes, hours and days of their forty-day isolation at a predictable rate, inside, the volunteers began to perceive time in a dramatically different way.

The full, extraordinary scale of this shift in time perception only became apparent when the experiment ended. Without watches or the sun to tell them when to get up and when to eat, when to work and when to sleep, they had settled into their own individual rhythms – rhythms vastly out of kilter with the normal twenty-four-hour cycle of daily life. On average, data later showed, the volunteers began living, on average, thirty-two-hour days, sleeping for twelve hours and spending twenty awake. Some slipped into a mind-boggling sixty-hour cycle. But while the participants went about life at their own, seemingly steady pace inside the cave, time was passing far faster than they imagined.

'When people came to tell us the forty days had finished, it was impossible for us to accept it,' Clot told us in an interview. 'We were sure they were lying to us. In my mind, only twenty-nine days had passed.' Clot's experience was replicated throughout the group, with one volunteer estimating that they had spent just twenty-three days in the cave. On average, the group thought approximately 25 per cent less time had passed than actually had. 'Even now, some of us still can't accept it,' added Clot. 'They have the facts, of course, but they still think someone stole those ten days.'

On the face of it, this may sound familiar – we have all experienced time appearing to speed up or slow down in extreme situations. But what causes these radical fluctuations in time perception – and how can it affect the way we think more broadly? Time isn't just one thing – we *measure* it and *perceive* it in two very different ways. The time we measure with a watch (let's call it 'clock time') essentially marks Earth's predictable passage around the sun. It takes a year for the Earth to orbit our star and a day for it to rotate on its axis. Coming up with a universal theory of time that can be defined on a cosmic level is more complex. Einstein's Special Theory of Relativity, for example, shows that *all* time is relative. But few of us are likely to travel close to light speed, orbit a black hole, or encounter the cosmic phenomena that, dramatically, can warp measurable time, so let's assume that the time on our watch is a constant – at least in our everyday lives.

The way we *perceive* time, however, is very different. In fact, we are all time travellers of sorts. Even as the hands of our watch sweep round the dial at a constant rate, we may feel that time is moving faster, or slower, depending on our mood, what we're doing and how old we are. In a scary situation, such as a car accident, for example, time can seemingly grind to a near standstill, as if the event is being played in slow motion.[3] Conversely, time often appears to speed up as we age – a phenomenon that dramatically affects how we think.[4] This sense that time is passing more quickly as we get older may make us anxious and regretful, trigger a mid-life crisis and result in impulsive behaviour, from buying a sports car or quitting a job to having an affair.

As a child, even a brief car journey can feel like like an eternity. But by middle age, the years seem to whizz by. Psychologist Peter Mangan tested this difference in time perception by asking people of different ages to count out three minutes.[5] The younger participants, aged nineteen to twenty-four, were surprisingly accurate with their estimates – for them, 'felt time' and 'clock time' were roughly in sync. But three minutes and forty seconds whistled by before the older subjects, aged between sixty and eighty, reached their 'three minutes'. In other words, time felt like it was passing more quickly than it actually was; from their perspective, 'clock time' was 1.22 times faster than their perceived time.

One explanation for time accelerating as we age is that a year becomes an ever-smaller fraction of our total lived experience, making it seem increasingly insignificant. As Kit Yates, a senior lecturer in mathematical biology at the University of Bath, has explained, from this logarithmic perspective the period between your fifth and tenth birthdays would appear to pass at the same rate as the decades between your fortieth and eightieth birthdays – gulp![6]

But another intriguing theory, which is supported by early data from Clot's cave experiment, suggests that time perception is closely related to memory.[7] After all, we don't just experience the passage of time as we live it – 'prospectively' – we also experience it 'retrospectively', through our memories.[8] This is why, paradoxically, it can feel like time is ticking by incredibly slowly while you are doing something boring, but extended periods of mundane activity can seem to have zoomed past when you look back at them. You may have noticed this through the COVID-19 lockdowns, which many described as living in an 'eternal present', during which an hour, spent bored at home, seemed like an eternity. In retrospect, however, 2020, a year relatively bereft of memorable moments, seemed to have flown by.

The relationship between time perception and memory is important because it offers clues as to how we can feel more in control of our time and, crucially, how we can feel that we are living a fuller, more rewarding life. In our early years, we are bombarded with dazzlingly novel experiences. Think of all the 'first' experiences you had as a child – smelling, touching, seeing, hearing and learning the skills needed to make sense of those experiences. And all this new information requires memory. As we age, however, life becomes ever more familiar and we settle into predictable routines, placing fewer demands on our memory.[9] The science suggests that time appears to slow down – at least retrospectively – when we are subject to more sensory inputs and make more memories, such as during childhood, a thrilling holiday, a first date or a car crash.[10] But it speeds up as we get older, life becomes more mundane, we encounter fewer novel situations and the richness of new memories reduces. Indeed, MRI scans showed that the participants in Clot's experiment experienced a shrinking of parts of the brain, such as the hippocampus, related to immediate memory. In the bland confines of the cave and cut off from all the information we must normally process in the outside world, the volunteers began to remember less. And with fewer memories to mark its passage, the time they spent in the cave felt like it had passed more quickly.

The disturbing sense that we're running out of time can affect us all and lead to poorly thought-out decisions. That so many people often feel this way, despite being surrounded by more and more time-saving technologies, is one of the great modern paradoxes. But we can do something about it. One approach is to be more 'childlike' – to resist needless routine and seek out unexpected and unusual experiences that will establish more numerous, high-definition memories. Thankfully, this needn't mean adrenaline-rich experiences like freefalling (another proven way of slowing down time),[11] nor do we have to move countries or change careers and partners every few years. This can be as simple as making small tweaks, like avoiding the same old routines (which we cover in another chapter), such as taking the same route to work or eating the same lunch every day. That won't work for everyone, of course, and routines have their own benefits. But it could have a positive impact on those who are troubled by a sense of life slipping through their fingers. For others, the need to just relax from a stressful life without having to read maps or learn new recipes may be more valuable than slowing down time.

We can also create adventure and novelty in life without travelling to exotic locations, paying anything or putting ourselves in peril. Creative projects – writing a book, taking up a new instrument or learning a new language – can be hugely rewarding and take us on great journeys in our minds, far away from routines and schedules. Research also shows that being more mindful can help, paying attention to the here and now rather than just getting through the day on autopilot. You don't need to start meditating to achieve this, even a (perfectly safe) walk in nature can slow down our perception of time.[12] Cannabis has also been shown to slow down time perception – though you should familiarise yourself with local laws first.[13] Overall, the more our minds need to process new information, the more time will appear to expand – the longer and richer our lives will seem in retrospect.

It's not just about slowing down, or speeding up, time either. We should also reconsider our broader relationship with the clocks that dominate modern life. At first, many of the volunteers in Clot's Deep Time experiment found the prospect of being locked in a timeless cave deeply daunting. But as they settled into their new environment, they began to feel happier and more liberated. So much so that, when the experiment ended, most didn't want to leave. 'It's not a question of environment. It's really a question of putting away the obligations we have in normal life, which can cause a lot of stress, and finding suddenly that your brain is free to think and to see things,' said Clot. Perhaps our obsession with time is the real prison and we can think more freely in its absence. As Clot's fellow Deep-Timer Marina Lançon said in a media interview after leaving the cave: 'For once in our lives, it was as if we could press pause. We are always in a rush in our lives. Left, right, we don't have time, we don't take our time. For once in our lives, we had time and could stop to live and do our tasks. It was great.'[14]

In fact, Clot claimed those in the cave didn't just become happier – they also became more productive. Without alarm clocks to buzz them awake and the nine-to-five to dictate their working days, the team simply woke up, ate and went about their jobs when they felt like it. And when the data was analysed later, it showed that they had often been working for far longer than they thought. They were able to pay more attention and to focus more fully on what they were doing. 'We are not all designed to work at the same time and perhaps this is something we should now think about as a society,' said Clot. 'What I will now teach to companies and to people is the idea that you should take one day a week when you cut off everything. Of course, you have a life, you have a job, but just try to take at least one day a week, just without any phone, any email, any clock.'

So rather than always watching the clock and worrying about the next appointment, the next commitment, give yourself the time to pay attention and focus on what's happening right now, to explore new places, try new things and think new thoughts. A life containing more of these novel experiences, and fewer nagging diary entries, will seem longer and more vivid – and gift you the precious space to think more clearly.

2

Are you stuck in the past?

On 20 January 1987, Terry Waite, the Assistant for Anglican Commun-
ion Affairs for the Archbishop of Canterbury, was taken hostage in
Beirut, Lebanon, by the Islamic Jihad group, and kept captive – often
in total isolation – for 1,763 days. He was in Lebanon to negotiate the
release of several hostages when he was betrayed and taken prisoner
himself. He went on to suffer extreme loneliness, the daily threat of
torture and mortar attack, and a terrifying mock execution when a
gun was held to his head, but the trigger was never pulled. But as he
was bundled into his underground, white-tiled cell, seven feet wide
and ten feet long, one of the first things his captors took from him
was his wristwatch. And for Waite, the loss of his watch wasn't just an
inconvenience, but something that left him living 'outside time'.

Like Clot and the other participants of the cave experiment
detailed in the previous chapter, Waite noticed how time in captivity
appeared to move at a different, highly disorientating pace. But it
wasn't just his perception of how time was passing that changed. He
was also forced to rethink how he *oriented* himself in time. We all
view life through the prism of time. We experience the world and
make our decisions in the present; the past contains the memories
that establish our identity and inform our thinking; and the future
is the canvas onto which we sketch our hopes, fears, ambitions and
motivations. Our sense of time passing from the past, through the
present, to the future gives us our awareness of cause and effect, of
agency, of what makes us, us.

Waite's immediate present was a relentless limbo, a seemingly
endless monotony of captivity. Faced with the threat of imminent

death or torture, he also deliberately avoided thinking about the future and being reunited with his family. And so rather than focusing on his present predicament, or fragile future hopes, Waite began to time travel – exploring his memories in elaborate detail. 'Time took on a new meaning for me,' he recalls. 'It was almost the past and present, merged together.'

Waite revisited the lines of the first song he heard on a gramophone: *Run rabbit, run rabbit, run, run, run.* His isolation in hospital, aged three, with scarlet fever. Marching alongside the singing soldiers as they strode past his childhood home en route to the Second World War. The names of all his classmates in primary school. Jane, the girl whose hand he wanted to hold as a teenager, but never did. These journeys into the past were more than just idle escapism; by exploring his memories, Waite was also able to maintain his sense of self, even his sanity. Indeed, they became the basis for the autobiography, *Taken on Trust*, which he wrote in his head during his nearly five-year captivity.[1]

Waite's hostage experience is an extreme example. But it highlights how we can change our orientation in time so that we live more in the present, past or future, a phenomenon that can radically change the way we think. It can trigger emotions such as boredom, fear, anger and contentment, make us dangerously over- or under-confident, or alter our life prospects, leading us to engage in dangerous behaviours or save for a financially secure future.

In 2016, twenty-five years after Terry Waite was finally freed, two events shook the Western world, blindsiding most pollsters and pundits. First, in June, the UK voted to leave the European Union. Then, in November, Donald Trump beat Hillary Clinton to become the forty-fifth president of the United States, beginning one of the most turbulent periods in American history. Ask people what the two have in common and you'll get some familiar answers: dissatisfaction with the ruling 'elite' and a desire for greater national 'sovereignty', the rise of populism, racism, perhaps Russian interference. But they were also closely linked by something more surprising: the past. For while both events appeared revolutionary, they weren't so much about looking forward as focusing backwards, to an imagined golden age. While the UK's Vote Leave campaign relied on new technology and data-mining techniques to push its message, the message itself was tinged with nostalgia for a time when Britain still had its empire and made its own rules.[2] The Leave campaign's focus on the past, and an empowering return to it, was nowhere clearer than in the key central word of its slogan, 'Take *Back* Control'. Trump similarly appealed to nostalgia, pledging to turn back the clock on globalisation's more damaging consequences and promising on millions of red baseball caps to 'Make America Great *Again*'. Ultimately, Brexit and Trump weren't just populist triumphs, they were also textbook examples of 'past orientation'. Indeed, in general, language used on conservative websites references the past more than the future, while language on liberal websites does the opposite.[3]

For Waite, the past offered solace, security and sanity. It helped him survive his terrifying experience. For many of those who voted for Trump or Brexit, the past offered something similar: a nostalgic antidote to the modern world's turbulent, complex realities. But we all focus to different degrees on the past, present and future, something explored in detail by psychologists Philip Zimbardo – perhaps best-known for his controversial Stanford Prison Experiment – and John Boyd, authors of *The Time Paradox*. They argue that time orientation 'is a pervasive and powerful yet largely unrecognised influence on much human behaviour'.[4] But how exactly does focusing on the past, present or future change the way we think and feel?

Focusing on past experiences can inform better decisions and solutions based on acquired knowledge. Echoing the observations of Waite – and doubtless the Trump and Brexit campaigns – research shows that nostalgia can give us an increased sense of meaning in life. It can also make us feel more connected to others and perhaps less lonely.[5] But while our past is a mental library of experiences and memories – some good, others bad – which we can use to inform the way we think, feel and act in the present, we should be cautious.[6] Our memories are highly subjective, malleable and sometimes completely fictional, as we will learn in the next chapter. And our past is also subject to – and can reinforce – our biases. Looking backwards can lead to an unhealthy preoccupation with past mistakes and regret. Waite discovered this dark side of the past for himself, saying: 'The danger, the difficulty, I recognised of making that deep inner journey into the self is that you come across the negative side of personality, which exists in all people . . . And the danger, when I came across that, was whether I could fall into deep depression or even into psychosis.' Past broken relationships can haunt our present, while concentrating too much on what has happened may make us more prone to holding grudges (you just can't let go of prior wrongs) and less likely to make new friends.[7] A past orientation may also make us more conservative and less open to change, new experiences and novel ways of thinking (the very things that allow us to feel in control of time).

But what if we focus instead on the present? Mindfulness has made the present a fashionable global movement. Central to its philosophy is the idea that we should spend more time focusing on the present moment without letting in nagging distractions. Jon Kabat-Zinn, the inventor of Mindfulness-based Stress Reduction, has claimed in an interview with Insights at the Edge that it 'has the potential to ignite a universal or global renaissance' and it certainly has an international following.[8] Around 70 million people in 190 countries subscribe to Headspace, which offers mindfulness exercises, and the mindfulness movement has starred on the cover of *Time* magazine and been endorsed by medical professionals, including the UK's NHS.[9]

Mindfulness has its critics, but it has popularised the idea that we could all benefit from being more present-oriented.[10]

That's great if you're in a state of mindful contemplation, which can paradoxically help you to be more responsible and aware of future consequences.[11] But *mindlessly* living too much in the moment may make you more likely to engage in impulsive, risky behaviours, such as unsafe sex, drug misuse and gambling. Present-oriented people may be more likely to offer immediate assistance to those around them, but less likely to focus on their own long-term health and well-being.[12] Present orientation can encourage us to focus on immediate actions, rather than future consequences. It is the YOLO* way. We'll have plenty of experiences, but we may not live long enough to tell the tale.

Novel experiences make life rich and memorable and research shows we're more likely to regret long-term *not* doing something than saying 'yes' and indulging in life's pleasures.[13] We just need to be aware how present orientation can impact the way we think. Most of us, for example, are subject to 'present bias', which means that we'll often opt for a smaller reward now, rather than defer gratification and hold out for more later. Think about those companies who offer a 'buy now, pay later' option. It's a tempting offer, because it allows us to follow our immediate impulses and enjoy the benefits – a five-star holiday, a new car, the latest iPhone – while conveniently shifting the unpleasant consequences (like the huge bill) – into the future. But as you're filling up your gas-guzzler you might be thinking, 'Did I even really want, or need, a new car, or was it the offer that made it compelling in the first place?' Studies have shown that if offered, say, £100 now or £125 in a week, most people will choose the smaller amount because they apply a discount to the larger sum purely because it is further away in time.[14] This may make sense if it's nearly Christmas

---

* 'You Only Live Once'.

and you need some immediate cash to fill your children's stockings. But we should also consider whether our present orientation is short-changing the future us.

So, what about future-thinkers? According to Zimbardo and Boyd, 'future oriented people are the most likely to be successful' – they're able to delay gratification and reap the rewards.[15] Perhaps we imagine our future self as happy and comfortable in a four-bedroom home with a partner, two children and a lucrative pension – and do today the things we believe are required to get us there. That may well mean sacrificing a few, immediate pleasures. But so be it. It is the middle-class way, espoused by many free-market leaders. Predicting what will happen and improving future outcomes is the driving force behind science and our greatest leaps forward – indeed, without one eye on the future we may not have one at all. To tackle the climate crisis, for example, we'll need to think long-term – though it's worth noting that future-thinkers are also, according to Zimbardo and Boyd, 'the least likely to help others in need'.[16] You only need to read about Silicon Valley billionaires building underground bunkers in New Zealand to see this in action . . .

Most people are future biased in some way and like to think the good times are still ahead of them. But novel experiences in the present make memories, and denying ourselves those experiences can lead to dissatisfaction, boredom and the feeling that happiness is always just out of reach. We can never be sure what our future selves will want anyway. We often believe our current tastes and beliefs will remain constant over time, but you just have to look at photos of your teenage self's idea of style to see that that belief is often wrong.[17] Instead, we shouldn't assume our futures are certain – we should plan for today, not just tomorrow.

* * *

Past, present and future orientations all come with their rewards – and costs. To think clearly, we must understand how each can influence our decision-making and beliefs and ensure that we maintain a healthy focus on all three. Looking backwards can make us feel safe and connected, while critical analysis of past decisions and experiences can improve our thinking in future. But to focus too much or too negatively on the past may make us closed-minded or fatalistic. Living in the now, and being more mindful, meanwhile, will ensure we benefit from colourful new experiences and gain greater control over time's passing, but may also make us dangerously impulsive, damaging our prospects. And a future orientation can improve our prospects but could also cause us to forget to live fully today. When we make decisions, we should ask our future selves what they'd want and consider how our thinking might be disproportionately motivated by past experiences or present whims. But we should also question whether we're deferring too much gratification, turning down exciting opportunities today because we're too focused on tomorrow.

If you think you are particularly biased toward the past, present or future, there are structured ways to ensure you're not trapped in one mindset. Psychology offers three interventions, dubbed 'best possible self', 'gratitude' and 'nostalgia', linked to the future, present and past, respectively. To enhance your future focus, imagine your best possible self, perhaps by sketching out your dream plan for the next five years – this intervention proved particularly effective at improving people's well-being during the COVID-19 lockdowns.[18] To become more present-oriented, take a moment to write down the things you are grateful for today. And if you want a better relationship with your past, embrace nostalgia and devote some time to thinking about a happy memory each day. It worked for Waite, but beware: your memories aren't always what you think they are, as the next chapter reveals.

3

Can you trust your memories?

At an uncle's ninetieth birthday celebration, leading memory researcher Elizbeth Loftus experienced for herself how easily memories can be manipulated. She was talking to a relative about her mother, who had tragically drowned in a swimming pool decades earlier, when Loftus was just fourteen. The relative claimed that Loftus had found her mother's body, something she couldn't recall. But the relative's recollections sowed a seed of doubt – and Loftus's own memory of the tragedy began to change. 'This relative was so confident about it that when I went home from the celebration, I could visualise it – I could almost see my mother in the swimming pool,' she told us. 'I started thinking of other things I did remember about her death. And that seemed maybe consistent with the idea that I had the horrifying, additional experience of finding her body.' A week or so later, the phone rang. It was the relative calling to say they had been mistaken – Loftus's aunt had actually found the body. For Loftus, however, this harrowing experience brought a sharp and vivid life to her work: 'I thought, this is what it's like for the people I've been studying.'

We often think of memories as high-quality video clips, safely archived in the brain to replay on demand. But this couldn't be further from the truth. Our mood and physical state during an event can influence how we remember it. Every time we think or talk about past experiences, we doctor our own recollections, creating distortions by exaggerating certain details that are relevant to our current beliefs and emotional state. We may, somewhat paradoxically, *forget* aspects of an event every time we *remember* it, making our memories less accurate over time. Not only do memories fade and morph into new ones, we also pick and choose what to remember. This is even the case for our own, personal histories, which ultimately shape who we are. We remember the things that enable us to have the identity we most desire.[1] If you want to be a nonconformist, for example, you'll remember more clearly the times you challenged the norms than those when you followed them. And this can change if you later decide you want to be more of a team player.[2] And we are also capable of constructing completely false memories of things that never happened.

Despite this enormous room for error and discrepancy, we put a huge amount of trust in our own memory. Whenever we are faced with a choice, we rely on it to guide us, providing us with similar choices we or others have made in the past, and their outcomes.

Take your first memory. How old were you and what were you doing? If you were younger than about three or four years old, chances are it isn't real. The infant brain simply isn't capable of forming and storing long-term memories – an effect dubbed 'childhood amnesia'.[3] Despite this, many people claim they can actually remember being pulled into the world. Even later childhood memories can be inaccurate, and we can easily confuse early memories with photographs, or our parents' stories. More than a fifth of people will remember childhood events that never happened, such as attending a birthday party with a clown entertainer, if a researcher claims they did.[4] Loftus remembers the day she realised that her own first memory was false. She used to think it was being taken to the movie *The Greatest Show on Earth*, at the age of around four. But decades later, she flicked through a film history book and to her surprise, the movie wasn't released until she was about eight. Clearly, what she had thought of as her first memory, wasn't; she could, in fact, remember plenty of other events that had occurred before the age of eight.

The intimate link between memory and identity raises an intriguing question: if you lost your memory, would you remain the same person? In one sense, it's a philosophical question. But we can glean insights from those who have experienced just this. Take people with Korsakoff syndrome, a dementia-like condition that is caused by vitamin B1 deficiency and linked to heavy alcohol consumption. Sufferers can lose their ability to form new memories and sometimes the capacity to recall old ones – making them unable to remember events that happened just a minute, or several decades, ago. Tellingly, this disintegration of memory comes with a parallel loss of identity, as the late neurologist and science writer Oliver Sacks movingly described in the case of forty-nine-year-old Jimmie G – aka the 'Lost Mariner' – from his book *The Man who Mistook His Wife for a Hat*. Jimmie G could barely remember anything after his late adolescence, which made it impossible for him to connect with the people around him. As a result, he lost his sense of self, telling Sacks that he hadn't 'felt alive in a very long time'. Like Jimmie G, many people with Korsakoff syndrome suffer from apathy, and are prone to fabricate past events to fill the void.

But how can people with healthy minds also be so bad at remembering? Every memory has a specific, physical representation in the brain, linking various groups of neurons to one another as explained by Julia Shaw in her book *The Memory Illusion*.[5] If you encode a memory of a wonderful skiing holiday, for example, your brain strengthens connections between existing neural networks representing concepts such as snow, cold, schnapps, mountains and happiness. Some of these networks represent uninteresting details that you didn't pay much attention to, such as the colour of the walls of the local ski rental store. Connections with these groups can weaken over time – until you forget them. But other networks can be added. Perhaps, years later, you read about the same alpine resort in the news, this time being described as the ground zero of Europe's coronavirus outbreak. Now, every time you think of the holiday, you annoyingly also think of COVID-19. Our brains constantly make associations between memories, new experiences and ideas, which makes them powerful and highly creative. But the cost of this is false memories.

The consequences of false memories are often relatively benign, but they can be triggered by interests and beliefs that skewer our perception of important things. A 2019 study investigated false memories among 3,140 voters in the week before the 2018 Irish referendum on legalising abortion.[6] The participants were told they were taking part in a survey about attitudes to abortion and were presented with short summaries of news stories related to the campaign – two of which had been entirely fabricated by the researchers. One concerned either the Yes side (those in favour of legalising abortion) or the No side being forced to destroy campaign posters that had been purchased illegally using foreign funds. The other was about events related to a sexual assault trial that took place that year. Almost half the voters said they remembered at least one of the two fabricated stories they were shown actually happening. Interestingly, voters were more likely to remember a fabricated scandal regarding the opposing campaign. So, while most of us like to believe we think rationally about politics, our memories are easily manipulated – providing us with false evidence.

This reveals how easily false information can stick in the mind. In the run-up to the UK's 2016 referendum on EU membership, an eye-catching message was daubed by the Vote Leave campaign on a red bus. It claimed £350 million a week was paid by Britain to the EU, and that this would be redirected into the NHS following Brexit. The real figure, however, was actually much lower, and there were no guarantees that the NHS would receive the cash. The claim was therefore widely debunked. But two years later, in 2018, nearly half of people in the UK who had heard the claim still believed that the UK paid £350 million a week to the EU.[7] We remember the things that fit our values. So, if you want to think clearly, be sceptical of your memories, especially when it comes to highly emotive issues. The consequences can, after all, be dire, especially when it comes to the justice system, which often relies on witness testimonies. The Innocence Project, a non-profit organisation that has helped exonerate hundreds of people who have been wrongfully convicted with the help of DNA testing, estimates that faulty memory was involved in nearly 70 per cent of the cases.[8]

If we can't trust our memories, how can we ever think clearly or know the truth about the past? And what can we do to prevent false or distorted memories? Sadly, there aren't any quick fixes – these biases are a natural consequence of how our brains work. Through our evolutionary history, our species has been forced to make quick decisions. And our ability to form rapid associations by strengthening connections between memory fragments in the brain and new ideas or experiences allows us to solve problems creatively. But it helps to be aware of the tricks memory can play on us – the circumstances when these distortions are more likely to arise, and the things we can do to catch them.

We know, for example, that people with high cognitive ability, which includes skills such as reasoning, planning, problem solving, learning from experience and abstract thinking, are less likely to develop false memories due to misinformation.[9] This may be partly down to the fact that intelligence is linked to flexibility. People who are persistent and rigid in their thinking will be more closed to questioning their own judgement, potentially resulting in more false memories. It seems one of the most useful things you can do to limit false memory is being curious and open, rather than just trying to be right all the time. But intelligence isn't everything. If you've got great perceptual abilities, such as being able to spot tiny changes made to images, you may also have some protection against creating false memories from misinformation. And perhaps more surprisingly, being grumpy can also help reduce false memory – good news for Eeyores. Why? It may be that people who are pessimistic, worry prone and fearful are simply more vigilant than others, concerned about getting things wrong. Good moods, on the other hand, make us significantly more likely to falsely remember things than bad moods – perhaps because they make us overconfident.[10]

So, if you're arguing with a sibling about who got the most birthday presents from your parents growing up, you may want to reflect upon how your memories have been constructed. If you want to remember something a certain way – be it positive or negative – there's a good chance you are manipulating your memories. The same goes for recalling events when you are worry-free, happy and optimistic. But ultimately, there is no foolproof way of knowing whose memory is correct, other than actual evidence. The more important lesson here is therefore one of empathy. Rather than accusing people of lying about the past, be open to the possibility that they are genuinely misremembering. This approach may actually help you get a better grip on what's going on – seeing shades of grey in the world rather than just black and white.

And while the past is out of our control, the future isn't. If you worry about forgetting aspects of your life, why not keep a diary? Or at the very least, write down special events you are keen to remember in detail as soon as they happen, making them less likely to get further distorted over time.

4

Have your parents fucked you up?

They fuck you up, your mum and dad.
  They may not mean to, but they do.
They fill you with the faults they had
  And add some extra, just for you.

Philip Larkin's famous poem, 'This Be the Verse', explains how *nurture* can shape our destiny. It suggests we can all too easily end up being just like our parents, by copying their destructive behaviours and ways of thinking and passing them on to our own children. But the poem could just as well describe *nature* – your parents have literally filled you with their genetic 'faults', and you have no choice but to do the same to your children.

We are all dealt a genetic hand, which predisposes us to think, act and feel in certain ways. That means that the extent to which you can think clearly is partly programmed in your DNA. Some of us simply like thinking more than others, and some find it more comfortable to think critically. Our upbringing and early experiences then affect how these propensities develop, giving rise to a (hopefully) stable personality and level of cognitive motivation and ability – further cementing individual differences in thinking. This may sound like it's depressingly out of our control, like we have a biologically determined destiny. But if you look beneath the surface it is actually quite empowering.

Scientists have discovered that genes can explain about half of all individual differences between people. For physiological traits, such as height, the genetic influence tends to be much higher than for mental or behavioural traits, such as motivation. But the process is often misunderstood. If we are told that motivation is 40 per cent heritable, for example, we tend to think that 40 per cent of our own motivation is down to our genes. But what it really means is that 40 per cent of the *differences* in motivation between *different people* can be explained by DNA, while 60 per cent is down to other factors. It is the difference that remains when you've accounted for variables such as education, socioeconomic status and other environmental influences. It is a statistical measure. *Your* level of motivation may be almost entirely down to that one amazing teacher you had in primary school. As Yulia Kovas, a professor of genetics and psychology at Goldsmiths, University of London, explains, 'Genes are important, but it's difficult to quantify the effect of genes for a specific person.'

So to what extent can the ability to think clearly, on average, be explained by DNA?

How we think is largely determined by two key features: cognitive ability and personality. Determining the genetic heritability of such traits often relies on studies of twins, in particular monozygotic (or identical) twins, who share the same DNA but may differ in their life experiences. The website MaTCH estimates the heritability of 17,804 traits based on 14,558,903 twin pairs – nearly all the twin studies published in the past sixty years.[1] It shows that higher-level cognitive functions – including IQ, verbal intelligence, speed of information processing, working memory and general knowledge – are, on average, 51 per cent heritable. A further 24 per cent can be explained by the shared environment of twins, such as their childhood home and schooling, and the rest by other factors – including events that take place later in life. Clearly, our environment can substantially impact our cognitive ability. If we grow up being encouraged to learn and challenge ourselves intellectually, we may become more confident about doing so and interested in pursuing it – creating a positive cycle, helping us to seek out more situations in which we can learn and develop.

But people with identical IQ and working memory can differ in how they think. Other higher cognitive abilities, which may have a bigger impact on thinking, include cognitive flexibility (the ability to switch between tasks and perspectives), creativity and critical/ rational thinking.[2] While these traits tend to be correlated with IQ to some extent, they are essentially separate, though can compensate for 'deficits' in IQ or other cognitive skills. To think well and make good decisions, we need to be able to change strategies when necessary and come up with new ideas when old ones aren't working – rather than being fixed on one approach – and that's exactly what cognitive flexibility enables. It also offers intellectual humility and protection against certain cognitive biases.[3] The ability to think critically is also crucial: helping us sort facts from beliefs and protecting us from falling for misinformation or useless fads. Indeed, one study found that people who had a high critical thinking ability had fewer negative life outcomes, such as credit card debt, than people with high IQ.[4]

High cognitive ability doesn't guarantee razor-sharp thinking – you can still think in muddled ways if your personality motivates you to do so. You can be a sharp critical thinker and yet fail to apply that criticism to your own thinking. In fact, one study has shown that intelligent people may in fact be particularly bad at changing their own thinking by updating their beliefs.[5] As David Robson shows in his book *The Intelligence Trap*, highly intelligent people can actually be worse at recognising their own thinking flaws and biases than others. They are also very average in their ability to consider alternative points of view.[6] Having very strong views in combination with being good at spotting patterns might make it easier to find 'evidence' to support your beliefs and fall into the trap of confirmation bias. Intelligence also doesn't make you immune to being influenced by what your neighbours, friends or family members think. And traditionally smart people (those with high IQs) can also fall into the trap of being extremely pessimistic or overconfident. Being closed-minded, lacking in creativity or having poor empathy, emotional intelligence or social insight can also get in the way of accurately understanding the world around us. So, 'thinking clearly' isn't just a factor of the measures you might expect, like IQ; and indeed a diverse range of mental and behavioural characteristics profoundly affect how we think. Many of these traits are related to 'temperament and personality', which is just 44 per cent heritable according to MaTCH.

Personality traits themselves are often described by the 'Big Five' model, which divides them into five distinct groups: extraversion (how social you are), agreeableness (how friendly and compassionate you are), conscientiousness (your sense of duty), emotional stability (your level of depression and anxiety) and openness to experience (your curiosity about new things). All these traits can affect how we think – or sometimes how we don't think – in different ways. If you are emotionally unstable, for example, you are more likely to be pessimistic, perhaps lacking in motivation and being biased to focus on negative events rather than positive ones. If you are extremely happy, with high emotional stability and extraversion, on the other hand, you may be prone to optimism bias and overconfidence. And if you *are* extraverted, your thinking may be more motivated by social factors, such as making others feel good or having interesting stories to tell at dinner parties. Introverts, on the other hand, can be deep thinkers but may also be at risk of rumination and negative bias.[7] And agreeable people often have great capacity for empathy.[8] But for some people, the desire to fit in may make them easily influenced by what others think, and so less able to think independently.

Conscientiousness, meanwhile, can help you do analysis, paying attention to detail and instruction, and working hard until a task is finished. As it involves a hefty dose of self-discipline, it can also protect against destructive habits and addiction[9] – which can ultimately hijack our thinking. However, if taken to an extreme, conscientiousness can lead to rigid thinking and mindless schedule-following.

Finally, openness to experience is linked with creativity, an appreciation of thinking and intellectual curiosity.[10] Crucially, people who are high on this trait prefer the big picture to details, new experiences to routine and are more likely to be cognitively flexible.[11]

We spoke to several experts about which personality traits are the most helpful when it comes to thinking well, and most cited openness to experience and conscientiousness. In other words, as Mathias Allemand, a psychologist at the University of Zurich, explains, 'Openness is the personality trait that is most strongly related to cognitive functioning.' In the recent book *Noise*, Daniel Kahneman, Oliver Sibony and Cass R. Sunstein show that open mindedness is linked with better judgement – in particular, people with high levels of cognition and a high 'need for cognition' (this means you enjoy thinking, which is related to openness and conscientiousness) were found to be less biased and have more consistency in their decision making. They also show that the people who are most likely to be good at forecasting are those who score highly on 'actively open-minded thinking' – which is linked to actually seeking out information that contradicts your views. Needless to say, though, high levels of anxiety or depression can also substantially cloud our ability to think clearly.

But personality traits are still fuzzy concepts, warns Kovas. This is particularly because they are assessed by questionnaires asking people about their own thoughts, feelings and behaviour – things they may not necessarily have good or honest insight into. Scientists have developed the concepts because they seem useful and can explain and predict behaviour to some extent. But they may be replaced by more accurate terms in the future. Nevertheless, there is curious evidence from eye-tracking research to show that people with different personalities literally perceive the world differently – as evidenced by their eye movements.[12] Things like our gaze and blink rate can therefore help predict personality traits, too. Happy, optimistic people, for example, spend less time looking at negative images, such as those of skin cancer, than pessimistic individuals.

To understand how nature and nurture each shape personality we met with Alex and Helen,* identical twins in their late thirties, and asked them to take a personality test. They grew up in a loving home in London, with parents who gave them equal amounts of support and attention. They had similar temperaments, obtained similar grades in school and were enrolled in almost identical activities. This suggests their personalities should be fairly closely aligned. It wasn't really until university that their lives diverged substantially, and they lived in different cities and even countries for the next fifteen years. Alex went to a quite conservative university, while Helen attended a more liberal one. After this, they both lived abroad for some time, with Alex working in a conflict zone. Helen instead moved to continental Europe, where she met her wife. Today, they are both living in London, where Helen works as a journalist and Alex is employed in the public sector.

The personality test revealed plenty of similarities, but there were a few moderate differences, with Helen scoring slightly higher on agreeableness and openness to experience, and Alex scoring higher on extraversion, particularly on its facet of assertiveness. Both had impressive scores on conscientiousness and emotional stability, though Helen had a higher score on the facet of anxiety whereas Alex scored higher on anger. None of this surprised them, and they both believe the differences are mainly down to their experiences

---

* Alex's and Helen's names have been changed here to protect their identities.

as adults. 'When you are a twin and you leave home, you become an individual,' explains Alex. 'I'm a very strong and assertive person, and I think I've got stronger because of the jobs I've done,' she says. 'Being in a conflict zone toughened me a bit.' Meanwhile, Helen thinks living abroad and getting married has 'mellowed' her. She also thinks her higher score on openness to experience is down to her being slightly less conservative – with a small c. Whereas Alex has more sympathy for Britain's traditions and institutions, something she was taught to value at university and, later, at work, Helen feels differently. 'I get very irritated with tradition. I am much more willing to question that. I think a lot of it is a bit silly.'

Their story shows that the things we learn, the jobs we do and the people we surround ourselves with can all impact our personality – and therefore how we think, down to our biases, tolerances, likes and dislikes.

Personality, then, isn't set in stone from early adulthood, which researchers traditionally believed. Indeed, studies have shown that personality traits vary throughout our life, meaning we may think slightly differently at different stages of our lives. This is likely to be mainly due to changing habits and social roles – holding down a job requires conscientiousness, for example, while long-term romantic relationships can make us more emotionally stable. Over time, such changes in behaviour may become integrated into our personality, though this is still something that needs to be proven. Nevertheless, researchers have observed that, on average, people increase in all five personality traits between the ages of twenty and forty.[13] Over those twenty years, we become more emotionally stable, extroverted and conscientious. After sixty, however, as we approach retirement and may come across fewer new people and challenging tasks, we reduce in openness and extraversion, but continue to become even more conscientious. Our personalities may also shift slightly depending on what situation we find ourselves in – we may be more assertive in certain environments and with certain people, for example.

So how can we harness this knowledge to think better, or at least limit the impact of personality-based thinking biases? Fledgling research is beginning to show that people are actually able to shift their personality in a direction they want by simply changing their behaviour and acting as if they had a different personality. That may sound too simple and easy to be true, but in 2021, an impressive study asked 1,523 Swiss people to pick a trait that they wanted to change.[14] For three months, they were then coached by a smartphone app called PEACH (PErsonality coACH), which gave them specific tasks to do, such as talk to new people if they wanted to become more extraverted or organise their lives more if they wanted to become more conscientious. The researchers discovered that the participants did manage to change in the ways they wanted, as judged by personality tests and reports by friends and family. But how much can people really change? A statistical measure of change in psychology is 'standard deviations', showing how spread-out numbers are. The difference between a maximally introverted person and a maximally extroverted one, for example, is about three standard deviations. During a lifetime, people tend to change about one standard deviation in a particular trait. The personality tests showed changes of between a third and a half standard deviation in three months among the study participants.[15] That's pretty significant.

If you want to become more conscientious, for example, you can train yourself to become more organised and attentive to detail. You can, for example, try to set yourself daily tasks: write down important birthdays, proofread emails before you hit send and volunteer to organise things for others. To become more open, make an effort to understand the views of other people. Ask your friends about their opinions on controversial subjects, for example, and really try to take them in. Make an effort to read news outlets or listen to music or podcasts you wouldn't normally go for.[16] In fact, each of us tried this scheme for four weeks and we managed to slightly increase our levels of conscientiousness and emotional stability.[17]

Whether you can boost IQ, however, remains hotly debated among scientists. One study from Norway, which looked at the effects of lengthening compulsory education in the country in the 1960s, found that education seems to be linked to IQ. As adults, the IQ of people who went to school at this time was, on average, 3.7 points higher for every extra year of education they received.[18]

Education is also linked to improved rational and critical thinking, although possibly mainly in the specific areas studied.[19] One study, albeit based on a small sample, found that rational thinking was only 34 per cent genetically heritable, showing that the experiences we go through have a huge impact on our ability to act rationally.[20] And while we can't do much about the level of education we receive as children, we can continue to actively train our critical and rational thinking abilities – slowing down our thinking in areas where it is important to be rational, such as when dealing with numbers. We can also educate ourselves about our own weaknesses, for example the biases and other thinking traps that affect us – covered in this book and others – and try to apply them to ourselves. It is still unknown to what extent cognitive flexibility can be trained. Barbara Sahakian, a professor of neuropsychology at the University of Cambridge, is currently investigating this, and there have been promising results.[21] Similarly it seems people can boost their levels of creativity through 'divergent thinking training'[22] – resulting in actual brain changes that are associated with enhanced creativity.

There are, of course, general things we can do to look after our cognition, especially as we age.[23] Physical and social activity can help protect our minds – boosting blood supply to the brain and strengthening neural connections. There are also various techniques and brain training games – commercial puzzles, video games, memorisation techniques and other tasks – designed to boost functions such as attention, processing speed and memory.[24] The evidence for such training is mixed, however, and it remains to be proven that improvements in memory, for example, make you better at thinking in general. But some well-designed studies have shown that brain training can help older adults boost memory, reasoning and processing speed.[25]

While there isn't a pill or other simple solution that can make us substantially smarter, it *is* possible to boost cognition temporarily with pharmaceuticals in certain domains as you'll see elsewhere in this book (Chapter 20: 'Are you hangry?'). But the best approach remains being conscientious and open-minded – training yourself to critically take in many conflicting bits of information. People can, and do, improve. Regardless of our DNA or early life experience, we are all blessed with brains that are amazingly malleable. As this book shows, by seeking out new habits, behaviour and intellectual challenges, we can rewire our brains to think more clearly. Of course, thanks to the genes we inherited from our parents, this may be easy or hard. That doesn't mean we shouldn't keep trying, though. Cycles of rigid thinking and destructive behaviour that have persisted within our blood line for generations are at stake. It is up to us to take charge and break some of them.

5

Do your emotions rule your mind?

Gunilla was an exceptional wordsmith, her razor-sharp wit spliced with an infectious enthusiasm and penetrating intellect. She could persuade virtually anyone of anything. An ambitious journalist and editor, she once successfully campaigned to stop politicians from backtracking on their promise to build a new school in her local area. On another occasion, she managed to secure her family's ideal home by showing up unannounced on the owner's doorstop after hearing it would soon be on the market. She launched organisations, investigations and demonstrations – energetically thinking about how she could improve the world and then working tirelessly to make that change happen.

So as Gunilla sat in her psychiatrist's office one afternoon, her daughter, Kajsa, struggled to believe she was listening to the same person. As the young doctor eagerly explained to her the benefits of cognitive behavioural therapy, Gunilla looked disdainful and absent at the same time. When asked simply to describe her day, she struggled to find the words. 'She was like a little girl,' explains Kajsa, who had to help her answer the questions.

Gunilla had suffered bouts of severe depression since her early teens, and had tried to kill herself several times. Kajsa knew the signs well. Her mother would be increasingly on edge – critical, short-tempered and anxious. Her attention turned inwards, leaving her unable to register any positive cues from her environment. Her usual, unbridled optimism would turn inside-out, with a dark, pessimistic worldview taking over – one in which she was ultimately a failure. She would ruminate on her faults as well as others' hurtful actions and comments, and the creativity, curiosity and empathy that normally bolstered her thinking would seemingly shut down. It was as if her mind was operating on a shred of its former capacity. Kajsa says the evidence was partly in her language, which became not only sparse and self-centred, but also impoverished – lacking in both colour and nuance.

As Gunilla descended deep into her depressions, she would become a 'shell of her former self', her scrawny body, motionless face and 'dead eyes' making it visually striking to anyone. At this point, it was hard to know what, or even *if*, she was thinking – she would be on strong medication, appear slightly confused and sleep through the day. When she finally came out the other end weeks later, her positive personality would appear to regenerate, and she'd talk only of hope, gratitude and plans for the future – suggesting she'd some-how erased the memory of the dark hole she'd just climbed out of.

But as Gunilla grew older, the more severe and lasting her depressions became, with just diminishing moments of respite between. And at the age of sixty, she tragically chose to end her own life – leaving behind a note outlining what she saw as her life's failures and some supportive and loving words for her family. 'I never blamed her for what she did,' says Kajsa. 'Nor did I think it was our fault.' Indeed, according to Kajsa, the depressive periods had left her mother with such distorted cognition that it seemed logical to her to end her life.

Emotions are often seen as the enemy of thinking clearly – there's sense and there's sensibility. But this is often far from the truth. If our mind is like a house, then our emotions are the lively flames that flicker in its fireplace. Fluctuations in this fire can ultimately help us to think clearly and make good decisions – giving much-needed information about what we want or even know. It's the rapid heartbeat that helpfully shifts our attention to the long, slithering object in the tall grass and allows us to avoid the snake's bite. The feeling that a partner is wrong for us, even though we can't rationally determine the reasons. The sense of joy that reminds us to keep doing something we enjoy or find rewarding. Logical thinking is not the only way to be right.

But, sometimes, the fire can burn too hot, causing our minds to overheat, resulting in rage or panic. While on other occasions, the flames can cool and die back, trapping us in a chilling spiral of formulaic and repetitive negative thought.

Emotions affect our thinking by influencing a number of cognitive processes. And that makes perfect sense. 'If emotion is telling you what matters to you, you should expect it to change your attention, perception, memory and decision-making – it *should* bias those things,' argued Elizabeth Phelps, a professor of neuroscience at Harvard University, in an interview with us.

When it comes to decision-making, for example, emotions affect our thinking in two key ways: 'integrally' and 'incidentally'. While integral emotions are triggered by a decision, helpfully telling us whether it is beneficial to us, incidental feelings are independent of our decisions but may nevertheless influence them. A sense of relief or calm after taking a difficult decision is an example of an integral emotion. This is useful to us as it indicates that we don't have to revisit the decision, and also helps us make similar decisions in the future. An example of incidental emotion is being annoyed because you've just missed a train, and heading straight to the nearest shop to buy a huge chocolate bar and eating it in one sitting – even though you're not hungry. Similarly, if you're feeling anxious because your mum is undergoing a medical test, you may be extra risk averse when making an unrelated financial decision. Research has shown that incidental emotions can influence thinking about a range of topics, including how much we are prepared to pay for products, how attracted we are to others and how content we are with our lives.[1] These incidental emotions can interfere with our thinking on a day-to-day basis.

Mental health conditions such as depression or anxiety, however, can have an extreme impact on our thinking. And they are common – roughly a quarter of us (though this number may be higher) will be diagnosed with clinical depression in our lifetime, while one in five will have suicidal thoughts and at least a third will struggle with an anxiety disorder.[2] And many of us will also feel down or worried over the course of a week, which can impact how we think, too. However, when we are trapped with feelings such as sadness, numbness or hopelessness for prolonged periods of time, this can be associated with significant changes in brain structure and function.[3] In depression, for example, activity of the prefrontal cortex, which is involved in planning and problem solving, tends to reduce, while the hippocampus (the memory centre) shrinks and the amygdala (which processes emotions, in particular fear) gets larger.[4] All this alters how we think. And as Kajsa, who now works as a counsellor, learned early on, language is an excellent tool for probing the content of these, often intrusive, thoughts.

Over the past few decades, researchers have trawled through poetry, essays, conversation transcripts and social media posts to show that people with depression and other psychiatric conditions use language differently – reflecting changes in their thinking. For example, it is well established that both people with depression or anxiety use first-person singular pronouns – such as 'me', 'myself' and 'I' – to a much greater extent. They also use fewer second- and third-person pronouns, such as 'you', 'they', 'her' or 'he'.[5] Understandably, they also use more negative emotional words, such as 'sadness', 'concern' or 'lonely'. And according to one recent study, people with symptoms of depression or anxiety use significantly more 'absolutist' words that convey absolute magnitudes or probabilities, rather than nuance – such as 'never', 'nothing', 'totally', 'always', or 'completely'.[6]

The study, which compared the language used on online anxiety and depression forums with that on neutral chat rooms such as Mumsnet, found that the use of absolutist words was about 50 per cent greater in anxiety and depression forums, and roughly 80 per cent greater in forums for people with suicidal thoughts. This line of research backs up Kajsa's impression that her mother's thinking became more black and white, self-focused and pessimistic during her depressive episodes.

Scientists don't currently know whether this way of thinking *causes* episodes of depression and anxiety or whether they are *symptomatic* of the conditions. We do know, however, that both conditions are linked to rumination about negative events. Depressed people often ruminate about the past, and their (negative) role in it, while anxious individuals focus more on bad things that could happen to them in the future. And it certainly makes sense that someone who is suffering in this way would be self-focused – in the same way that it's hard to think about anyone else right after you've stepped on a nail.

But in the chat room study, there were some signs that absolutist thinking may underlie the mental health conditions – that it be causal, rather than symptomatic – potentially making people more prone to them. The researchers also examined forums for people who had recovered from their condition and discovered that these individuals used more positive emotional words than the non-recovered groups. However, they were still significantly more likely to use absolutist words than those in neutral forums, suggesting that, though recovered, they were still thinking in a more black-and-white way than others, and potentially therefore maintained a higher risk of suffering from mental illnesses. Similarly, we know that both people who have depression and people who are at risk of developing it tend to be biased to think in a negative way – in other words, more pessimistic, on average, than those who are less at risk – having certain genes, lower levels of emotional stability, or previous depressive episodes.[7]

While negative, black-and-white thinking limits our ability to understand the world in a flexible, productive and nuanced way, it is worth noting that some with depression or anxiety do manage to harness their thoughts in creative ways. Many artists, from Sylvia Plath to Kurt Cobain, who both killed themselves after periods of severe depression and other problems, were insightful thinkers who produced poems, lyrics and music that captured something real and touched the hearts of millions.

So while psychological disorders can inhibit our thinking, highly intelligent people aren't immune to developing them.[8] While many studies have shown that high IQ can protect against mental health problems,[9] one study surveying nearly 4,000 members of the high IQ society Mensa in the US found that they had much higher rates of depression (26.8 per cent) and anxiety (20 per cent) than the national average (9.5 per cent and 10.9 per cent respectively). The authors of the Mensa study argue this could be because they are psychologically and physiologically 'overexcitable', responding more strongly to threatening events and being more prone to overanalysing, worrying or ruminating. After all, if you are highly intelligent, you might just be better at imagining catastrophic – but possible – outcomes. But it's important to keep in mind that this is a rather biased group of people with a very high IQ – they have chosen to be members of Mensa.

Phelps's own research shows that emotion does two things in threatening situations.[10] 'It sort of heightens your perception for the highly emotional threatening thing, and it captures your attention so that you're really focused on it,' she explained. At the same time, 'Some brain regions that are important in moving your attention from here to there become less good at doing that.' So depending on whether you are sad, scared or happy, you will be attentive to different things around you, focusing more on some details while missing others – which in turn can affect your decision-making and thought processes.[11] Depression and anxiety, for example, can alter our attention so we become biased towards and give greater weight to negative information, making it difficult for us to think flexibly.[12] Even as we are on our way to the airport for an exciting holiday in the sun, we may obsess about all the things that could go wrong on the way there. This, no doubt, makes the world seem sad and menacing – and leads to further errors in interpreting our surroundings.

Perception and attention also affect how we memorise things. When we see the world in a negative light, we'll likely remember it that way, too. Our memories are stored through a process called consolidation, during which the brain actively forms connections between different neurons. And this is enhanced when we experience a relatively high level of arousal, such as fear or excitement. It's what helps you remember your first kiss from twenty years ago, but not what you had for dinner last Thursday. But this can also make us over-remember difficult life events, such as being bullied in school or dumped by someone we loved. As trauma expert Jennifer Wild explores in her book *Be Extraordinary*, these memories can haunt us decades later by manipulating our thinking. We can get 'stuck' feeling that people are trying to attack or abandon us when they're not, interpreting everything according to a false narrative based on over-remembered, difficult memories. And when we are in a negative mood, we are more prone to access negative memories. This can make us feel even lower, leading us to accept and record even more negative memories – creating a destructive feedback loop.

The longer we feel down and stressed, the worse we become at remembering. 'There comes a point when you have had persistent stress for a while, which boosts levels of certain hormones and cortisol, that actually hurts your ability to form new memories,' explained Phelps. Depressed people, for example, can struggle to remember specific and detailed events from their lives, having more general memories such as, 'I ate a lot of croissants when I was in Paris,' rather than, 'I had the best, buttery croissant of my life on that crisp, winter's morning in a Montparnasse cafe with the red chairs.'

This may have serious implications when it comes to threatening memories. In one experiment, Phelps showed participants pictures of various objects: either a type of animal or a type of tool.[13] For some specific images, say a bird, she gave them a mild shock to the wrist – creating a fearful memory of that object (as measured by their heart rate, level of sweating, etc.). The next day, the participants were invited back to the lab to have their memories tested. And it turned out that they remembered the shock-related objects better than the neutral ones. But they also remembered objects that were never paired with a shock better if they were from the same category as the shock-related object (for example, another animal). It seems the participants generalised their threatening memories – ultimately making them fearful of a greater number of objects than necessary. This suggests that threatening experiences may lead us to develop even more general, threatening memories – potentially making us feel more scared and prone to developing mental health conditions.

There is also evidence that people with depression are worse at forgetting negative information.[14] This can cramp our 'working memory', making it harder to remember a shopping list or hold numerous thoughts in our heads at the same time – and creating another vicious cycle. Other cognitive impairments can occur, too, including slower response time, planning and reasoning in depression, and problems with concentration, as well as working memory, in anxiety.[15] Some of these cognitive problems may persist even if the person has recovered.[16] This makes sense – prolonged periods of rumination and worry drain cognitive power.

It also matters whether we think in words or pictures. When we are relaxed, most of us tend to have a roughly even mix of images and words in our thoughts. But research shows that worry often plays out in words rather than images – it's a bit like talking to a friend about all the bad things that could happen, over and over.[17] If you are scared of riding a bike, for example, repeating the phrase 'I don't want to fall off' can make you stressed out. It is much more helpful to think in images, to simply picture yourself cruising down the street on the bike – after all, it is near impossible to picture the phrase 'don't fall off'.

In one experiment, Colette Hirsch, a professor of cognitive clinical psychology at King's College London, and her colleagues, tested whether worrying in verbal form could make it harder to concentrate on certain tasks.[18] She asked a group of study participants, some of whom were 'high worriers', to do a cognitive task involving pressing a key in short, random intervals. While they did this, they were asked to either worry about something in words or in images (which the researchers had trained them to do). The results were intriguing. 'People who were not worriers performed just as well under those conditions, but people who were high worriers ended up being able to press the key much less well when they were worrying in verbal form,' explains Hirsch. 'The lack of imagery when you're worrying leads to reduction in your cognitive control – it uses up more attention.' Hirsch believes the same thing applies to depression. 'Depressive rumination is more abstract and generalised than other thinking, and is therefore less likely to elicit imagery,' she says.

So how can we minimise the impact of feelings, and particularly negative emotions, on our thoughts? Luckily, it isn't just our emotions that influence our thoughts; it works the other way around, too. 'People tend to think of their emotions as reactions that they can't do anything about,' argues Phelps. 'I do think people underestimate the extent to which they can use their thoughts to create their emotional life.' And this is ultimately the key to improving your thinking.

Elsewhere in this book, we've described the enormous effect that even just basic feelings, such as tiredness and hunger, can have. But it applies to more complex emotions, too. Incidental feelings might make you unnecessarily harsh to someone you're interviewing for a job if you've had a row with your partner earlier that day, for example. The key to tackling this kind of undue influence is to understand it – and that takes some self-knowledge. Several studies have shown that people who have a good grasp of their emotional lives make better decisions. In one study, researchers made their participants anxious by telling them that they had one minute to prepare a three-minute presentation about why they were a good job candidate.[19] They were also tested on how nervous they felt and how well they could understand their own emotions, before being asked to make either a high- or low-risk financial gamble. The researchers found that anxious individuals who had a poor understanding of their emotions were much less likely to make a risky gamble than other groups. But they also discovered that this effect disappeared when informing the participants what the source of their anxiety was. Of course, it is not always ideal to take risks, but being aware that unidentified anxiety could make it harder to do so can only help our thinking.

Another study on 118 traders in the City of London showed that the most successful, experienced group tended to consider and include their feelings and hunches when making decisions, combining them with analytical thinking.[20] They also seemed more willing to think critically about their emotions. The less successful and experienced traders, meanwhile, often ignored their emotions. Rather than contemplating why they had a strong, sudden emotion, they might walk away from their desk or try to think purely rationally when it struck.

So, it seems that emotional intelligence can help us make better decisions. And there's no doubt it is a valuable quality in leaders.[21] After all, the less you know about the sources of your irritation or anxiety, the less able you will be to resolve them or even account for them. Paradoxically then, to common perceptions, people who are more in touch with their emotions might be less driven by them. So the next time you are making an important decision, do consider how you're feeling at the moment and what the source of that emotion is.

This is difficult to do if you are depressed or anxious, though. For serious cases, it is near impossible to 'think yourself better' – and

43

professional help is the best solution. Both cognitive behavioural therapy (CBT), which can help shift unhelpful thinking patterns, and antidepressants have been shown to reduce the negative biases that are at the heart of the depressed or anxious brain.[22]

But if you're just a bit anxious or feeling a tad blue, you may be more able to 'treat' yourself by reframing your thinking. For example, while a bit of self-criticism is good, it is unlikely that every single 'failure' in your life is entirely down to you. Sometimes, things are simply out of your control. If you fail to meet a deadline at work, for example, it isn't necessarily because you are bad at your job. Maybe you had to look after a sick child that week or perhaps the deadline was unreasonable or the task poorly explained to start with. Constant negative thoughts about yourself can be draining, and take up space that we could use for more creative thinking. If you can stop constantly jumping to conclusions about your own fallibility and sometimes reframe failures in terms of circumstances, it can lead to what researchers call 'post-traumatic growth' – helping you to become more resilient after facing hardship.[23] When you're anxious, also try to remind yourself that worrying can in fact be helpful in reasonable amounts[24] – making us perform better on tests, for example. Making an effort to try to visualise rather than thinking in words can also help.

This sort of reframing isn't easy, and needs to be done when you're in a positive headspace. 'When worry invades your head, that isn't the best time to think about that issue,' explains Hirsch. 'It's actually better for you to be able to choose when you think about it'. Consciously choosing to do things that create worry-free moments can enable space for you to reframe your thinking: reading, karaoke, exercise or meditation, for example.

There is research indicating that negative memories can be reframed, too. Ultimately, the key is to try to break the link between the past and the present intellectually, and realise that whatever we went through ended, and does not need to continue into the present or future. So if you're anxious about public speaking because everyone laughed at you when you gave a speech in high school, realise that there's no reason why that should happen today.

Excitingly, further in the future, scientists may even be able to edit out fearful memories. Phelps has shown that very simple fear memories, created by a mild shock to the wrist when participants see a certain geometrical shape, can be extinguished if people are later reminded of the fear memory and are shown the shapes again without getting the shock.[25] But this needs to happen in a relatively brief period of time as the memory is being 'reconsolidated' – a process that helps us maintain and tweak our memories, taking into account new information. Whether it is possible for psychologists to help people rework their traumatic memories, which are much more complex, remains unclear, but nevertheless it's an exciting prospect.[26]

Emotions are helpful, especially when we are open to them and can understand them well. It makes sense that they should fluctuate. Constant positive, cheerful feeling and thinking isn't necessarily the answer – such a disposition can in fact sway us to become so over-confident that we fail to rethink what we know or learn from our mistakes. But in serious clinical disorders, such as depression, anxiety or bipolar disorder, our thoughts and feelings change in complex, unhelpful ways that we can't control. Indeed, the powerful negative thinking that hijacks our minds when we're severely depressed is downright dangerous. As Gunilla tragically experienced, it can make us lose all hope. It's hard to think of anything that could influence our thinking in a more destructive way.

In the UK, Samaritans can be contacted on 116 123 or by email – jo@ samaritans.org.

6
Are you an optimist?

When Cayle Royce emerged from a forty-eight-day coma, after stepping on a Taliban improvised explosive device (IED) while serving with the British Army in Afghanistan in 2012, he found it 'difficult not to be pessimistic'. He'd survived a near-death experience, but had awoken from one nightmare to find himself in another. He had lost both legs, most of one hand, nearly half of his body weight and the blast had severely scorched his lungs, leaving him weak, in agonising pain and attached to an array of wires and machines. But one of the hardest things was coming to terms with the hospital staff having to do virtually everything for him. 'I couldn't sit up, I couldn't roll over, I couldn't feed myself, I couldn't clean myself,' recalls Royce. And in this hellish, disorienting world, he found it almost impossible to stop dark thoughts from hijacking his mind.

Royce, who grew up poor on a South African farm and had battled his way through several firefights as a serviceman, had faced hardship before and had always remained positive and resilient. But this loss of physical independence was a deep and debilitating trauma, not least because of his love for physical challenges and the outdoors.

'For people who don't suffer severe trauma, whether that be mental or physical, and the desperate lows that it brings, I think it is easier to maintain an optimistic mindset; having your health and a fully functioning body naturally gives you a certain confidence in yourself,' he says. 'I believe it is only when you discover just how fragile you are that you really re-evaluate risk in a different manner.'

Over the following months, however, things slowly began to change for the better. Both in the hospital ward and later on at Headley Court, the UK's main rehabilitation centre for seriously wounded servicemen and women, he met people in a similar position. 'These guys would come up to have a chat and they were Paralympians and ocean rowers and just people getting by with no concerns really.' The community became a real inspiration for Royce and enabled him to talk openly about his fears and concerns – the pain, everything being slow, the frustration of prosthetics. 'We could be comfortable around each other. It didn't matter whether Derek shat himself again, we knew it wasn't his fault – he was shot in the stomach and there was nothing you could do about it.'

Royce's rehabilitation progressed successfully and, a few months into it, he received a call from his close friend Captain James Kaylle that would further boost his outlook. Kaylle suggested an epic challenge. Would Royce be willing to row across the Atlantic in a 29-foot boat? And after spending months worrying that he would be seen as a liability on such an adventure, Royce decided to join. In December 2013, the team set off on their journey, rowing 3,000 miles across the shark-infested, volatile ocean, where towering waves can reach 62 feet. It was just the motivation Royce needed, and he has since broken numerous records, including being in the first all-amputee team to row across the Atlantic and becoming the first double amputee to fly a solo, powered paraglider across the UK from John o' Groats to Land's End.

As Royce discovered, positive thinking can be a lifeline. It has no doubt helped us as a species – if we don't believe we can achieve the seemingly impossible, why even try? Optimism has also been linked to better physical health, medical recovery and well-being; although, it's unclear whether optimism directly causes these things or whether it is down to genetics or healthcare systems responding better to optimists. Either way, it is no wonder that countless self-help books and leadership conferences argue that positive thinking is the key to a good life and a healthy mind.

The truth, however, is more complex. Optimism isn't the same as happiness – if we always expect positive events to occur, we will occasionally end up being disappointed, depressed even (see Chapter 8: 'Are You Happy?', page 139) Nor does it work for everyone in every situation. As Royce knows too well, it can be difficult to think positively if you have gone through a trauma or are lacking social or financial support. Thinking, after all, doesn't happen in a vacuum; our environment influences it. An overly positive attitude can also seriously bias our thinking – just like pessimism. In fact, roughly 80 per cent of people have an optimism bias, although this varies slightly across cultures.[1] This means that we overestimate the likelihood of positive events happening in our lives, and underestimate the possibility of bad things occurring. It also means we learn more from positive information than we do from negative information. We may know smoking harms health, but we don't believe it will *kill* us.

Tali Sharot, a professor of cognitive neuroscience at University College London, has explored this phenomenon in depth.[2] Her team scanned the brains of a group of people as they each estimated the likelihood of a number of future scenarios happening. The results highlighted our natural tendency to look on the bright side and ignore life's more uncomfortable realities. If someone first estimated that their risk of getting cancer was 50 per cent, for example, they were relieved when the researchers told them their actual risk was just 30 per cent. Tellingly, when they were then asked again about their cancer risk, they considerably lowered their estimate in line with the facts. But if they initially thought their risk was just 10 per cent, and were disappointed to find out it was 30 per cent, they updated their estimation at the second time of asking – but only by very little, perhaps guessing it was 14 per cent. In other words, we are quick to update our thinking based on good news, but far less so based on bad news.

Sharot and her colleagues showed that the culprit was an area of the brain called the inferior frontal gyrus, which is involved in language and information processing. Whenever the participants received positive information, their left inferior frontal gyrus, which responds to good news, lit up brightly on the scan – in virtually everyone. But in optimistic people receiving negative information, the right inferior frontal gyrus, which responds to bad news, didn't react as fiercely. In fact, the more optimistic the participant, the less active their right inferior frontal gyrus.

But can we really divide people neatly into optimists and pessimists? Sharot thinks not. 'Optimism bias is not set in stone, it is quite flexible and it can come and go,' she explains. For example, it tends to change over a lifetime. While children and teenagers have a large optimism bias, this drops dramatically in midlife, only to rise again in the elderly.[3] The amount of bias can also change from one day to the next or from one situation to another. Sharot has shown that when you stress people out – telling them they have to give a talk in front of people and be judged on it, for example – their optimism bias disappears completely, and people start learning more from negative information.[4] For example, young people in California understandably lacked an optimism bias about their risk of being hurt in an earthquake a few days after one occurred in 1989.[5] But three months later, their optimism bias had returned.

While studies involving twins show that genetics can explain up to 40 per cent of differences in optimism, experience plays a crucial role.[6] If you have a lot of negative experiences in a certain area of life, such as being bullied at an early age, you may start developing negative social expectations. But that needn't stop you from being optimistic about your intellect or physical abilities.

Optimism bias can be harmless, helping us take risks and be happy. It may enable us to apply for a job we're not technically qualified for, and end up getting it. But it can also sometimes lead to bad decisions.

It can get in the way of accurately assessing risk and failing to take necessary precautions, with consequences such as unhealthy lifestyles, failed relationships or financial problems. Similarly, optimism bias is the reason why so many big infrastructure projects run over budget and take longer than planned. It was also widely blamed for the US and its allies being caught off guard when the Taliban rapidly advanced through Afghanistan, recapturing the capital, Kabul, in 2021.

Optimism is linked to something called overconfidence – a type of optimism about yourself.[7] 'Optimists tend to interpret positive events that have happened to them as related to *them*, as their traits,' explained Sharot in an interview. When an optimist does really well on a project at work, for example, they think this happened because they have great skills, concluding they are likely to succeed again and again. But if they fail, they will blame external circumstances, such as being allocated insufficient time for the project. Pessimists, on the other hand, do the opposite – they blame themselves for failures and give circumstances or other people credit for their successes.

Countless studies have shown that most people think they are better than the average person at almost everything – from work and driving to grammar, reasoning and making people laugh.[8] We are guilty of this when we shout at the football player who misses a penalty, honk the driver who doesn't move immediately after a traffic light turns green, or grumble at the partner who doesn't season the pasta sauce correctly. This well-documented sense of superiority can clearly influence how we think and make decisions. Students, for example, are often overconfident about their exam performance and the grades they'll get.[9] If they don't get what they expected, they may be quick to blame the examiner for unfair questioning when over-confidence itself was the culprit – leading to a false sense of security and less time spent studying.

Companies with overconfident CEOs are also 33 per cent more likely to face class-action lawsuits, which can be costly.[10] 'We reward these individualistic, self-confident CEOs in the US,' argued Julie Norem, a professor of psychology at Wellesley College, in an interview with us. 'So we find correlations between their individual optimism and their individual success, but around that, people are left picking up the pieces.' Overconfidence can also get in the way of relationships, leaving us to big up our own contributions while minimising those of our partner.

However, being a pessimist has its own downfalls. According to Sharot, of the 20 per cent who don't have optimism bias, half tend to be either mildly or severely depressed. It is easy to see why. If we always expect negative outcomes, then why try to achieve anything? And if we always blame negative outcomes on ourselves, it is easy to feel hopeless – believing we are unable to chart our own course in life. 'One reason optimists are optimists is because they have a sense of control,' says Sharot.

Norem, however, believes pessimism and negative thinking can be handy in certain situations and tasks, as it tends to come with a very detail-oriented, critical and risk-averse style of thinking – potentially explaining why it hasn't been eradicated from the human gene pool. She has also shown that, for highly anxious people, embracing 'defensive pessimism' – using a negative outlook on life to try to overcome obstacles and ultimately improve it – may sometimes be a good strategy. This involves allowing yourself to set low expectations, seeing the challenges and risks in all their glory, and finding ways to overcome them bit by bit – rather than being paralysed by fear. Anxious students preparing for an exam can use this approach to ensure that they are sufficiently prepared, lowering their anxiety and boosting their performance. Research has shown that anxious people are more successful when they adopt this approach than when they try to be optimistic and cheerful.[11] In countries such as the US, this allows them to achieve on a par with optimists. In countries such as China and Japan, however, where optimism isn't as celebrated as in the West, it seems defensive pessimists in fact have an edge.[12] Norem has also shown that defensive pessimism was linked with taking more precautions and fewer risks during the COVID-19 pandemic, ultimately benefiting others.

So, what can you do to tackle optimism bias? While it can be difficult to *think* your way out of it, an awareness can help you manage it and check your thinking. Many governments have put in place guidance for how optimism bias can be accounted for in infrastructure projects, such as by comparing cost estimates with evidence from other projects.[13] Similarly, you can check facts. If you are taking a big risk, such as quitting your job to become an artist, it makes sense to interrogate what the odds of success really are – do your research rather than optimistically relying on the one success story you heard on the news. As Royce knows too well, planning for some pretty terrifying situations can be a matter of life and death if you are going to row across the Atlantic – enabling a healthier, more cautious optimism. Ultimately, it can be hugely rewarding to take risks by leaping into the unknown, but being aware that you are doing it can allow you to take a few parachutes with you – increasing your chances of success.

This needn't just apply to yourself. You can also try to spot optimism bias in your loved ones. If your children have unrealistic expectations about getting their dream job, for example, help them work out a plan B. Tempering optimism bias and overconfidence could even help your romantic relationship. If your partner claims they do a disproportionate amount of housework, but you are (over)confident you do, why not keep a tally? It may not sound very romantic, but being open to the fact that we aren't as great as we think we are, especially when there's a lot at stake, could save your relationship.

If you are deeply pessimistic, on the other hand, perhaps even depressed, it is likely that you suffer unnecessarily by imagining horrific things that may never happen. Perhaps you are sometimes right, and that may give comfort in the moment, but this approach could end up entrenching your negative expectations and make you even more depressed. In addition to talking to a professional, you could try to train yourself to think in a more balanced way – reframing how you interpret the world around you. If you didn't get a job, perhaps it wasn't because you are worthless, but rather because the employer prioritised someone who previously did temp work there. And if you did get a job, maybe it was because you are competent rather than lucky.

Not all pessimists suffer from clinical depression, however. As we've seen, people who struggle with anxiety can sometimes use pessimism defensively – as a powerful motivator in situations where they can actually influence the outcome. And of course, there are plenty of people who are just a bit pessimistic, but don't suffer too much from it. They may even enjoy being critical, spotting faults in the world around them. Although they may not be everyone's cup of tea, these grumpy individuals can sometimes be quite useful.

Many countries in the Western world worship positive thinking, and it's easy to fall into the trap of thinking that a sole change in attitude can transform our lives. Ultimately, society is full of structural problems, such as inequality, that can make it difficult for some people to remain optimistic. Proponents of positive thinking who blame lack of success or poor health on individuals' pessimistic thinking simply miss this point. In fact, the movement may leave many people feeling like failures because they can't reach their life goals with optimism alone. But as Royce discovered, when you find yourself in a major trauma, in particular, you can't just think yourself hopeful – you need realistic goals, a fair chance to succeed and the support of those around you to begin to see the light.

7

Are you really from
Mars or Venus?

Feminism is facing a backlash, with the hyper-masculine and misogynist alt-right gaining ground pretty much everywhere.[1] With links to online communities such as involuntary celibates (incels), pick-up artists and Men Going Their Own Way (MGTOW), this has created a 'manosphere' which celebrates extreme masculinity and calls for women to submit to their 'natural' roles as wives, mothers and home-makers. Many influential thinkers in the movement are even opposed to women voting, getting educated or having reproductive rights.[2]

Perhaps more surprising are the groups of women who are also yearning for outdated gender roles. TradWives, for example, is a group of women who want to be traditionally feminine and choose to stay at home to look after their husbands and children. In the UK, the author and blogger Alana Pettit has become the face of this movement, arguing women should 'spoil their husbands like it's 1959' and realise their men 'should always come first' if they want a happy marriage.[3] Like those in the alt-right movement, Pettit has a nostalgic view of the past. In a video for the BBC, she says the movement is about 'harnessing the best of what made Britain great, during that time when you could leave your front door open and know that you were safe, and you knew your strangers in the street.'[4]

Pettit and many other members of the TradWives community do not support the alt-right, and are making a perfectly respectable personal choice to stay home at a time when women are often expected both to have careers and do the lion's share of the housework.[5] Nevertheless, they are celebrated by the manosphere – which refers to them as 'tradhots' (a mix of 'traditional' and 'hot'). Liberated women, on the other hand, are dubbed 'thots', which stands for the derogatory 'that ho over there'. Charming!

The view that women and men are biologically different in terms of both thinking and ability, and are therefore suitable for different roles in society, is ancient and powerful. But does the idea that women are from Venus and men are from Mars stand up to scientific scrutiny? Or is it just a social construct the patriarchy has invented to create a world that ultimately serves a small group of men at the top of the hierarchy?

Our understanding of the male and female mind has gone through a quiet revolution in recent years, with researchers discovering a series of highly questionable assumptions that scientists have historically made when investigating sex differences in thinking and behaviour.[6] Research suggesting that testosterone-fuelled men are simply more rational, promiscuous, aggressive and risk-taking – all things that could shape thinking – are increasingly being questioned by psychologists, neuroscientists and even evolutionary biologists.[7]

Humans who are born male, with XY chromosomes, are, of course, biologically different to humans who are born female, carrying XX chromosomes – they have different genitalia. This isn't a binary, though, as a small proportion of humans are intersex, while others strongly identify as being the opposite sex. There are other differences too, such as biological males being, on average, taller and having more facial hair, body mass and muscle mass. There's a huge amount of variation, however, with some women being taller or stronger than some men; all of these characteristics exist on a spectrum after all.

Since the eighteenth century, we've also known that human biological males have, on average, larger brains than females – something that was historically taken to be a sign of male superiority.[8] Today, however, we know that there are barely any overall differences in general intelligence between men and women, as measured by IQ tests.[9] And we also know that when it comes to brain size, 'bigger' doesn't mean 'more intelligent' – after all, several animal species, such as orcas, have far larger brains than humans, yet are generally not considered to be more intelligent. The physicist superstar Albert Einstein had a smaller brain than average.[10] Brain structure and connectivity, rather, seem to matter more than size.

Yet ideas about men being more logical or women being more nurturing live on. This is partly fuelled by cherry-picking brain scan studies, which may not be representative of neuroscience research overall, showing sex-dependent activity in certain brain regions. Using such studies to promote ideas about what men and women are suitable for has been dubbed 'neurosexism'.[11] Ultimately, whatever a brain scan shows, we know very little about how various brain areas or structures actually relate to function and behaviour in the real world – they certainly can't be used to predict someone's thoughts or actions.

The myth that men and women have dramatically different brains is increasingly being busted, even though small, overall differences in features and connectivity have been identified. In 2015, researchers analysed MRI scans of 1,400 people's brains and discovered that most brains are 'unique mosaics' of different features: some of which are more common in men and some of which are more prominent in women – but are largely overlapping.[12] Indeed, only 6 per cent of brains had only 'male' or 'female' features. Another study in 2021 used machine learning to place brains along a male–female scale based on what we know about average differences in brain connectivity. It found that half of the 9,620 brains were somewhere in the middle of this continuum.[13] According to this study, some 25 per cent were clustering around the distinctly 'male' region and 25 per cent at the opposite 'female' end. Interestingly, however, women's brains shifted increasingly towards the 'male' end of the spectrum after middle age, although this effect was small.

We know that brains are changeable. Many studies have demonstrated that the experiences we go through, and the hobbies and jobs we choose, can change the structure of our brains.[14] Importantly, if we treat girls and boys differently from the day they are born, their brains are likely to develop slightly differently in response. And this doesn't seem to be a good thing. The 2021 study which used machine learning also revealed that the people whose brains were at the extreme ends of the 'male' and 'female' spectrum reported more mental health problems than the people with more 'androgynous' brains. This may be a result of conforming to oppressive social expectations about what men and women should be like – and therefore developing more distinctly 'masculine' or 'feminine' brains – but at a price.

Gina Rippon, a professor of cognitive neuroimaging at Aston University and author of *The Gendered Brain*, suspects that the differences we see between men and women are more down to social expectations than biology. 'If evolution has done anything, it's wired the human brain to make us social,' she told us, arguing that cooperation is ultimately the biggest factor in our species' success. 'But the downside of that is that the drive to belong is very powerful. You have to identify your in-group and make sure you fit in with that group. And if there are very strong messages that members of your own group wear pink and like being princesses, for example, then you'll go along with that.'

Rippon has spent decades trying to educate people about sexism in neuroscience. But she often receives pushback from those arguing that their personal experience indeed shows that men and women think differently. When she asks for examples, however, she often discovers they rely on assumptions. 'It's clear that they are attributing characteristics in individuals *because* they're male or female as opposed to people with a particular way of solving a problem or responding to a crisis,' she explained. As shown elsewhere in this book, our beliefs have a powerful impact on our thinking. If you think men are more logical and women are more nurturing, that's ultimately what you are likely to see when you look around you.

Some studies have shown that women tend to be, on average, slightly better at language, non-verbal reasoning and recognising facial expressions than men.[15] Men, on the other hand, have, on average, a tad better motor skills and visuospatial processing, which can help you rotate objects in your mind, for example.[16] This may mean that men, on average, use slightly more visual information to inform their thinking, while women potentially think more in words, for example. But there's little evidence to suggest that such differences are innate – social expectations, in combination with genetics, are more likely to be at play. 'We know that women who play video games have better visuospatial skills than those who don't,' explained Rippon. 'So I think the visuospatial story is a good case study; we believe it is inborn, but if you look at the facts you discover it is trainable.' While women are nearly as likely as men to play video games today, this hasn't been the case for very long – potentially giving middle-aged men today an advantage. And there is evidence that teenage boys spend more time playing video games than teenage girls.[17]

Many researchers, in fact, don't even believe there is sufficient evidence to back up these findings of sex differences, with two meta-analyses of a large number of research studies finding vanishingly small psychological or cognitive sex differences.[18] What's more, average differences by demographic are a poor indicator of how an individual is likely to think or what they'll be good at – there will be more variation between individuals than there will be between a group of women and a group of men.

When it comes to personality, which is often self-reported, men tend to score more highly than women on assertiveness, self-confidence, risk-taking, anger and dark personality traits such as psychopathy.[19] They are also at greater risk of substance abuse problems. Women's personalities are, on average, higher in agreeableness (how friendly and empathetic you are) and lower in emotional stability. This may make men, on average, more vulnerable to blaming others and being selfish and overconfident in their thinking – missing opportunities to learn from their mistakes. Women, on the other hand, may try harder to fit in and 'internalise' negative events by blaming themselves for perceived failures – and increasing their risk of mental health problems such as depression and anxiety in doing so. However, we know that personality traits change in response to life experiences, so it is likely these changes are also to some extent down to social expectations.

Simon Baron-Cohen, a professor of psychology at the University of Cambridge, believes there are some differences between males and females – on average – and that these are likely to be biological to some extent. Researching what characterises the minds of autistic people, he developed a scale called empathising–systemising, reflecting an aspect of how our brains work. People who score highly on empathising tend to take great interest in what people around them think and feel, while people who score highly on systemising are more interested in analysing 'systems' according to specific rules – be they engines, the weather, recipes, algebraic solutions, syntax or electronic devices.

In 2018, Baron-Cohen and his colleagues asked nearly 700,000 people to fill out a questionnaire about their thinking, with questions such as 'I can tell if someone is masking their true emotion' or 'If I were buying a stereo, I would want to know about its precise technical features'. He has identified five distinct cognitive types. People who score more highly on empathising than systemising are classified as E-type, while people who score higher on systemising than empathising are dubbed S-type. There are also two extreme versions of this: extreme E-type and extreme S-type – people in these categories score highly on one dimension and below average on the other. Finally, there is a middle type in which people score equally highly on both.

The results of his 2018 study revealed that more men than women had an S-type mind, although the differences weren't huge.[20] Some 40 per cent of men were classified as S-type compared to 26 per cent of women. Almost the opposite was true for E-types, which included 40 per cent of women and 24 per cent of men. A further 30 per cent of men and 30 per cent of women were in the mixed group, with only a small percentage of people classified as extreme types. Ultimately, nearly 56 per cent of men were neither S-type nor extreme S-type, and 58 per cent of women were neither E-type nor extreme E-type. So, if you assumed that most women are 'empathisers' and most men are 'systemisers', you would be wrong – according to this research. Among autistic people, however, 62 per cent of males and 50 per cent of females were S-type, or extreme S-type.

Importantly, these scores don't necessarily say much about ability – you can be more interested in people than systems, but still be better at solving equations than some people who are interested in systems. Your female author here, for example, was classed as E-type on the test, but has a background in physics. Similarly, people who are S-type may be better at empathy than some E-types. But it could nevertheless impact how we think about the world by making us gravitate towards certain things. 'In a way, these brain types are saying where you allocate your attention,' says Baron-Cohen. An E-type person in a restaurant might pay more attention to what the people around them are doing or saying than analysing the precise ingredients in the crab linguine they're eating so they can recreate it at home. 'I can see strengths and weaknesses associated with each type,' argues Baron-Cohen. 'The whole point of neurodiversity is we need all of these.'

It isn't clear, however, to what extent these differences are fixed or biological. Baron-Cohen is the first to admit that there may be a range of different factors influencing the results – from social to hormonal. When people fill out a questionnaire about their thinking, they might answer in a way that is socially expected of them. If you strongly identify as a very masculine man, you might not want to admit or even realise that you are in fact interested in people's feelings. And people may not notice how good you are at it, because they don't expect you to be. What's more, if you are a woman and you're rewarded for responding to people's emotions, you may take a greater interest in pursuing it. 'The trouble is when people believe that a stereotype is the truth, it becomes a self-fulfilling prophecy,' says Rippon.

Baron-Cohen, however, believes there may be a hormonal factor at play, too. His own research has shown that children of mothers who had high levels of testosterone and oestrogen in their womb were more likely to be diagnosed with autism later in life. 'And we know they are also likely to have a brain type S, which suggests that hormones are playing some role,' he says.

It is, however, far from proven as it isn't easy to do such research – it involves a procedure that carries a significant risk of miscarriage. Other research, however, has shown that girls with congenital adrenal hyperplasia, who have been exposed to very high levels of testosterone in the womb, are more interested in stereotypical 'boy toys' than 'girl toys'.[21] But recent opposing research has shown that these girls, who also tend to have other medical conditions which may contribute to differences in thinking, are less sensitive to socialisation – they aren't as keen to conform to norms or copy the behaviour of other women.[22] This suggests, though doesn't prove, that prenatal hormones may make girls more prone to follow social norms. But, importantly, it is society that determines what those norms are.[23] So rather than it being the case that women are biologically more nurturing than men, it may be that they are biologically more likely to be nurturing if society dictates they should be. If society told them to be more aggressive, they might be. If this is true, surely we should be treating boys and girls more equally to level out the playing field later in life.

Testosterone is often used to explain the fact that men are slightly more likely to be aggressive and risk-taking compared to women – although the sex difference in aggression, for example, is only about a quarter as prominent as that in height.[24] And while these traits are linked to testosterone in many animals, this hasn't been proven to be the case in humans. Nevertheless, aggression and risk-taking could no doubt have an impact on our thinking – a moment of rage may make us lose our sense of logic, failing to think through the consequences of our actions. Testosterone has, in fact, often been blamed for causing the reckless behaviour that led to the global financial crash in 2008.

Yet in the book *Testosterone Rex*, psychologist Cordelia Fine picks apart many of the arguments suggesting testosterone ultimately makes biological males different.

For example, while research suggests that biological males are more openly and physically aggressive than women, women are arguably more indirectly aggressive – engaging in menacing acts such as spreading rumours or harming someone's social status.[25] This may simply be because they are, on average, smaller than men and it wouldn't be advantageous for them to engage in physical aggression. But they may still feel aggression at the same rate as men. And as for testosterone, research suggests that levels may in fact be influenced by social or environmental factors – so that our thoughts, experiences and behaviour can alter our testosterone levels rather than purely the other way around. One study investigated a ten-year intervention programme in the US, which aimed to reduce antisocial behaviour in boys who were at risk of developing it, by teaching them social skills and how to stay calm when provoked.[26] When forty of the participants were invited back to the lab years later, in their twenties, they had their aggressiveness and testosterone response tested. When compared to a control group of other men, they showed less aggression in response to provocation and also a dampened testosterone response. Hormones, it seems, respond to the world around us – it doesn't make sense to blame them for our behaviour.

Scientists are even questioning whether risk-taking is really more common among men. According to Fine, studies of risk-taking often focus on activities such as skydiving or betting money on a football game, for example. But both football and skydiving are more traditionally accepted 'male' hobbies. If the studies had looked at risky 'female' activities, such as horse riding or cosmetic surgery, they may have produced different results. Similar results have been found for sex drive – with women being equally keen on casual sex as men, but only when society isn't judging or there's no risk of harm involved.[27]

All things considered, males and females aren't born with different brains, and they only differ slightly, on average, in their thinking. This doesn't mean that we should pretend that there are no sex differences at all or that we can't talk about things such as men's violence against women, or higher rates of suicide or substance abuse among males. But rather than blaming it all on a hardwired brain or a hormone that we have little control over, we should ask what social and structural factors are allowing or even encouraging such behaviour. Just because fewer women than men choose to pursue science careers, and especially so in more egalitarian countries, doesn't mean they're less interested or capable, but perhaps rather that many scientific establishments are male-dominated and even sexist – putting women off from the get-go.[28]

It doesn't seem surprising that a patriarchal society that celebrates extreme masculinity and even violence (under the 'right' circumstances, like a hero killing off baddies) would produce a world in which many men get away with some pretty horrific acts. Others, meanwhile, are pushed towards substance abuse or suicide, perhaps because they can't live up to macho expectations and haven't had an opportunity to learn to deal with their emotions. Similarly, the societal pressure on women and girls to be perfect, self-sacrificing and caring – while constantly scrutinising themselves – can make it difficult for them to speak up and refuse to do what's expected from them.

What's more, as we shall see in Chapter 13: 'Do you stereotype people?' (p. 104), being stereotyped in terms of our sex can actually have a negative effect on our achievements. Studies has shown that when researchers remind people of stereotypes such as 'men are bad at being socially sensitive' or 'women are bad leaders', men actually perform worse on tests for decoding non-verbal cues and women are put off leadership roles.[29]

So, what's the solution?

Be aware of the damaging power of stereotypes and social expectations, and realise that gender roles can produce thinking traps. If you are a woman, chances are you've been raised to pay attention to other people's feelings and care what they think – potentially at the expense of your own happiness. You may also think of yourself as less capable to pursue careers in science or policing, and you may end up feeling that you are somehow biologically destined to take on the main responsibility for childcare. Similarly, some men may feel unable to pursue careers such as teaching or nursing, or lack the confidence to ask for parental leave to look after their kids. This is a shame, as men are fully capable of loving and caring for their children. But you need to get an opportunity to practise a skill to become confident at it – and reap the benefits.

The stereotypical choices that many of us make suggest we are hugely influenced by what society thinks – whatever we like to believe. The majority of men aren't systemisers and the majority of women aren't empathisers. So how come women are so extremely overrepresented in care jobs? Why do women do so much more of the childcare than men? And why do nearly 90 per cent of British women taken their men's surnames after marriage, with the opposite being almost unheard of?[30]

If families were purely making rational decisions based on their desires and ability, the science suggests you should expect a slightly more even distribution. Some women would spend more time in the home, and some men would, too. We may be free to make our own decisions, but the fact that there is such disparity suggests society is manipulating us – both in terms of its structure and values. And it is likely that those things impact our thinking much more than our biology.

We all want to be accepted and appreciated, and to do that we live up to what's expected of us. The good news is that the brain is malleable; it can learn new skills relatively easily – no matter what society has taught us so far. But it ultimately takes a bit of courage to stand up against the system and make the best choices for ourselves – and indeed for our loved ones and future generations. Sure, some people may giggle at stay-at-home dads, female naval officers, or families taking a woman's surname. Others may worry that if men and women were too similar, this could 'kill the romance' in a relationship. For what it's worth, they would be wrong.[31] Research shows that people in more egalitarian relationships report greater stability, lower divorce rates and more sexual satisfaction.

But unless we can change social norms by speaking up and putting up with a bit of disapproval, things aren't likely to change and we'll continue to believe and perpetuate the old adage that women and men are from different planets.

8

Are you paying attention?

It sounds like a magic trick. And Petter Johansson, a cognitive scientist at Lund University in Sweden, and his colleagues actually consulted a group of magicians to create the experiment. In fact, it is science based on a simple card trick. This is how it goes: an experimenter briefly holds up two cards with a face on each and asks the study participant to quickly decide which they find more attractive. When the choice is made, the cards are expertly swapped as they are placed on the table face down, without the participant noticing. The experimenter then holds up what appears to be the card the participant chose, when in reality it is the other one, and claims this is the face they selected.

Would you notice such a swap? You probably think you would – you know what you like, right?

But the truth is that a staggering three-quarters of people don't actually spot such a swap.[1] What's more, when study participants are asked to explain why they picked the face they didn't actually choose, many will even start justifying their 'decision'.

The participants' surprising reactions to the switch are genuine. Indeed, the faces in the cards are often quite dissimilar: they may have different hair colour and one may wear glasses while the other doesn't. In one striking example, a male participant was shown two female faces, one with big earrings. He initially picked the face without earrings, but when the cards were switched and he was asked why he made his 'choice', he stated that he really loved the woman's earrings.

This effect, known as choice blindness, doesn't just work for rating the attractiveness of faces – and here's another example. Do you agree with the following statement?

The legal age for criminal responsibility should be lowered.

Again, answering this seems easy enough. But experiments have shown that when people answer questions such as this as part of a wider survey, they are also choice blind. When handed back a doctored version of the questionnaire they just filled in, suggesting they have an opposite view on, for example, the legal age for criminal responsibility, the vast majority don't notice, and start defending the view they've just been fed by someone else.[2] It seems we aren't as aware of our own thought processes as we believe, potentially making many decisions without much conscious deliberation at all. What's even more astounding is that when participants who are fed political views they didn't previously have are invited back to the lab a week later, they will continue to argue for the doctored view.[3] This appears to suggest that most of us don't always think for ourselves – we allow others to do it for us.

Johansson and his team have tried many different versions of the tests, most recently on groups of people. Perhaps two minds are less fallible than one? Sadly not. When pairs got to select a flatmate based on seeing two faces, they were similarly tricked into arguing for the one they had rejected. Johansson is now moving on to problem-solving, asking people to work out how much information you need to solve a certain problem, and then swapping their solution for someone else's. And the initial results, yet to be published, suggest people can be tricked in this way too.

So what's going on? The phenomenon remains something of a mystery, but some clues are starting to emerge. Our first thought was that it could be a consequence of people placing trust in an authority figure – in this case a scientist – and feeling insecure about their own thinking. Or perhaps they do notice the swap, but don't want to embarrass the experimenter and so play along instead. But Johansson's research shows that these explanations don't hold up. In experiments with students, for example, the researchers pretended to be fellow students, explaining to the participants that they didn't really believe in the experimental set up, and that it was dumped on them by an unseen experimenter – the results remained the same. And there is little to suggest people are just pretending to be tricked – by tracking participants' eyes, the researchers noticed a significant pupil dilation in people who did spot a swap. This suggests it was a genuine moment of discovery, which didn't appear in people who failed to detect the manipulation.

Humans' relatively poor visual memory is partly to blame, but it doesn't quite explain how we can be tricked into justifying a view we don't have. The culprit, perhaps, is attention – or our lack of it. Clearly, we don't always pay attention to the choices we make and the views we form, but research has shown that a lack of attention can make us more than choice blind – it can make us quite literally blind. In their book *The Invisible Gorilla*, Christopher Chabris and Daniel Simons describe a jaw-dropping example of this. You may recall having seen this video yourself (or do you?). When people were asked to count the number of basketball passes by a certain team on a screen, about half didn't notice a woman wearing a gorilla costume crossing the court halfway through the video – despite being on-screen for nine whole seconds. The video, which also fooled us when we first saw it, has had over 25 million views on YouTube. And the takeaway is simple: we are good at counting basketball passes if we focus on them, and we are good at spotting a gorilla if we are looking for one – but we can miss just about anything when our attention is elsewhere.

Attention is a hugely important cognitive resource, but it can easily wander or be diverted, as magicians know all too well. The magic wand, for example, doesn't really contain a sorcerer's spells, but it can just as effectively be used to misdirect our attention while a spectacular manipulation happens elsewhere. When we're in control of it, attention helps us to concentrate on specific tasks or bits of information while ignoring others. But when we are overloaded and distracted, we can struggle to pay attention and think rationally and critically as a result. Many people suffer from deficits in attention, and conditions from depression to ADHD can interfere with our ability to focus. But even if we don't have such a condition, attention is a limited resource that is in constant demand. Humans in general are relatively bad at multitasking – just try doing some mental maths while simultaneously playing the piano, for example. But this can become debilitating in a world full of clever technology that is constantly asking for our attention, distracting us by drowning us in message alerts, push notifications, calendar invites and social media updates.

In fact, we all fall victim to focusing our attention on the wrong things. An anxious person, for example, will often be on the lookout for threats in the environment, such as how contaminated the handrails on the Underground might be. This can feed the anxiety and cause us to focus attention even more on such cues, while missing others, such as that guy who is about to pick our pocket. The same applies to addicts who become hyper-vigilant to cues relating to their addiction: the advert showing a refreshing glass of wine, the bleep of a gambling machine. But we're all fallible. With our limited cognitive resources, we don't always take in and think through everything we see, say and do profoundly.

While the role of attention in choice blindness is contentious, it is possible that we fail to notice manipulation and doctored evidence because we don't pay enough attention, or take enough care when making our decisions.[4] We know that when people do detect a manipulation in such studies, it can boost the chances of them detecting further tricks because they then look out for them.[5] This correlation fits with other research showing that people who have higher analytical skills, as measured on a cognitive reflection test, are less likely to be choice blind.[6]

Enthusiasm and expertise can also act as antidotes to this kind of misdirection. Johansson has discovered that people who answer questions about something they know a lot about or have very strong views on are more likely to detect when their results have been warped. The same goes for people who have accurately solved a problem. So, if you lazily subscribe to an opinion without thinking much about it – perhaps it's just what everyone else at work or down the pub believes – then you are more likely to be choice blind when asked about it. 'Knowing what you know and knowing what you think is helpful,' Johansson told us.

But how does all this affect us in everyday life? After all, if someone swapped your partner at the wedding altar, you'd no doubt notice. But while it is unclear exactly how and when we suffer from choice blindness while going about our lives, there are countless scenarios where it could be a problem. An eyewitness picking out a perpetrator from a line-up, for example, may be vulnerable to corrupt police officers misdirecting them or altering the evidence after they have made their choice. And if at a dinner party you are asked about your political view on a specific issue you don't care much for, you may end up defending the view someone else suggests you have, rather than thinking through what you really believe. And the idea that we could be manipulated into having certain views should concern us all.

The lazier we are, then, the less we pay attention and the less likely we are to spot tricks and manipulation. So how can we prevent these mistakes from happening? Of course, we can never fully pay attention to everything, but we can choose to focus on the task at hand and put down our phones while we're doing it. A good night's sleep is vital for being attentive in general, and some findings suggest that mindfulness, meditation and brain training can also help boost focus. Another option is to train your analytical skills, making sure you think slowly and resist going with quick, intuitive answers where rationality matters.[7] This will make you more vigilant and could mitigate against some of the traps set out in this chapter. And keep in mind that curiosity and knowledge are helpful. You can fake your way into sounding clever by imitating the views of smart people, but ultimately thinking deeply and openly about the world for yourself seems to confer an advantage when it comes to this sort of manipulation.

So next time someone asks you to make a snap decision, take a breath and have a proper look, ensuring you're giving it your full attention. But while attention might be one reason for failing this test, there could be another. Perhaps you just didn't want to change your mind – something we explore in the next chapter.

9

Can you change your mind?

'Hence the ways of men part: if you wish to strive for peace of soul and pleasure, then believe; if you wish to be a devotee of truth, then inquire.'

So wrote the then twenty-year-old German philosopher Friedrich Nietzsche in an 1865 letter to his sister, Elisabeth, explaining why he had given up on religion, despite having studied to become a Lutheran minister.[1] It was the first of a series of U-turns – not to mention outbursts, fall-outs and psychiatric problems. But it is unlikely that Nietzsche would have come up with his radical and influential theories without these dramatic changes of heart and mind.

Embarking on a career as a philosopher, he soon discovered the ideas of Arthur Schopenhauer, whose work he adoringly described as 'dynamic, dismal genius'.[2] He essentially became Schopenhauer's disciple.[3] But it wasn't long before he started to change his mind again. Schopenhauer had a rather gloomy view of the human condition, believing we are all doomed to a life of misery as the world can never fulfil our greedy desires – promoting Buddhism-inspired asceticism and a rejection of the self as the best ways to cope. Nietzsche, however, came to dismiss this view, proposing instead that we should embrace and, crucially, *overcome* suffering in order to create meaning through life-affirming action.

Nietzsche continued to change his mind on many topics, including the quest for 'truth' itself that had originally attracted him to philosophy (declaring that there was no such thing as objective reality or 'truth' at all). This was a radical view at the time; it surely would have been simpler for Nietzsche to stick with the beliefs he'd initially had.

While it may seem that history is full of assertive and consistent thinkers and actors, many profound theories, discoveries and even political events have involved radical shifts in thinking. Mahatma Gandhi, for example, was once a supporter of the British empire.[4] Encountering racism in South Africa and elsewhere led him to question his belief – a shift that was ultimately instrumental in bringing independence to his native country, India.

But while we are all capable of changing our beliefs, we often hold on to the views we already have and seek out evidence to support them rather than trying to prove them wrong – further entrenching them over time. Even the sharpest, most critical minds can struggle to accept that this applies to them and to reconsider what they know, which can be a major obstacle to improving our thinking.

In his book *Think Again*, psychologist Adam Grant shows how our inability to rethink our views can have huge, real-life consequences. He argues, for example, that the downfall of the once hugely successful communications company BlackBerry was a consequence of its founder's inability to rethink its mission as technology progressed. People didn't just want a secure device to make calls and send emails, they wanted a full-on pocket computer packed with apps and entertainment – and would often be willing to trade in their privacy and security for more access to fun and convenience. The inability to change one's mind can have many consequences, minor or drastic. But when we do take a step back and take the trouble to think again, the benefits are clear. So why don't we do it more often?

There are many reasons why we struggle to change our minds. One is confirmation bias, a common tendency to search for, interpret or even remember information in a way that is consistent with what we already believe. It can be easy to spot in others, such as the former classmate who always posts conspiracy theories from highly dubious sources on social media. But while we may be adept at identifying it in people we disagree with, chances are we'd be less likely to spot confirmation bias in the people who have similar views to ourselves – because of our own confirmation bias.

Confirmation bias runs incredibly deep. Consider the sentence below and verify as quickly as you can whether it is grammatically correct.

'*The internet has made people more sociable.*'

As you probably guessed, the grammar is indeed correct. But a recent study has shown that people take longer to verify sentences like it if they disagree with them.[5] So if you agreed with the statement above, you might take a little longer to evaluate the grammar of the sentence 'The internet has made people more isolated'. The result, which also holds for assessing the grammar of factually incorrect statements, suggests that it simply takes us longer to process information we don't agree with – a sort of involuntary confirmation bias.

Most of us, including scientists, can succumb to confirmation bias without even knowing it – to prove your theory right, after all, you have to gather evidence to support it. And being clever doesn't really seem to protect against it, though an ability to think rationally might.[6] In one study, participants at a US university had to decide whether a dangerous car should be banned. Their 'intelligence' was also measured using a US college admission test (SAT). And it turned out that these people were more willing to ban a risky German car driving in US territory than an equally dangerous American car driving on German streets – with their SAT scores having little impact on their choices.

Confirmation bias even clouds how we perceive information – for example, we often hear what we want to hear – and how we remember past experiences. If we think a politician is stupid, for example, we are more likely to remember the times when they said something incoherent or irrational than when they said something coherent and rational. This also applies to our own decisions. If we choose to remain living in our current location, rather than moving somewhere else, there are likely to be both positive *and* negative outcomes. Perhaps by staying put we get to be near our friends and family, but by not moving we may also forgo our dream job. Thanks to a cognitive bias known as choice-supportive misremembering, however, we tend to focus on the positive aspects of the decision and ignore the negative ones.[7] If we go through life remembering all our decisions in such a favourable light, it is no wonder that we become bad at rethinking our choices and changing our minds.

There are many different reasons why we are this way. One is simply that most people (at least in the West) are biased towards optimism and positive thinking – especially about themselves – as explored elsewhere in this book (Chapter 8: 'Are you an optimist?', page 46). We believe in evidence that chimes with our views because it makes us feel good about ourselves.

Another is that heuristics save us time and energy.[8] They're short-cuts that enable us to make sense of the world quickly and allow us to avoid treating every thought as a hypothesis that we must aim to prove scientifically. And there's often nothing deficient about this. Humans need to survive and thrive in social settings. Sometimes, stability or cooperation are more important than truth. If you are in a new relationship, for example, you may try to work out whether you can trust your partner. And if your hypothesis is that you can trust them, it is likely to be costly for you to set about disproving it – and becoming suspicious and jealous. To simply accept it, and look for signs supporting this belief, even if there's a chance it may be wrong, is therefore quite rational in this particular case. Yet it can be downright dangerous in other areas, such as when it comes to medical treatments. If there's a chance that a procedure may harm us in some way, it makes sense to search for information that allows us to weigh up the pros and cons of having it.

Another factor is our intrinsic need for consistency. When we become aware of inconsistencies in our beliefs, perhaps because someone presents a strong piece of evidence that suggests our views are wrong or outdated, we become incredibly uncomfortable, experiencing what scientists call 'cognitive dissonance'. Rather than using such moments to reach better conclusions, most of us cling even tighter to our initial belief – doubling down on our outdated world view, ignoring the new theory or piece of information and even blaming others for our mistakes. You may have erased it from your memory, but chances are you've been guilty of this yourself, perhaps fuelled by the energy of an audience or a few glasses of Pinot Noir. [9]

Consistency of opinion is also highly valued in many societies, meaning we could be particularly keen to appear consistent when others are watching. Just think of the outrage politicians face when they make policy U-turns. In Chapter 8: 'Are you paying attention?' (page 66) we introduced Petter Johansson, a psychologist, who, in a series of mind-blowing experiments, showed that most people don't notice when scientists swap a choice they've just made for something different – be it claiming they found a certain face attractive, or doctoring their questionnaire to indicate they had a certain political view. When scientists alter questionnaires and hand them back to study participants, people not only fail to notice the swap – suggesting, for example, that they think petrol tax should be raised when they initially said it should be lowered – they also start defending the view they didn't have. And when the same people are invited back to the lab a week later, they are still more likely to defend the doctored view – because they want to appear consistent. As Johansson told us, 'There seems to be an especially strong effect of having heard yourself say it.'

So it seems that if we spend a lot of time lecturing others about what we think, we risk becoming more attached to our views and less likely to rethink them.

Another problem is that many people simply spend a lot of time believing they are right and more knowledgeable than others. Such an attitude will inevitably make us less likely to rethink our opinions. According to a well-researched psychological mechanism called the Dunning-Kruger effect, people with the least knowledge tend to be the most overconfident, although this mainly seems to be the case in the Western world. In four studies, Dunning and Kruger showed that the people who scored among the lowest on tests of grammar, logic and humour were the most confident that they were better than others at those very things.[10] And in another recent study, scientists discovered that people who felt their beliefs on a variety of political issues were superior to others actually had the biggest gap between their beliefs and their actual knowledge, assessed through multiple-choice quizzes.[11]

There are more subtle effects, too. Many people simply don't like change and prefer to stick with what they know – it's just easier. This 'status quo bias' is linked to a fear of regret – explaining why we often hold on to assets that are declining in value, stick with projects that aren't going well or stay in unhappy relationships.[12] Because we've made an investment, we convince ourselves that it is better to keep going and that changing our minds could lead to even worse outcomes. Brain imaging studies have shown that in addition to the hippocampus, the brain's memory centre, the neural circuits involved in fear also activate when we experience regret, which may explain why it is such an unpleasant feeling.[13] That said, regret ultimately helps us to learn from our experiences. If we keep avoiding it, we also lose out.

We don't want to spend our whole lives endlessly changing our minds. But how can we become more open to doing so if better evidence comes to light? Curing confirmation bias hasn't proved easy. That's because we are often motivated to believe in ourselves.

But if we are willing to challenge this approach, there are cognitive methods that can make us better at avoiding some of its consequences. Training programmes, for example, have been designed to reduce confirmation bias through various techniques, such as aiming to falsify, rather than verify, statements.[14] To what extent this transfers to real-world outcomes is unclear. But a thirty-year-old experiment showed that people can indeed overcome confirmation bias if they are prompted to think in a certain way. Participants were asked to review the methodological quality of studies that either supported or challenged their views about the efficacy of the death penalty. As expected, the participants demonstrated confirmation bias in their assessment, even when told to be as objective as possible. But when they were asked to specifically consider whether they would have made the same assessment if 'exactly the same study had produced results on the other side of the issue', the effect disappeared.[15]

Tom Stafford, a psychologist at the University of Sheffield, warns against painting too dark a picture of people's ability to rethink. In a new study, which is yet to be published but replicated the results of a previous one, he and his colleague recruited vaccine sceptics for a ten-minute intervention – short Q&A-style dialogues answering questions such as how scientists establish that vaccines are safe, and whether you can trust the scientists.[16] While the participants didn't change their minds completely, they were more likely to get vaccinated after the intervention – an increase of 16 per cent. Stafford believes it is incredibly important to consider this, not least if you are trying to change someone's mind. 'If you let your image of people who are vaccine hesitant be captured by anti-vaxxers, you might think, "These people are crazy – they are never going to change their minds,"' he explains. 'But people *are* responsive to new information; they don't just throw out their old beliefs completely; they weigh the new and the old.'

We can all help create a better climate for rethinking by realising this. Stafford credits the philosopher Daniel Dennett with a useful way of challenging someone's view as well as your own in a debate: listen carefully to what your opponent says, and then restate their argument in the strongest possible way – one that will make them exclaim, 'That's *exactly* what I mean!' Only when you have that endorsement from your opponent should you offer your critique. 'It forces you to see the strength of the different points of view.'

Ultimately, as demonstrated elsewhere in this book, being flexible, humble and open by actively seeking out information that challenges our views can help protect against many biases. To achieve this, however, we have to challenge our habits: relying on the same old sources of information, having the same experiences and talking to the same people. 'If you listen to people who've changed their minds, they often say, "I thought it was like this but then I met this guy . . ."' says Stafford. 'People have experiences and that's what changes our mind.'

So when you hold opinions that you feel strongly about, such as 'children are best off in a nuclear, heterosexual family' or 'conservatives are greedy', keep an open mind – even if you believe you've seen an abundance of evidence to support your view. An online search or conversations with people you don't normally speak with, for example, will likely reveal plentiful examples of children thriving under different circumstances or Tories with a human heart. It may not be enough to radically change your mind, but you could, at least, learn something new.

When it comes to status quo bias and fear of regret, meanwhile, accept that sticking with your current situation isn't risk free. By staying in a career or relationship that is making us miserable, we may avoid the niggling regret that could come with change, but it won't solve the current problem. Stafford suggests trying a technique called 'distancing'. This involves either thinking about how

79

you'll feel about something in the future or imagining it in a different situation. So while we may not want to change careers because we'd face an immediate period of change, uncertainty and possibly unemployment, how would we feel about staying, or leaving, five years from now? And if you're struggling to get rid of your old boxes of stuff, worrying you'll regret it, ask yourself whether you'd pick it up if you saw it in a charity shop today. We can also try to focus on aspects that will remain unchanged after we have made the decision, and listen to those around us – taking some of the pressure off our decision making.[17]

But perhaps the best way forward is to be more supportive of those who do change their minds as a result of new evidence. This applies to society as a whole but also in relationships between individuals. Just because someone was a vegetarian last year, doesn't mean they still have to be one today. As George Bernard Shaw once wrote, 'Progress is impossible without change, and those who cannot change their minds cannot change anything.'[18]

10
Do you trust your gut?

Magnus Carlsen, the current world chess champion, hasn't always played by the rules. As a LEGO-obsessed four-year-old, he would often deviate from the instructions when building, his father and manager Henrik Carlsen recalls. Magnus had to learn the hard way that if you want to assemble the toy intended by the manufacturer, you have to stick to the specifications. But while he came to appreciate and use this approach, he never stopped experimenting and combining designs in innovative ways. One day, after six hours of intense LEGO-building, Henrik spotted his son lying in bed, staring at the ceiling and still assembling structures in his head. 'At that point, I think I told my wife that maybe he could become a good chess player.'

When Magnus first tried chess, however, his father wasn't impressed – severely underestimating how difficult it is for a young child to master such a complex set of rules. But Magnus kept playing and by the time he was seven or eight, he was hooked. A keen chess player himself, Henrik soon realised that Magnus showed promise, and encouraged him to develop his skills. Magnus wasn't interested in learning in a structured way, however. He used his imagination to create patterns on the chess board that he thought were intriguing, even though it would require one side to be less cautious than the other. He didn't even read chess books in the 'right' order, from front to back. Instead, he would flick through them and read the pages that sparked his interest, one by one, until he had covered the entire book in his own way.

By the age of thirteen, Magnus was a chess grandmaster, winning the Norwegian Chess Championship two years later and dropping out of high school to keep up with the tournaments. Today, he is one of the best players of all time, holding a series of records and top ratings. But he is different from many other chess players. Often described as the 'Mozart of Chess', Magnus has raw talent and impressive intuition. Sometimes he just feels that a certain move is right, without exactly knowing why. Chess players often do this, but they are also very good at calculating what will happen in a game. Henrik, however, believes Magnus relies less on such computing than many of his opponents. He recalls a post-match conversation between the then seventeen-year-old Magnus and a grandmaster twice his age who explained all the variations he had seen and calculated during the game, leaving Magnus gobsmacked – he hadn't thought about these things at all. While Magnus today has deep knowledge and experience, he still relies substantially on his intuition when he plays chess. According to Henrik, it is when Magnus overthinks a situation or engages too much in long, complex calculations that things can go wrong.

But how can intuition be of any use in a game that is mainly about computation? After all, if you can accurately calculate all the possible moves of a game of chess, you will win it – that's why computers are unbeatable. While the human brain is remarkable, it does have limited processing capacity and must also ensure it works as efficiently as possible, so it doesn't use up unnecessarily large amounts of valuable energy. Consequently, it simply cannot accurately perform that many calculations – it must instead rely on shortcuts known as gut feelings, or intuition. This is a type of automatic, rapid mental processing that we aren't aware is taking place. It's that hunch you get to turn left to get back to the main road when you are lost in the woods with no phone reception. Or that feeling that a first date just isn't going the right way and you'd better make your excuses and leave. It can help us instantly realise which bits of information to disregard when making decisions. While we typically can't explain gut feelings, they aren't supernatural. In reality, intuition simply draws on past experiences and observations that we aren't paying close attention to in the moment, such as which way the sunlight falls in the forest or a pattern of behaviour we have spotted in earlier personal encounters.

Intuition has a sketchy reputation in science. It is often portrayed as the flawed and irrational enemy of logic. And as we will discover in further chapters, it can give rise to astonishingly faulty decisions and prejudiced views. But does that mean we should always keep intuitive thinking in check? And is it really the opposite of analytical and rational thinking? Gerd Gigerenzer, a director emeritus of the Centre for Adaptive Behaviour and Cognition at the Max Planck Centre for Human Development in Berlin, told us he believes there is a 'war on intuition' in the behavioural sciences. But he argues that intuition and the mental shortcuts it involves aren't irrational. Instead, they are a form of intelligence that is necessary to make sense of an uncertain and changing world, in which logic and probability theory aren't always suitable.[1]

We often believe that complex statistical and mathematical models always produce superior results to flawed human quick thinking. In 2009, for example, engineers created an algorithm – Google Flu Trends – that used 50 million queries that people had put into the Google search engine to predict the number of flu-related doctor visits across the US. It often worked well, but the unpredictable complexities of the real world also made it fallible. For example, the AI model failed to predict the 2009 swine flu pandemic. It was then updated to become even more complex, but still overestimated doctor visits nearly every week between 2011 and 2013, in some cases by more than 50 per cent.

So, would a more intuitive model that relied more on shortcuts – making predictions based on very few, simple data points – than on the mathematical crunching of vast amounts of data prove more effective? A common human bias is that we judge situations based on the most recent available information, disregarding much of what came earlier. This can lead to problems. But in a 2021 study, Gigerenzer showed that relying on this simple rule of thumb – using only how many people saw their GP *last* week to predict flu rates *this* week – was more reliable than Google's big data algorithm.[2] As we explore in Chapter 11: 'Are you good with numbers?' (page 88), intuition can often mislead us when we are dealing with (even simple) numeracy or statistics. Uncertain and rapidly changing situations, where it is hard to apply strict rules, can be an exception though, sometimes benefiting from simpler, more intuitive ways of thinking than lengthy and complex statistical analysis.[3]

Gigerenzer isn't alone in thinking this. In 2015, American researchers showed that analytical and intuitive ways of thinking don't seem to exist at opposite ends of a spectrum, so that we always use either one or the other.[4] Instead, we could well apply them at the same time. So even when you are certain that you are thinking completely rationally, intuitive processes may be going on without you noticing. This suggests that the idea that intuition is the opposite of logic is a myth. A lot of intuitive knowledge, say putting on a tie or doing your shoelaces, starts with analytical thinking. We actively learn how to do it at some point, but over time it becomes automatic, intuitive, and it is often hard to explain the process. Intuition helps the brain save cognitive resources for hard, new decisions, rather than wasting it on the mundane.

Intuition is often believed to be involved in creative invention. This makes sense intuitively, and some research supports the idea. In science, for example, many hypotheses start from intuitive hunches, which are then developed and tested analytically using the scientific method.[5] Even Einstein reportedly once told a friend that all great achievements of science must start from intuitive knowledge. But how do we know that a purely analytical approach wouldn't produce even better results? Research reviewing previous studies on creativity and intuition in professionals, ranging from top chefs and film producers to Nobel Prize-winning scientists, suggests that intuition is primarily at work when ideas are generated.[6] A chef looking to create a new dish, for example, clearly can't test everything logically. But because of their experience, they have strong intuition about what may work, which helps them choose ingredients that will complement each other in a recipe. According to this view, a world-changing idea can't be logically derived, because it is so new – it starts with a gut feeling or sudden thought. The creator then combines separate bits of gradually acquired information and uses associations to form a coherent idea of what's going on. To evaluate whether their idea is any good, they again use their expert intuition, often alongside analytic, rigorous testing. So intuition isn't necessarily dumb. Clearly, you can't accuse a scientist who has just discovered an entirely new way of looking at the world of not thinking clearly, just because gut feelings were involved.

This doesn't mean that relying on gut feelings is always a good idea. Intuition is an evolutionarily old process, which enabled our ancestors to make rapid decisions in high-stakes situations – such as deciding whether a new person is a friend or foe. That is also why it is packed full of prejudice and bias; themes this book will explore further. So, when is it safe to trust your gut feelings and when is it better to cross-check them with rational thinking? And at what point can you use intuition to think more creatively?

If there's a chance that a damaging cognitive bias could be at play when you have a strong gut feeling, it may be worth questioning your intuition.[7] For example, you may have a strong intuition that an argument is wrong because it disagrees with your worldview. If you dismiss it without considering why it is a bad argument and what its consequences are, you aren't really thinking well or learning anything. Chances are you are simply falling prey to good, old-fashioned confirmation bias. So, if you are aware that you have a vested interest in an area when you get a hunch, it makes sense to be wary of it. Similarly, if you know you are hugely overconfident, for example, and you are trying to work out how much to study for an exam, your gut feelings may suggest you don't need to do much revising when you in fact do. Likewise, relying on a gut feeling that suggests that people who are different from us are threatening reveals our prejudice more than anything else. In fact, when it comes to hunches about people in general, always ask what's at stake if your intuition is wrong. Other areas in which intuition can lead us astray include numeracy and statistics, such as figures expressing risk.

Our intuitions generally tend to be better in areas where we have lots of experience. If you are a GP and spend all your time listening to what symptoms people are experiencing, you will have a good intuition for when something isn't right, based on small cues that you aren't always conscious of. And as Magnus discovered, when you have played thousands of chess games, you have a lot of experience to draw on. According to Gigerenzer, over 50 per cent of the decisions made by top executives are ultimately based on gut feelings, informed by years of experience.

So do go ahead and trust your intuition at times – but be wise about when and how. Gut feelings relating to your professional life or your favourite hobby, for example, could be hugely helpful. If you've played lots of football games, you are likely to have strong gut feelings about when you should try to score a goal and when it is better to pass the ball to a teammate. And if you are interested in fashion, you would probably be wise to trust your intuition when it comes to working out whether a product is authentic. In one study from 2012, research in fact showed that people who have a lot of experience in shopping and buying designer items were 20 per cent better at assessing whether a handbag was counterfeit using their intuition than people who lacked such experience.[8]

But be aware: just because your intuition is sharp in one area doesn't mean it won't be poor in domains where you're less of a pro. Some of us are also better at intuition than others, which can be measured by tests such as the Iowa Gambling Task – in which participants have to use their intuition to establish which decks of cards are more profitable (as the rules are too complicated to easily work out analytically).[9] And research has shown that people who have high emotional intelligence excel at this game.[10] This makes sense – if you are to trust your feelings, you need to be able to perceive them accurately and understand what they are. So if you know you have strong intuitive ability, it is probably relatively safe to trust your gut feelings in certain areas. And if you're not, there is some burgeoning evidence that we could train our emotional intelligence, and thereby our intuition. For example, researchers have created online course modules that, when taken twice a week for three weeks, can improve both emotional intelligence and intuition.[11]

Intuitive knowledge should not be dismissed, but it should be used selectively and cautiously. Ultimately, knowing when to trust your gut will make you a better player – in chess and in life.

11

Are you good with numbers?

The tiny village of Miejsce Odrzańskie in south-west Poland was largely unknown to the world until 2019. That year, it made headlines globally because of a striking 'population anomaly' in the words of the *New York Times*.[1] For over a decade, not a single boy had been born in that village. Does that seem odd to you? According to the village's mayor, there was even 'scientific interest' in the case. Perhaps it was down to genetics? Or maybe the drinking water had been contaminated?

It's not until you start looking at the details more closely that the eyebrow-raising nature of the anomaly begins to wear off. Does the fact that the statement 'no boys born in a decade' could have been phrased as 'twelve girls born in a row' change the way you think about it? Certainly, the odds of getting twelve girls in a row are small. But how unlikely does something have to be before we consider it an anomaly? Mathematically, there are two possible outcomes for each birth, meaning that the probability of having a girl is: ½, or a 50 per cent chance. The odds of having two girls in a row are: $\frac{1}{2} \times \frac{1}{2} = \frac{1}{4}$ (or a 25 per cent chance). Using this method, you can work out that the probability of getting twelve girls in a row is 1/4096. That's roughly a 0.024 per cent chance, or in other words, very unlikely.

But, as statisticians have pointed out, this is, in fact, the wrong way to think about it.[2] Or at least, it just doesn't have enough context.

If we assume there are about 200,000 towns in the world (this is difficult to estimate), that actually means that this 'anomaly' – of twelve girls being born consecutively – should (statistically speaking) have also occurred in nearly fifty, not just one (1/496 × 200,000).

What's more, Miejsce Odrzańskie is tiny, with a population of under 300. Which means that twelve girls in a row becomes much more noticeable than in a larger town, where twelve children may be born in a day, or even an hour, rather than in a decade. Ultimately, small samples can be incredibly misleading – it is only when we have a large enough sample that we will see a roughly equal distribution of boys and girls. Yet we erroneously believe small samples to be representative of larger ones.

We are also drawn to storytelling and biased to think in terms of cause and effect, making it difficult to spot simple statistical coincidences. 'We are hopeless at things which require huge amounts of scrutiny and evaluation, because that is tough,' explains Magda Osman, a psychologist and head of research at the Centre for Science Policy at the University of Cambridge. 'We want to do the fun stuff, such as inferring things, because predicting and explaining what we see can take us beyond what we observe.'

The human brain has evolved to make predictions that help us survive. It is therefore biased to spot patterns, even when there aren't any. 'Bias is a side effect of the way the mind works. If you have a mind that is working with imperfect information and limited time and resources, it is going to take shortcuts,' explains Daniel Kahneman, who won the Nobel Prize in Economics for his work on biases and heuristics. 'The shortcuts are going to be associated with predictable mistakes – that doesn't mean that the mind is flawed.' As Kahneman has shown in his book, *Thinking, Fast and Slow*, when we are faced with problems involving numbers or statistics, we often rely on intuitive reasoning. But this can go badly wrong.

There are obvious and avoidable thinking traps when it comes to numbers. One is known as the 'gambler's fallacy', which is the belief that something that has happened often in the past is less likely to happen in the future.[3] If we are flipping a coin, for example, and we've had heads five times, we believe we have a higher chance of getting tails next time. But in reality, that's not the case – there's always a 50:50 chance that the next throw will be heads. The same goes for a game of roulette, and many others, yet we struggle to accept it. Research has shown that when a certain number has been drawn in a lottery, the amount of cash bet on that same number in the next couple of rounds falls – even though it's statistically still as likely to be drawn as any other number.[4] It is this kind of reasoning that can even lead us to wrongly assume that we are more likely to give birth to a girl next if we've already had three boys.

Thinking errors of this kind can have huge consequences for our behaviour – just ask the citizens of Miejsce Odrzańskie who, according to the town's mayor, were advised to boost the amount of calcium in their diet to try to conceive boys.

Probabilities, for example, often play a key role in how we assess risk. But if a risk is small, we tend to either over-inflate or ignore probability altogether – resulting in a bias dubbed 'neglect of probability'.[5] This can help explain, for example, why many people feel safer driving a car than flying. While both have a relatively low risk of death, flying is statistically safer than driving. But many people nevertheless hugely overestimate the risk of flying, while neglecting the risk of driving. This tends to happen when there's emotion involved, explaining why we irrationally over-inflate the risks of unlikely but terrifying events, such as shark attacks, when, statistically speaking, falling coconuts are far more dangerous to us.[6]

There are many other cognitive biases affecting our ability to deal with numbers, probability and risk. The availability bias, for example, can make us estimate risk, or reward, based on something we've seen recently that's stuck in our minds.[7] If it's breast cancer awareness week, and we've heard lots of stories about people getting cancer, we may perceive the odds of getting cancer as larger than we otherwise would. In fact, after the reality TV star Jade Goody died from cervical cancer in 2009, there was a surge in the number of women getting screened for the condition.[8] But sadly, the effect didn't last as people's memory of the tragic event faded. Similarly, if our neighbour was recently in a car crash, we might worry about our loved ones driving. In reality, the actual probabilities of those events happening remain unchanged.

Recent numbers can also inform and 'anchor' our thinking. If you walk into the supermarket and notice the price of a pack of expensive cereal, all the other cereal brands suddenly seem cheap. So if you are trying to sell a product, it makes sense to put it next to a similar, but more expensive, product – creating an anchor in the customer's mind. It is the reason it works well to start with a high price if you are trying to sell something – making all lower offers seem generous. Interestingly, even random numbers that we come across seem to be able to influence subsequent number estimates. If you have to state your age before guessing how many Mentos could fit in a glass, this could influence your guess. In their research, Kahneman and Adam Tversky asked participants to play a game of 'wheel of fortune' before guessing the number of UN countries located in Africa. And it turned out that the people who had obtained a high number in the game guessed a higher proportion of such countries.[9] This finding was repeated when participants were asked to make guesses about a number of other quantities too.

Values and beliefs can also influence our interpretation of numbers. In 2015, a study which surveyed all published cosmological research between 1996 and 2008 showed that the statistical spread of the results were small and inconsistent with what would be expected mathematically – suggesting the cosmologists tended to agree with one another more than they should.[10] This could be down to confirmation bias, in which the researchers interpreted their data according to their prior, shared beliefs.

To avoid falling into intuitive ways of thinking about numbers, we need to become aware of such risks, and challenge our immediate instincts with 'slower', rational thinking. This is hard, and people differ in their ability to do so. One test that tries to capture this skill is the 'cognitive reflection test'. There are many different versions of this, but the first one, developed by Shane Frederick in 2005, involves just three questions. Take a moment to try to answer them.

1. A bat and a ball cost $1.10 in total. The bat costs $1.00 more than the ball. How much does the ball cost?
2. If it takes five machines five minutes to make five widgets, how long would it take 100 machines to make 100 widgets?
3. In a lake, there is a patch of lily pads. Every day, the patch doubles in size. If it takes forty-eight days for the patch to cover the entire lake, how long would it take for the patch to cover half of the lake?

How did you find it? The correct answers are five cents, five minutes and forty-seven days, respectively. But if you think intuitively, you will end up with the incorrect answers of ten cents, one hundred minutes and twenty-four days (though if you're reading this book, chances are you are taking the time to not rely on your brain's shortcuts when it comes to numbers). As Kahneman showed in his book, many people get this wrong, including 50 per cent of students at the universities of Harvard, MIT and Princeton.

Chances are you occasionally make errors of these kinds – we often simply don't have the time or bandwidth to think carefully. And luckily, intuitive thinking can be rather efficient in an area in which we have a lot of expertise. If you are an epidemiologist, for example, you may have quite reliable instincts about the risks of contracting various diseases. But that doesn't mean you can't be tricked in a negotiation when trying to buy a car. Ultimately, it is impossible – and arguably unnecessary – to completely erase intuitive thinking about concepts such as risk. You can't start each day by sitting down and accurately calculating the risks of everything that might happen to you over a day. Shortcuts are often useful, and computation and mathematical models aren't always foolproof.

Is it even worth, then, trying to boost your cognitive reflection ability and knowledge of statistics? According to Osman, there are perks to slowing down your thinking when it comes to numbers, but what matters more than proficiency is confidence. Having an insecurity about numeracy can make us feel unempowered and unable to ask tough questions of whoever is presenting numbers to us, be it a doctor or a politician. Making an effort to scrutinise numbers, and slow down our thinking when we're making tough decisions, can therefore be worthwhile – even if we continue to make mistakes from time to time.

Take medical decisions, for example. If we are told that we are at 'low risk' of developing a certain condition, it makes sense to question what low really means. Is it 1 in 100,000 or 1 in 100? And if we are told that our risk of a rare condition will increase by 100 per cent if we have a certain medical procedure, we might, understandably, be alarmed. But that's just what's called a 'relative risk', and it doesn't tell the whole story. If the 'absolute risk' of the condition before the procedure is 1 in 100,000, that means that the risk after the procedure is only 2 in 100,000 – still negligible.

Ultimately, the risks we perceive in life can shape our behaviour and sometimes limit our happiness. So, it may be worth asking ourselves what we base our fear on – and interrogating what the actual odds of them happening are.

An awareness about numbers and the tricks they can play on us can also come in handy as a consumer or negotiator. Rather than falling for 'anchoring' – and judging prices by comparing them to one we've just seen – we can just do a bit of research. In fact, if it's an important purchase, we could set our own anchor based on how much we are prepared to pay – and then compare any offers against it. It can also empower us as consumers, when we are at the mercy of the marketeers that design food labels. We might be told, for example, that a product is '70 per cent fat free', which sounds good. But this also means it contains 30 per cent fat. Is that a big or a small number? There are countless such tricks – a label may highlight that the product contains a lot of healthy omega-3 and vitamins, but when you look carefully at the list and percentages of ingredients you could discover it is also packed with salt. 'Numbers can be a distraction,' explains Osman. 'When you look at the claims made on a label, where market forces are working, don't trust that.'

No matter how number savvy you are, it makes sense to be humble. In fact, being good at maths doesn't guarantee that you'll draw the correct conclusions, particularly if you are tired, dealing with time pressure, or are strongly motivated by certain beliefs. As Kahneman highlights in his book, even researchers make mistakes when it comes to statistics – with psychologists often choosing such small samples of participants for their studies that they run a 50 per cent risk of failing to confirm their hypotheses. Psychologists, argues Kahneman, would therefore be wise to mathematically compute the risk of error for a given sample when designing their studies.

We also weigh risks differently depending on a variety of factors. A given risk may seem lower when you're feeling optimistic than when you are pessimistic, for example.[11] Say you love paragliding. If there's a one in a thousand risk that the carabiner on your harness will open during a flight, causing you to potentially tumble to your death, that may seem negligible. But if you intend to continue flying throughout your lifetime, making up to 1,000 flights or more, those numbers start to look less reassuring.

Ultimately, we are all vulnerable to erroneously spotting patterns, confirming our beliefs and misjudging probabilities. Beliefs and storytelling ultimately activate the emotive parts of our brains, often at the expense of rational thinking, which is yet another obstacle to interpreting numbers. This has been particularly obvious during the pandemic – with people with different values and opinions clashing over the exact same statistics. 'You can't isolate the conditions and the human element of behaving from the numbers themselves,' says Osman. Let's say you are passionate about stopping the rise of synthetic chemicals being released into the environment and have read somewhere that this is affecting global sperm counts. If you then hear that twelve girls have been born in a row in a small village in Poland, it might be tempting to assume this must be down to the chemical environment. But that needn't be the case. As Osman puts it: 'Once we come up with a narrative that can explain a set of numbers, no matter how crazy it is, we're not very good at letting it go, especially if we then start layering it with value systems and beliefs.'

That we struggle to separate numbers from beliefs is understandable when you consider humanity's long tradition of assigning to numerals mystical or supernatural qualities. From numerology in ancient Greece to China and India, numbers, and their combinations, have been linked to words and letters, and taken to represent luck, meaning or even the divine. So when we are making important decisions based on numbers, we ultimately need to challenge our long-lived and deep intuition about them and engage in effortful thinking.

12

Are you a creature of habit?

Take a moment to consider these statements:

1. *I find comfort in regularity.*
2. *Whenever I go into the kitchen, I typically look in the fridge.*
3. *I always try to get the same seat in places such as on the bus, in the cinema or in church.*
4. *I generally eat the same things for breakfast every day.*
5. *I often find myself running on 'autopilot', and then wonder why I ended up in a particular place or doing something that I did not intend to do.*

These statements – which you may find yourself relating to on some level – are taken from a twenty-seven-item questionnaire dubbed the Creature of Habit Scale, which is designed to measure individual differences in our reliance on habits.[1] The more you agree with these statements, the more you are likely to be a creature of habit.

The test was developed a few years ago by Karen Ersche, a professor of neuroscience at the University of Cambridge, and her colleagues. It measures two different aspects of habit: routine – a preference for regularity – and automatic behaviour – the things we do seemingly on autopilot, such as mindless eating in front of the TV.

Routine is essentially a repetition of actions that we find rewarding, such as washing our face in the evening, flossing, placing our pants on top of our other neatly folded clothes and finally flopping into the right-hand side of the double bed, in that particular order.

Automatic actions are typically triggered by the environment: when you enter your kitchen, for example, you may unthinkingly open the fridge and gaze longingly into it. Similarly, if you are driving to a shop and it happens to be en route to your office, you may miss your turn because you automatically continue to your workplace.

'What characterises habits is that they're not deliberate,' explains Ersche. 'You may start going to the gym deliberately. But when you develop a habit, you do this automatically – at a certain time of day, you feel compelled to go.' New research shows that you don't need an overall goal or strategy to develop a certain habit or routine.[2] Instead, they typically arise naturally because we tend to repeat things which have been rewarding in the past – be it having a certain cereal for breakfast or going for a morning run to clear our heads.

Everyone has habits. Take the artist Francis Bacon, for example, who was famous for his late-night carousing, chaotic personal life and workplace pandemonium. Even he had routines, kicking off each day with a cup of tea and some work – before starting the boozing around lunchtime.[3] But some people are less prone to habits than others, typically craving more novelty and variation in life. In her neuroscientific work, Ersche has discovered that people who are keen on habits also tend to be comfortable with multitasking – when they do something a few times, they immediately go on autopilot so they don't have to actively think about what they're doing. 'I count myself as a creature of habit,' explains Ersche. 'When I go to the gym, I have my preferred locker. I get up at the same time every day, like the same things for breakfast, and I have my preferred seat at the dinner table.'

Routine may sound like a major obstacle to thinking well – turning us into robots rather than free thinkers. But that's not necessarily the case. Routine and habit have ultimately evolved to free up the brain's processing power and save it for novel and challenging tasks or decisions – falling back on automatic, habitual behaviour in mundane, predictable and repetitive situations. You can even see this on a brain scan. When we actively make decisions, weighing pros and cons or exerting willpower, the prefrontal cortex of the brain, which is involved in complex cognitive tasks, activates. But when people instead make habitual choices, activation happens mainly in the back of the brain,[4] in areas that are more to do with automaticity – relieving the prefrontal cortex of work.

And this makes sense. If you're dealing with a taxing work crisis, you may want to focus on that rather than spending half an hour trying to figure out what you want for lunch and where to get it. Instead, you can just go to the same old sandwich shop across the road and order the 'usual'. 'It's very efficient; efficient people are often creatures of habit,' Ersche states.

Relying on habit can also help reduce anxiety, as it diminishes uncertainty and makes life more predictable. It can also be useful for people who have cognitive problems, such as dementia. Ersche believes this may be why people tend to become more prone to habits with age – it reduces the pressure on the prefrontal cortex, which is vulnerable to shrinkage as we age.[5]

But there are also downsides to being a creature of habit. If we go about our lives on autopilot, we may not think very much at all. In fact, this can happen when we're extremely stressed, precisely because we prefer to act rather than think. It can also lead to a lack of creativity. 'You can't think outside the box if you keep repeating what you're doing,' says Ersche. There is also a risk that you become stuck in your thinking or a prisoner of echo chambers – if you always rely on the same old sources of news, have the same experiences and talk to the same people, it is hard to be open and flexible.

As Ersche has shown in recent research with hundreds of German study participants, creatures of habit tend to be worse at managing their emotions and behaviour (self-regulating) across a wide range of, often uncertain, situations.[6] They are also more prone to becoming compulsive and rigid – and unable to resist doing things a certain way. 'Habits are good and beneficial as long as you can adjust when they become inappropriate,' explains Ersche. 'If you don't adjust, if you overdo things and you don't stop, then it's not functional anymore, it becomes compulsive.' Autistic people or those living with obsessive compulsive disorder (OCD) are particularly vulnerable to getting 'stuck' in a habit. In the latter, the brain is essentially hijacked by an urge to do things a certain way, be it turning off the lights in a certain order, or washing your hands for a specific amount of time. Habits are also at the heart of addiction, with certain cues in the environment creating irresistible cravings for the substance.

When you first read the statements at the start of this chapter, on the other hand, you may have found that they didn't feel particularly familiar to you at all. If that is the case, then you probably aren't prone to habits – but instead crave novelty and variation. For such individuals, taking a different route to work each day may feel energising rather than cognitively draining. People who are low on the Creature of Habit Scale tend to be younger, slightly less anxious and potentially score highly on the personality trait 'openness to experience'.[7] These people simply get bored with too much repetition. And that can be a good thing, making you more flexible and less prejudiced. You are also more likely to be creative, open to different perspectives and willing to rethink what you know. But it can come at a cost. 'If you like to change all the time, there's more uncertainty,' says Ersche. 'So you are more exposed to positive and negative outcomes that you haven't predicted.' If you are clever and good at dealing with uncertainty and negative experiences, you can reap a lot of benefits from seeking variation in life. But if you are suffering from cognitive decline or struggle with uncertainty, it can be counterproductive.

That being said, the feeling of craving constant change can also become a habit in itself – a mindless avoidance of repetition that, ironically, becomes repetitive. This can get in the way of becoming skilled at something; for example, anyone who can play a musical instrument properly knows how much repetition it requires to get to that point, but if you're the type of person who jumps from one experience to the next, then you may never fully develop a specific skill. It can also prevent us from being conscientious and detail-oriented – perhaps occasionally skipping steps in a process or leaving a job half done – qualities that can ultimately help us to slow down our thinking and prevent us jumping to conclusions. Being a creature of non-habit could even get in the way of forming deep, lifelong friendships. If we are constantly looking for new people to socialise with this could come at the expense of nurturing and deepening the relationships we already have. Extreme novelty seekers can sometimes also be impulsive, which is common in conditions such as ADHD. This may result in us making rapid and haphazard life changes without any trace of logic or motivation – at least to an outsider – behind them. 'If you are impulsive, you change unpredictably,' asserts Ersche. 'You don't stick with a thought and that is a negative thing – you don't think things through until the end.'

Luckily, it is possible to create or break habits. But to do that, it's important to understand what fuels them in the first place. As described in *The Power of Habit* by Charles Duhigg, some of our understanding of the mechanics of habit relies on research carried out by Wolfram Schultz, also a professor of neuroscience at the University of Cambridge.[8] He once worked with a macaque named Julio, who had a tiny electrode inserted into his brain. Julio sat in front of a computer screen, and whenever a colourful shape popped up, he could receive a drop of blackberry juice – if he pulled a lever. It didn't take him long to realise this, and each time he got his juice, a spike in his recorded brain activity suggested he was experiencing a reward.

After a while, the behaviour started becoming habitual: a cue (colourful shape) resulted in a routine (pulling a lever), which led to a reward (juice/happiness). This is exactly what happens when we see our cycling gear (cue) and go for a ride (routine) to feel good afterwards (reward). But once Julio's behaviour had become habitual, the reward signal mysteriously shifted – coming straight after he saw the cue and before he had even pulled the lever. The pure anticipation of the juice became rewarding itself. At this point, Shultz started interfering with the set-up, occasionally withholding the juice once Julio pulled the lever – which understandably made the macaque feel a bit disappointed. The cue had created a craving in his mind, and a compulsion to receive the reward. As Duhigg shows, it's similar to how we feel when we hear the ping of an incoming email – craving the distraction and entertainment we could get from opening it.

This is exactly how a habit is formed: cue, routine and reward interact to create a craving. And it is only when the craving emerges that we develop an automatic behaviour – habit – to achieve the reward. If there's a bag of crisps on your coffee table, you will crave it and eat it. To stop a bad habit, you either need to remove the cue or create a different routine that can also create a reward. This can be as simple as banning chocolate biscuits from your home, or changing your environment at a time when the craving usually starts. Schultz explains that, 'Habits are triggered by external stimuli. If you eat lots of cookies at your desk, go to another office or another desk.' This is why we often easily break habits when we go on holiday – the novel environment may distract us from the habitual cravings we have at home.

Of course, if the cravings are so strong that they have become an addiction, simply changing the environment or removing the substance might not work. If you wish to smoke less weed (routine), and you realise you typically do it whenever you feel sad (cue), a better option may be to change your routine, such as talking to a friend instead. As Duhigg shows, this element of changing routine is part of what has made AA so successful, designating a sponsor for each participant to confide in instead of using a substance.

To create a new habit, such as going for a vigorous stroll each evening, perhaps set an alarm or place your hiking shoes where you can see them. Over time, these cues may make you feel compelled to go. And to make it extra rewarding, take a good friend with you, record and chart the number of steps you've managed, or treat yourself to something you love afterwards.

This may all seem straightforward, but a deeper question remains. What is the right amount of routine? According to Ersche, 'a balance' of habitual and novelty-seeking behaviour is good, 'but you can't negate your nature'. So, while we can all try to overcome bad habits or create helpful routines, our success will ultimately depend on our personality. For some sporty people, waking up next to their folded running gear will trigger a desire to go to the gym. But for others, it simply won't, leaving them having to rely on sheer willpower instead. One approach isn't necessarily better than the other. In the pandemic, for example, most of us experienced a total disruption of our normal routines and struggled with a lot of uncertainty. Some responded to this by creating new habits – such as tuning in to Joe Wicks's daily exercise routine, hosting a family Zoom quiz on Saturday nights or endlessly improving – and sharing online – their sourdough bread recipe. But others didn't need to, they just decided what to do one day at a time, using deliberation rather than automaticity to ensure they got enough exercise or social support.

Knowing yourself, then, is a good place to start, and one easy way to learn more about yourself is simply by taking the Creature of Habit test. If you are a creature of habit, you can use that to your advantage – creating helpful habits that save cognitive power for when you really need it. But you might also want to consider breaking habits that push you too far into autopilot mode, or trap you in an echo chamber. Finding the right balance can help you make the most of your cognitive power, having habits that encourage a healthy lifestyle and efficient day-to-day activities while enabling you to be open-minded and retain energy for the big decisions.

If you're a novelty seeker, you can exploit that quality instead to find the best balance for your brain. If you struggle with uncertainty or negative experiences, for example, deliberately creating a bit of routine may be helpful for your mental well-being – which in turn helps prevent negative thinking biases. And if you crave change to such an extent that you are bordering on being impulsive, you may want to identify a few areas of your life that are actually worth repeating for maximum gain in the long term – be it learning new guitar riffs, staying in a career for a while longer or speaking more of that second language you half know.

Schultz believes it is important to challenge habits from time to time, especially when it comes to the information we rely on and the social experiences we seek out, as these can ultimately lock us into echo chambers. A certain amount of change is ultimately necessary for us to learn and rethink what we know and be more open-minded – if you always go to the same restaurant, pub or nightclub, you'll never discover the much better one two streets down. We can all strive to make sure that our lives involve both a bit of routine but also enough random exploration to help us keep learning, whether it's meeting new people or discovering music we didn't know we'd like. The benefits are countless. Even if you're not interested in broadening your mind, a bit of risk-taking could help you discover an even more rewarding morning routine or a more efficient way of doing something. 'It sounds ironic, but make it a habit to change your habit occasionally,' argues Schultz.

13

Do you stereotype people?

Imagine you have a new neighbour moving in across the street. As they arrive, you strain to discern any details about who this new-comer is. Perhaps they're a middle-aged white woman, a young Black man, an Asian couple in their seventies. Perhaps the new arrivals are wearing suits and silk ties, a tracksuit, fake eyelashes, a sari or a hijab. Maybe they have an accent. Maybe they're unloading their well-worn heavy metal record collection, or clutching a copy of a scientific journal, the Bible or *The Anarchist Handbook*. This initial, fleeting glimpse of the new arrival doesn't offer you much to go on. In fact, it tells you nothing about *who* a person is. But depending on who they *appear* to be – and indeed, who *you* are – you will likely form a powerful first impression, based on nothing more than these sparse characteristics, which will significantly impact how you think about them and often how they feel around you.

This is stereotyping – and our world is rife with it. For while stereotypes may allow us to make snap judgements about people and things in the absence of more detailed information, they are often informed by ugly, lazy and entrenched biases that disadvantage certain groups more than others – particularly ethnic minorities and women. The fact that these shortcuts are so established in society makes them hard to undo. But there is a multitude of data and research to demonstrate where these stereotypes are at work, how they can manipulate our thinking (often in negative ways), and how we can identify and address them in ourselves.

Research shows that police, for example, view Black children as older and less innocent than white children.[1] Meanwhile, several studies show that UK and US employers are less likely to call people with names that are not typically considered 'Western' to job interviews than peers with 'white-sounding' names, even if they have identical CVs.[2] Many people would also rather take fashion advice from a gay man than a straight one – the very premise of the hit TV series *Queer Eye*. And some don't trust female scientists or politicians, while others feel uneasy when they see people in Islamic dress on an aeroplane.

It is obvious that stereotyping limits our ability to think clearly – hindering us from making friends, feeling safe, hiring the best person for the job or electing the most competent leaders. This is especially true when we are driven by fear, which can paralyse our minds and prevent us from thinking self-critically.

It isn't just stereotyping that can infiltrate our thinking, though. *Being* stereotyped can have a huge effect on both thinking and performance, too. If you belong to a social group that is often stereotyped in a certain way, this can create high levels of stress in certain situations.

Social psychologists Claude Steele from Stanford University and Joshua Aronson at New York University first discovered the phenomenon, dubbed 'stereotype threat', back in the 1990s. In their seminal study, they showed that Black people performed worse than white participants on verbal ability tests when they were told that the test was 'diagnostic' of intellectual ability.[3] The effect, however, disappeared when that description was excluded. Clearly, the Black participants felt threatened and stressed by a stereotype suggesting they were somehow intellectually inferior.

A large number of studies over the past few decades have found similar effects. For example, when Asian women are reminded of the stereotype that men are better than women at maths, they underperform on math tests.[4] But when they are instead reminded of the stereotype that Asians are better than Caucasians at maths, they do better. Same test, different stereotype, different result. Meanwhile, disabled people suffer from stereotype threat when they are informed that able-bodied people are going to score their test. Older people do worse on timed categorisation tasks when they are reminded that memory declines with age.[5]

It isn't just minority groups that suffer, though it seems self-evident that these groups experience stereotype threat more often – perhaps even constantly. When men are told that a task that involves decoding facial cues is a measure of social sensitivity, which they are stereotypically bad at, they do worse than when they aren't told so.[6] And as Steele explains, if you are a white person in a predominately Black classroom, you may feel stereotype threat when debating issues such as slavery or racism – thinking others may associate your social identity with being racist.

The effect isn't limited to cognitive tests. Researchers have even showed that players in the English national football team may suffer from a stereotype that they can't win a game on penalty shootouts.[7] Interestingly, this may have been at play in the final of the Euros 2021, when England lost in the final against Italy on penalties. But there may have been a racial stereotype at play, too – three Black players missed their penalties while the white players did not. Sadly, it wasn't long before racist abuse against them erupted, a possibility that the players were likely acutely aware of, having experienced similar mistreatment in the past.

When people feel anxious about their identity in this way, it can exhaust their cognitive resources – negatively affecting their performance. Sadly, this can also make them believe in the stereotype even more fiercely, and see their anxiety levels escalate – creating a vicious cycle.

Steele is today working on a book that aims to condense the complex emotions involved in stereotype threat into a single word:

churn. 'If you're in an important situation, but you could be negatively stereotyped, you churn,' he explained in an interview with us.
'That means there's a lot of thought going on. "What should I do? Is
it really true? I don't know if it's true. Maybe it's true. What does that
mean?"' And this paralysing onslaught of rumination can hijack our
thinking entirely.

Steele is no stranger to churn himself, having suffered racist discrimination growing up in an interracial family in the 1950s and
1960s. His mum, a white, educated woman, married his dad, a Black
truck driver, in 1942 – a time when such a union was utterly taboo.
As a result, his mother essentially moved into an entirely Black community. 'There were some interesting circumstances and it brought
race right into your face,' explained Steele. 'You couldn't ignore it.
And so, like a lot of Black people, you talk about race all the time
because you're dealing with it all.' One of those experiences was
churn. Steele believes churn may have even influenced his choice of
education, putting him off a career in the hard sciences. 'I enjoyed
math, and physics is kind of cool, but you don't have the bandwidth
for that when you've got all this churn going on,' he told us. 'You're
constantly trying to sort through the churn. So I've made the churn
my life's work.'

Studying psychology didn't make the churn go away, though.
When he started the social psychology graduate programme
at Ohio State University in the late 1960s, he was the only Black
American there. This was also a time when several researchers
were still arguing that African Americans had genetically inferior
IQs views that have since widely been discredited both inside and
outside the academic community. But the myth lives on in the form
of stereotyping, in the form of insecurities, in the form of churn.
Even though Steele has had a distinguished career, he still churns
all the time.

* * *

The research on stereotype threat is politically charged, as it challenges the myth that there are equal opportunities in society. As a result, it has had a lot of scientific scrutiny, and some have accused the field of suffering from various biases of its own. For example, it has been argued that studies that do find a significant stereotype threat effect are more likely to be published than the ones that don't. Critics have also highlighted that some studies have failed to be replicated by other researchers, a common problem in the field of psychology. And it's easy to see why. Humans aren't perfect lab specimens; our thoughts and feelings differ across cultures and even situations. As you can't put millions of people into one single lab experiment, it is understandable that results differ slightly across different studies. The more studies you have, though, the more reliable your findings will be.

Nevertheless, recent analyses looking at many different pieces of research suggest that the effect of stereotype threat on performance is indeed real, although the exact size of it is harder to determine.[8] The assumptions you make in a study matter, too. As Julie Norem, a psychologist at Wellesley College, says, 'I think some of the failures to replicate [the studies] are failures to understand the specifics of the process. [Stereotype threat] isn't always out there for everybody, and some of the research that has failed to replicate it has sort of assumed that. The research that finds reliable effects is specifically focused on people who value an aspect of their identity and that aspect of their identity is under threat.'

Given the hundreds of studies that have been published on stereotype threat, we should be confident it exists. So how do you actually tackle it?

One approach is simply to challenge stereotypes; consciously try to highlight a diverse set of role models when possible and make an effort to fight your own biases (although this can be tricky as we may be unaware that we even have them). Researchers have developed things like implicit bias association tests and implicit bias training, which aim to measure and, in the latter case, reduce unconscious racist, sexist or homophobic attitudes. The trouble with these, however, is that they aren't that reliable when you just take them on a one-off occasion. It is possible to be biased in favour of white people one day, and in favour of Black people another day, perhaps depending on recent social interactions. As for the training, researchers haven't been able to show that it can directly improve people's behaviour, making them less racist or sexist in a certain aspect of their everyday lives. But perhaps a one-off training session isn't going to overturn a lifetime of behavioural and thinking patterns. That doesn't mean it wouldn't help if we did it over longer periods of time.

A more serious problem is that many people don't want to do unconscious bias training – they don't want to admit that they are prejudiced – but end up being forced into it by their employer. This may, perhaps ironically, create churn about being a bad person, making them defensive. In fact, Steele believes this churn on both sides is one of the reasons that Western societies are so polarised at the moment. Black people and other ethnic minorities who have suffered churn their whole lives, and are perhaps better at dealing with it, are rising up and asking for equality. When white people, who may not have suffered churn to the same degree historically, react defensively to this it can paralyse debates, such as about the past. If you are called out for defending a subtly racist view or action, you may be more outraged about people being 'snowflakes' or how the accusation affects freedom of speech than by the existence of racism in society. That doesn't mean that freedom of speech isn't important, it just means that we can over-focus our attention on things like it because we struggle with churn. Clearly, this can get in the way of moving on to a more constructive engagement with the future.

Ultimately, it is extremely difficult to undo stereotypes. They are basically summaries and shortcuts – rooted and long-learned, established neural circuits in the brain,' Steele told us. But having an awareness about our own thinking biases isn't useless, it can make us humbler and more open to new perspectives. If you've ever kicked an addiction, made a decision to become a morning person (or a night owl), taken up mindfulness practices, or decided to learn an instrument or new hobby, you have rewired your brain. This flexibility, openness and willingness to learn means that it is likely that you should also be able to reduce your prejudices. But it isn't quick or easy. Surrounding yourself with a diverse set of people can also help, with several studies showing that people who live in diverse areas are less likely to be prejudiced.[9] Indeed, mixing between different groups, be it by ethnicity, sexuality or degree of disability, seems to make people less anxious and more trusting and forgiving.

In the meantime, there are some things we can do to reduce the *impact* of stereotypes – on ourselves and on others. For example, we can interrogate their validity. If you don't find evidence to suggest that men are somehow biologically superior to women when it comes to maths, it is less likely to bother you – even if the stereotype itself lives on. Research also suggests that 'self-affirmation' may be an effective way to tackle negative feelings due to stereotype threat for some people. As David Robson shows in the book *The Expectation Effect*, we can actually boost our performance on a variety of tasks if we take a moment to focus on qualities about ourselves that we are proud of, be it our sense of humour or altruism, and reflect on how these have helped us get by in life.[10] One study found that when women were tested on their spatial skills (a stereotypically male quality) they did substantially better – nearly on a par with men – if they had completed an exercise in self-affirmation first.[11]

But according to Steele, the most promising way forward is building trust, in institutions and relationships alike. When people know and trust each other, what stereotypes they have may not matter so much, he suggests. How do you do that? 'Show up. Listen. Listen again, and then help,' he explained to us. 'If you do that, people will trust you.' This is something he has experienced himself. 'Churn goes away if I'm in a situation where people know a lot about me, even irrelevant things – then they are less likely to use race,' he said, suggesting this was the case, for example, when he chaired a small, close-knit psychology department. 'But if I walked across the hall to the history department where they didn't know me, they might say, "Is that guy an affirmative-action baby or something?"'

Institutions, such as universities, could also do more to boost trust by putting certain systems in place to encourage that trust. For example, when hiring or evaluating staff or students, they could signal that they are using high standards, or even doing blind grading, leaving little room to rely on stereotypes. They could also have clear standards and protocols for how they go about promoting or remunerating staff, and take issues of discrimination seriously. And although it is controversial, there are certain monuments that are hurtful, such as statues of slave traders. If an institution is really serious about building trust with its Black employees, it may want to consider removing such items.

A fair society isn't just a question of socioeconomics or law. Stereotypes aren't only hurtful in an obvious and direct way, they also genuinely hinder people's right to a level playing field by sending them into a state of churn. So the next time you make a snap judgement about a new neighbour, work colleague or person next to you on the bus, consider how this might affect them. Maybe initiate a friendly conversation instead, and listen carefully to what is being said. As Steele put it to us, 'If the problem is churn, the answer is trust.'

14

Are you in love?

The rest is complicated but this is simple: I haven't stopped thinking about you. Nearly two years and it's still you.

Time to move on. Heart and brain are not on the same page. I am going with the brain. Good luck heart!

He left like a hurricane . . . Now I'm alone on this island – a child unmoored.

These are just three of the hundreds of anonymous confessions posted to Lockdown Love Stories, an online project by artist Philippa Found that enabled people to share their romantic highs and lows during the recent pandemic.[1] And they evocatively capture a truth – that love is wonderful, all-consuming, sometimes downright heart-breaking and often utterly baffling. It can build us up and it can break us down. Eventually, we all experience, and fall in and out of, love in our own way. But however its course runs, love certainly can have a major impact on how we think and behave.

Love is a kind of delusion.[2] If we went about selecting our ideal partner on purely rational terms, our search for love would never end – there are just too many possibilities and variables among the billions of people that surround us. And our biology doesn't have time for such analytical thinking – ultimately, it just wants us to get on with the important work of making and nurturing the next generation. So, our brains instead play all sorts of tricks on us to encourage us to believe that we have found 'the one', making us biased, blinkered and, in the eyes of some, completely mad.

This is most evident during the early stages of a romantic relationship when passions run high, love may seem overwhelming and we are sometimes driven to act in some famously silly ways.[3] This often-uncharacteristic behaviour is a big part of the fun, but it can have a serious impact on how we think (or perhaps more accurately, how we simply fail to think at all!), from irrationally believing our partner can do no wrong and letting other important obligations slip in our euphoric fug to becoming needy and jealous for no good reason. Love can make us more energetic, more attentive to our partner and more obsessive.[4] It can also make us more creative. But while many will personally recognise these profound changes in thinking, science also provides some intriguing insights into the social, psychological and biological mechanisms behind them. Some of the underlying changes can even be spotted in brain scans.

In the first months of a new relationship, for example, it is normal to find ourselves thinking obsessively about our new partner. Often, this will be accompanied by a blinding sense of euphoria. The brain chemicals dopamine, oxytocin and vasopressin have all been implicated in triggering this, as well as in helping us to form a close bond with our partner.[5] While evidence exists for oxytocin and vasopressin boosting monogamy in voles – some vole species are considerably more promiscuous than others (yes, that's you, meadow voles)[6] – their contribution to human love is much less certain. Nevertheless, many brain regions associated with romantic attachment are rich in receptors for oxytocin and vasopressin, not least the dopamine reward system, which plays a role in feelings of pleasure – but also in triggering addiction.[7] No wonder, then, that love can often feel addictive, causing us to think obsessively about the object of our romantic fixation.

Which isn't always a pleasant experience. Early-stage love may also drive our thinking in negative directions, leading to anxiety and sometimes depression, with all our thoughts hung up on that special someone. Obviously, those with control issues should seek professional help and there's no justification for any kind of abusive behaviour. But most of us will have experienced the occasional pang of jealousy or the feeling that a new relationship is hogging our thoughts. In fact, research shows that, in the early stages of love, levels of the brain chemical serotonin – associated with mood and appetite – get depleted, and reach similar levels to those in people with obsessive compulsive disorder (OCD).[8] This has even prompted some neuroscientists to suggest we might think of early love 'as a mild serotonin-depletion-related form of obsessive behaviour'.[9] How romantic!

What's more, serotonin levels tend to be inversely correlated with levels of cortisol, the stress hormone, so that a reduction of serotonin may also come with high levels of cortisol. Indeed, research has shown that levels of this stress hormone (which helps prepare the body for fight or flight by increasing blood sugars, suppressing non-essential bodily functions such as digestion and controlling mood and fear) do increase in the first months of a new relationship.[10] This, the researchers argue, is 'suggestive of the "stressful" and arousing conditions associated with the initiation of a social contact'. But while this stress response can make us deeply uncomfortable, it may also serve a more useful purpose, focusing our thinking so that we're vigilant to potential threats to our new relationship. After all, while fear in general gives us some unpleasant jitters and causes us to think obsessively about perceived threats, it can also be adaptive, helping us to safely bypass hazards. In a new relationship, then, it may work to make us more attentive to our new partner's needs, as well as rival suitors.

From a few months to a year into the relationship, however, love tends to evolve – along with the chemical drivers behind it. The dazzling, but often distracting and unsettling, form of early love will be replaced with something that feels far more secure and stable. Which isn't to say that love stops shaping our thinking – and we can continue to appear irrational, as anyone who has ever listened to a loved-up friend knows painfully well.

Brain imaging studies offer some further clues as to why that is, beyond hormones.[11] When we think about or see pictures of a romantic partner, many areas of the brain are activated, including the:

- medial insula (related to survival needs);
- anterior cingulate cortex (involved in attention, reward anticipation and morality);
- hippocampus (involved in memory, potentially explaining why our memories of passionate love are so vivid);
- striatum (involved in cognition and decision-making);
- nucleus accumbens (involved in reward and motivation);
- hypothalamus.[12]

The latter is associated with sexual arousal, which can obviously be distracting if we are trying to make a complex and rational decision – and it has been suggested that its lack of activation in maternal love is one of the key differences between the brain's response to these two different but related forms of affection.[13]

Even more interesting, however, are the areas which seem to be deactivated when we're in love. These include the frontal and prefrontal cortex (involved in planning complex cognitive behaviour, critically assessing people and negative thoughts), parietotemporal junction (involved in information processing and perception) and amygdala (which is involved in emotions such as fear and helps us detect threats).[14] In other words, being in love can likely make us more blind to flaws and red flags. Indeed, while early love may make us anxious, this deactivation of the amygdala may explain why more established relationships can make us less stressed and fearful overall, in turn contributing to better physical and psychological health – so not thinking *entirely* clearly could be beneficial in some ways.

The deactivation of these areas may also make us more positive, less critical when assessing social situations and worse at distinguishing between our self and our partner – meaning our ability to understand the emotions and intentions of others outside of our relationship may suffer. This no doubt influences how we think – and may explain why we are so quick to ignore others' opinions when they're at the expense of our partner. A positive mindset can also make us more gullible in general, leading us to miss potential warning signs in our relationships. The fact that we become worse at distinguishing between ourselves and others also enables that special feeling of 'becoming one' with our partner – the boundary between us and them is literally blurred by the brain. Ultimately, however, these brain changes help us to maintain our relationship, keeping us loved up and keen to have babies – arguably the brain's primary objective – rather than constantly identifying faults in each other.

The neuroscience of love is very far from complete or fully tested – and likely never will be. Love is far too complex to be cracked by an algorithm. But psychology offers further insights into how love impacts our minds, many of which tally with the neuroscientific findings explored so far. It also helps explain why love impacts our thinking processes. Whether in love or not, we are all vulnerable to the 'halo effect'.[15] This cognitive bias means that we give added significance to a positive first impression of someone – or something – which then excessively influences our judgements about their other characteristics. We are liable to expect that attractive people, for example, have other positive traits, such as being likeable and intelligent, whereas less attractive individuals are judged to be more disagreeable and socially awkward – perhaps even before we've even met them.[16] Essentially, we are biased towards believing 'what is beautiful is good', something which may be driven by how society in general interprets and values 'beauty'.

But research shows we are particularly liable to focus on positive illusions, rather than cold hard realities, about our romantic partners, a phenomenon that Viren Swami, a professor of social psychology at Anglia Ruskin University and author of *Attraction Explained*, calls the 'love is blind' bias, which makes us believe that our partner is less fallible and more attractive than an objective observer might think.[17] It may also make us believe that they are more attractive than us and that we are 'punching above our weight'.[18] On the upside, such positive illusions can improve our self-esteem and encourage us to put more effort into nurturing the relationship, potentially leading to better outcomes. One thirteen-year study into 168 newlywed couples, for example, explored the role played by positive illusions in marital relationships.[19] It found that the couples who thought about one another in idealistic ways were both more in love as newlyweds and less likely to see their love decline over time. Another study, meanwhile, found that people are happier in their relationships when both partners idealise each other.[20] So love encourages us to hold positive illusions about our partners, but these illusions, though far from objective, also then serve a purpose in maintaining the relationship.

This doesn't mean we should all go skipping off to forgive our partners for all their faults, and ignore red flags; we should also be wary of thinking about love in too romantic and unrealistic a way.[21] Our notion of romantic relationships has inevitably been shaped by the constellation of love poems, books, films and songs we have consumed from childhood, a mythology amplified by the self-consciously positive posts that so often fill our social media feeds.[22] Unfortunately, someone must also do the ironing and put out the bins. Squaring this circle can be hard – love's own kind of Rubik's Cube.

While having positive illusions about our partners can lead to longer-lasting relationships, they may also lead us to have unrealistic expectations – that can, conversely, lead to disappointment as the relationship matures beyond the honeymoon phase. And on top of that, if we are ignoring warning signs that may be blindingly obvious to everyone else, that doesn't exactly spell marital bliss either. Research has also shown that couples who idealise one another are less likely to use condoms during sex, suggesting you're less likely to think about unfortunate consequences not only when you're in the throes of passion – but also when you believe you're with the perfect partner.[23]

It's not all bad press for love though. In fact, love can change our thinking in other, positive ways, too. There is evidence, for example, that people in love think in a more long-term, holistic way, which may boost creativity and help us secure a happier future.[24] This is the opposite of what happens when people have more casual sexual encounters, which encourages them to be more focused on the present and potentially more analytical. There are, of course, limits to how much love can change the way we think about certain issues. Contrary to popular belief, opposites rarely attract; we tend to enter into romantic relationships with people who share similar values, personalities, interests and demographic backgrounds with us.[25] Consequently, longstanding biases, beliefs and ways of thinking will likely be confirmed. Racists, for example, will often pair up with other racists, while sexists will prefer someone who allows their sexist behaviour and attitudes. So our relationships may play a part in cementing confirmation bias (the tendency to take on and give more weight to new information that confirms what we already believe). But there is, thankfully, plenty of evidence to show that being in love *can* lead to personal growth, expanding and evolving our thinking.

'As an individual, you have your own attitudes and beliefs,' says Swami. 'But when you enter a relationship, the other person brings a set of new attitudes and beliefs and they merge. You become a unit rather than an individual and rather than thinking about your individual beliefs, it's the unit's beliefs and values that become more important.'

Lovers, then, may often be similar, but they can also help broaden one another's horizons. Studies have found, for example, that people who have recently fallen in love show a greater change, and more diversity, in their 'self-concept' – essentially how we think about and perceive ourselves – than those who haven't.[26] To a degree, we become a 'new' version of ourselves, accommodating novel ways of thinking from the one we love.[27] Not that this is always for the best. Unhealthy relationships can impact our thinking in more destructive ways, perhaps leading us to drink more, because our partner does, or become more aggressive or suspicious, because our partner is and our relationship feels insecure or unequal. Critically, while positive illusions can help support healthy relationships, they may also keep us in bad ones. By being aware of these factors, taking a step back and seeking with an open mind the advice of more objective friends and family, we may be better placed to think clearly about when to call time on a relationship.

But even broken relationships – once you've cleared away the tear-streaked tissues, pizza boxes and empty wine bottles – can offer an opportunity to change the way you think, allowing you to consider where you want to go in life and how you might behave around others. In psychology, this is known as 'stress-related growth' and research shows that individuals can change for the better – by developing the personality trait 'agreeableness', for example – following some post break-up reflection.[28] You do, however, need to be open and willing to change. Whether you're in a relationship or in the messy aftermath of one however, psychology shows that a degree of self-compassion – essentially treating ourselves in a kind way – is key. Research has shown that self-compassion is a better predictor of positive relationship behaviour than attachment style or self-esteem.[29] After all, if we think about ourselves in positive terms, we'll likely be better placed to be a good partner for someone else.

Most of us will recognise Shakespeare's observation that 'the course of true love never did run smooth'. It's a rollercoaster ride of highs and lows that is unique to all of us and affects our thinking in a starburst of different ways. But by understanding how love's biases may be manipulating us, appreciating that ideals and illusions are challenged by reality, showing some self-compassion, and ensuring our relationships are equitable and have space for growth, we may be able to think more clearly and level out at least some of those disorientating bumps and corkscrews.

15

What language(s) do you speak?

As soon as critics denounced her poetry collection – saying someone so God-less would be more suited to looking after pigs than writing – Jila Mossaed knew she was in trouble. So when five religious soldiers turned up at her door in Tehran, Iran, while her husband was away, she held her three-year-old daughter close and cooperated fully. The men searched every inch of her home, taking 'unsuitable' items with them, including records, a chess set and her artist brother's paintings of naked women. Was she not ashamed to have such filth on her walls, in front of her children? they asked aggressively. Having grown up in a non-religious and activist family, she refused to be ashamed. 'After this, I realised I didn't want to live in my country anymore,' she says. The year was 1986, and the war between Iran and Iraq was raging. Terrified that her fifteen-year-old son would be drafted, she contacted a smuggler, who explained that Sweden would be her best shot at asylum.

Taking off in a small, crowded bus, the family made it to Turkey on narrow, winding roads in the middle of the night. From there, they continued to Bulgaria, and then onward to Denmark and finally Sweden. But as she looked out at the leafy, serene landscape – noting that even the cows in Sweden looked happy, peacefully eating lusciously green grass rather than plastic bags and newspapers at the side of the street – she realised it wasn't going to be easy. While she had gained peace and freedom, she had lost something almost as important: her language. Mossaed was thirty-eight years old and had worked as a poet and script writer for Iranian TV and radio. What would become of her now?

It took ten years before she started writing poetry in Swedish, recalls Mossaed, although she never stopped writing in Persian. 'I didn't know if I would succeed. From the very start, I never used a dictionary. I thought, if I am a good poet, even if I only know ten words, I have to write.' It wasn't long before her poetry was published, and today she is a member of the esteemed Swedish Academy, which awards the Nobel Prize in Literature. But along the way, she changed. While Mossaed feels that poetry is something that happens to her, 'attacking my brain as abstract essences', the shape it takes on paper is influenced by the language she writes in. And Mossaed noticed that, in Swedish, she became a different poet: simpler, braver, more direct and economical. This was partly because Swedish was new to her, but also because she believes the Scandinavian country's language and culture are themselves more direct. Either way, it made it easier to write. 'When I write in Persian I am diving into an ocean of words,' she explains. 'When I write in Swedish, I am standing outside a swimming pool.'

Mossaed believes it is extremely difficult to meaningfully translate poetry into different languages, which is why she ultimately started writing in Swedish. The Swedish Academy, she explains, has to be very rigorous when reviewing authors of different tongues to select their Nobel laureate each year. After all, how do you compare works as different as the hallucinatory realism of the Chinese laureate Mo Yan with the poetic expressions of American pop icon Bob Dylan? She says the members of the special working group that is ultimately responsible for selecting the laureate are proficient in a number of languages, and also send translations of nominated works to various experts to ensure that the translation is of the highest quality.

Translation isn't everything though. Mossaed believes that language and culture also impact how people see the world, leading to another layer of complexity. She finds Swedes cold, lonely and anxious, for example – things she argues are reflected in the language and poetry. But they are also more direct and honest, allowing them to talk about things as they are. 'The Persian language is veiled,' she explains. 'Due to a fear of religion and those in power, poets have created a hidden language – certain words may symbolise something else, and there are messages between the lines.' A case in point is emotions. In Persian, it has long been taboo to talk about things like mental illness, and so a lot of words for negative emotions are somatic – referring to bodily aches instead of the emotion itself.[1] A common example in English, for example, is 'heartache'. For Mossaed, the ability to speak openly is freeing, but can sometimes be at the expense of a certain type of beauty and truth that a veiled language can offer when it comes to complex experiences such as love.

But does language really affect how we think, or is this all anecdotal? It's a question that linguists have long battled over. While some believe that thinking is ultimately independent of language – universal rather than relative – others believe it is the opposite. Arguably, the truth is somewhere in between. 'The way that the question has been posed has been misleading,' argues Panos Athanasopoulos, a professor of linguistics and English language at Lancaster University. 'Saying that thought and language are independent doesn't preclude the possibility that one is influenced by the other.' And while there is increasing evidence that culture and language do influence how we think, the exact mechanisms for how this happens, and how it affects people's behaviour on a daily basis, is still unclear.

One way for researchers to decipher how language is linked to thinking is to look at concepts that are abstract and naturally open to interpretation. In concepts such as time, do people who write from right to left think differently about time, for example? Research suggests people who speak languages that are written from right to left do indeed picture temporal events in a similar way – if asked to put pictures of their parents at different ages on a timeline, they might start with the young images at the right and move left. Mossaed, for example, still flicks through Swedish newspapers from right to left. This experience of time going in a certain direction depending on your language has been demonstrated in the lab several times.[2]

Many languages, including Spanish, also denote the future as being in front of us. The Swedish word for future, for example, is *framtid* – literally meaning 'front time'. But in Aymara, spoken by the Aymara people of the Bolivian Andes, the word for future means 'behind time'. They reason that, because we can't see the future, it must be behind us, whereas we can see the past very clearly, meaning it is in front. Research has shown that people who speak languages such as Spanish tend to make forwards gestures when they speak about the future, whereas Aymara people make backwards gestures.[3] For Chinese Mandarin speakers, time is even more complex, including a vertical time axis alongside a horizontal one.[4] For example, they use the word *xià* (down) when talking about future events – with 'next week' literally becoming 'down week'.

The future is one of three main tenses in the English language, alongside the past and present. 'I wrote yesterday', 'I write now' and 'I will write tomorrow', for example. But many languages – like Chinese Mandarin – do not use a future tense, requiring external circumstances to explain that an event is taking place in the future, for example 'I go on holiday *next month*'. Interestingly, economists have shown that countries with futureless languages, including Japan, Switzerland, Germany and the Scandinavian countries, tend to, on average, save more money than countries which don't – with a difference of 5 per cent of GDP saved per year.[5] 'The hypothesis is that if you speak a futureless language you tend to see the future as closer to you,' explains Athanasopoulos. 'There's no linguistic barrier between the present and the future, so you're going to save more money, you're going to be more frugal.' Importantly, it's not that speakers of these languages don't have a sense of the future. On the contrary, because grammatically the future doesn't seem as far away, they are likely *more* future oriented. Perhaps that is also the reason why Sweden, for example, is a comparatively progressive and climate conscious country. Then again, your Swedish author may just be a little biased.

As well as affecting how we think of time, language may also affect something as basic as our visual perception of the world. Take colour. Unlike English, Greek has two different words for light and dark blue, *ghalazio* and *ble*, respectively. Research shows that the brains of Greek speakers fire a bit more when they are asked to visually compare the two shades, which suggests they may pay more attention to the difference – even be able to distinguish between similar shades that English speakers could not.[6]

This is likely a crucial part of how language affects thoughts. Language doesn't determine what we think – research shows you can still do complex thinking without language – but it makes us pay more attention to certain things.[7] For example, the English language has a bias towards dishing out blame.[8] When English and Spanish speakers, respectively, view videos of accidents, English speakers are more likely to remember who did it. Why? Because in English it is more common to say 'she broke the plate' than 'it broke itself', which you can comfortably say in Spanish. In English we can even go as far as saying 'I broke my leg', which would be bizarre were you to directly translate it into Spanish – why would you do such a thing? Not only does this have implications for witness testimony, but perhaps also for how judgemental and punitive we are – crucial factors when it comes to our thinking.

Another quirk in the English language is that it is very action oriented. In one study, German-English bilinguals were asked to describe scenes involving motion they had just watched in video clips, such as a man walking towards a car.[9] While monolingual Germans would describe the scene holistically, including the goal of the action – 'the man is walking *towards the car*' – monolingual English speakers would just describe it as 'the man is walking'. Bilinguals, on the other hand, switch perspectives based on the language they are speaking and the country they are in. Whether you prioritise action or the bigger picture is going to change how you think – being action focused may be useful when you are building a shelter in the wilderness, but holistic thinking can help us plan for it. Also, while science often heavily relies on narrow disciplines of expertise, areas such as climate change have benefited from merging them into a more rounded view.

This can even influence how we think about space. Athanasopoulos reports that in one instance of spatial navigation, when Spanish or English individuals were asked to walk diagonally across a field, they found it easy – you just walk diagonally; it is about the action of walking. But when German or Swedish speakers were asked the same thing they got confused.[10] They understood that they needed to walk diagonally but the instruction didn't make sense to them without a start and end point. Another example is the Aboriginal Kuuk Thaayorre people in Australia, who use cardinal directions – south, north, east and west – to orient themselves, rather than the comparatively clumsy 'left', 'right', 'behind', 'next to', 'above' and so forth.[11] If they wanted you to move your luggage a bit to the left, they may ask you to move it north-east. Surely, this should make them better at navigating.

Another much talked-about feature of language is grammatical gender, which doesn't exist in English. In languages such as Italian, French and German, objects have a gender. And it seems this has some influence on how speakers of such languages think about the world, assigning masculine objects more stereotypically masculine characteristics, for example. New research suggests the distinction could even have life-and-death implications. Take the COVID-19 pandemic. In French, Italian and Spanish, the disease, COVID-19, is grammatically feminine, whereas the coronavirus that causes it is masculine. The study revealed that speakers of these languages feel more threatened by the pandemic when they are asked about the masculine virus than when asked about the feminine disease.[12] They are also more willing to take precautions when they are dealing with the grammatically masculine form.

It seems difficult to argue that language has no impact whatsoever on our thoughts. It also seems to follow that it should offer some protection to speak more than one language, making the mind more flexible to take in different perspectives. Athanasopoulos agrees, but says that research highlighting the seemingly endless benefits of bilingualism is so far controversial and far from proven. When bilinguals and monolinguals are compared, the bilingual group is often more educated or financially secure than the monolingual one, making it hard to prove that bilinguals are cognitively superior. That said, there is some evidence that language learning can protect our cognitive abilities, particularly as we age.[13]

You may be wondering what all this might have to do with you. After all, you speak the languages you speak; you're not going to become bilingual or trilingual (and so on) overnight. You're already locked in, for the most part, to the languages you speak. But understanding more about how language impacts our thinking can be illuminating and can also indicate what we can do about making sure our thinking is *less* clouded by the language we speak, simply by being aware of it. Awareness about findings, such as how English speakers may pay more attention to action or that Swedish speakers could be more future-oriented, could be the start to being more open-minded and clear-thinking. If you are curious, delve into the research and find out more about the quirks of the language or languages that *you* speak. And if you do speak more than one language, here is something quite concrete you can do to improve your decision making.

Ultimately, we seem to be more emotional in our first language.[14] If we are gambling, for example, we are more likely to think in terms of luck than probabilities, potentially leading to emotionally charged and impulsive decision-making. This makes sense when you consider that a first language is acquired during the formative childhood years – a time in life when we are extremely emotional. By contrast, we often learn second languages a little later in life and perhaps in an educational setting. So if you are facing a difficult decision that requires a rational perspective, perhaps think it through in a second language first.

If you don't speak another language, it may in fact be worth learning one – or even several. While it may not turn you into a superhero, it could help you more easily spot the attention biases of your first language, allowing you to shift your perspective and discover a different side to yourself. Mossaed has certainly developed a 'Swedish' side after thirty-five years in the country. Today, she lives a rather quiet and hermitic life, and is enjoying a newfound love of nature.

Her story is compelling, but do note that some things may have been lost in the translation of our original interview in Swedish. That said, the chapter itself was written in English, a second language to one of your authors – hopefully making it as rational and reliable as it can be.

16

Do you believe in evil?

In 1941, sixty years before he was awarded the Nobel Prize in Economics, Daniel Kahneman was a seven-year-old living with his family in Nazi-occupied France.[1] As a Jew, he had to wear a Star of David on his clothing and be home by 6 p.m. every night. So, when he played for too long at a friend's house one evening, he was well aware of the peril he faced. Turning his jumper inside-out to disguise his religious identity, he began his journey home – only to run into a German soldier in the dreaded black uniform of the SS.

The soldier called him over and clutched him tightly. Would the German notice the Star of David? Would he be arrested, or killed? Instead, the soldier seemed overcome with emotion, pulling out a picture of another young boy, perhaps his own son. He then gave Kahneman some money – and left. Speaking in a TED interview years later, Kahneman said the experience fitted with what his mother had told him as a child 'about people being very complicated and nothing being quite black or white' – that no one is all good or all evil.[2] Indeed, Kahneman's fascination with the human mind's nuances has driven much of his work in psychology and economics since.

As Kahneman's research shows, people don't always think rationally, assessing all of the evidence, but instead often rely on mental shortcuts, or heuristics, to make quick decisions. This process of simplification can be highly effective. But it can also lead to an array of cognitive biases, some relatively benign and others that may result in destructive stereotyping, such as sexism and racism.

Arguably one of the oldest, most overlooked – and potentially most dangerous – mental shortcuts is the tendency to divide the world neatly into good and evil. To be fair, this appears to make perfect sense. We use the word 'evil' to describe the inexplicably abhorrent and apply it to actions, individuals and groups that offend our moral code and what we consider to be 'human'.[3] But as Kahneman's childhood story suggests, labelling people in definitive, black-and-white terms can limit our ability to think clearly about individuals, groups and the wider world, which are often considerably more nuanced. After all, even SS soldiers – who committed some of the most horrific crimes of the twentieth century – were capable of individual acts of kindness. And countless 'ordinary' people – from Nazi Germany to Rwanda to Bosnia – have enthusiastically and knowingly committed 'evil' atrocities in the warped belief that it was, in fact, their victims who were 'evil' and that they were simply doing 'good'.[4] After all, violence against 'evil' isn't wrong – it's 'virtuous'. Right?

Evil is primarily a moral and philosophical, rather than a scientific, notion – although the concept is explored by social psychologists and sociologists. It is also highly relative, both culturally and across time. As Simon McCarthy-Jones, an associate professor in clinical psychology and neuropsychology at Trinity College Dublin, explained to us in an interview: 'You can't see *evil* in a brain scan. Nor is it a word that is used in [clinical] psychology or neuroscience.' But whether we like it or not, we do all have measurable 'dark traits' that can influence our thinking in destructive ways – and these can, to some extent, be mapped in the brain.

Consider the following statements. Do you 'strongly disagree', 'strongly agree', or do you fall somewhere in between?

I tend to manipulate others to get my way.

I tend to lack remorse.

I tend to want others to admire me.

130

Don't worry, agreeing with any of the above doesn't make you 'evil'. But these examples are among the twelve items that comprise the catchily named Dirty Dozen, a tool that measures three specific 'dark' traits: psychopathy, narcissism and Machiavellianism.[5] Known as the 'Dark Triad', these traits are significant, not only because they predict anti-social behaviour, but also because they influence how we think.[6]

Most of us will shudder at being labelled a psychopath, narcissist or Machiavellian. The traits have a reputation as the sinister drivers behind the 'evil' anti-heroes of films like *Halloween* or real-life serial killers like Ted Bundy. No one would add them to their dating profile. But while extreme versions of the first two traits may be diagnosed as clinical psychiatric disorders, differing levels of the Dark Triad exist in us all. 'In psychology, it's not a case of "you are a psychopath", or "you're not a psychopath" . . . you have degrees of these traits,' explained Adrian Furnham, a psychology professor at UCL. 'So you might be more psychopathic than me in the same way that you might be taller than me,' he told us.

Think of the Dark Triad, then, not as switches that are either on or off, but facets of our personality with their own volume settings. In some, all three may be cranked to maximum; in others, they may be muted. Most of us, however, will sit somewhere on the dial.

Since 2002, when psychologists Delroy Paulus and Kevin Williams introduced the Dark Triad, research in the area has boomed, offering detailed insights into how the traits impact our thinking.[7] And while there is considerable overlap between the three, psychopathy is considered the most 'malevolent'.[8] Diagnosed psychopaths make up about 1 per cent of the general population, but the condition is more prevalent in men and is present in nearly 8 per cent of male – compared with 2 per cent of female – prisoners in the UK.[9] But while there are established links between psychopathy and criminal and destructive behaviours, being high in the trait doesn't mean you are programmed to be 'evil' and doomed to commit inexplicably abhorrent actions.

Psychopaths (like narcissists and Machiavellians) are often skilled liars, who hide their motivations behind a façade, which - initially, at least - dupes others into believing they are something they're not. Perhaps because of widespread misunderstanding of the trait, research also shows that the general public are significantly worse at spotting a clinical psychopath (exemplified in the study by an unrepentant murderer serving a life sentence) than someone with schizophrenia or depression.[10]

Beneath the surface, however, those high in psychopathy tend to lack remorse, empathy, a conscience.[11] They're more likely to be racist, and much more likely to be impulsive and fearless, behaving in ways that are risky and destructive to themselves and others, by driving too fast, taking drugs, breaking laws, having unsafe sex or carrying a weapon.[12] This may deeply affect thinking. With reduced levels of empathy, you may be less likely to take on other people's points of view - potentially making you less flexible. Higher levels of impulsivity, meanwhile, can lead to rash decision-making. In general, psychopaths think more about their own interests than others', and prioritise present actions over future consequences.

For the general population, levels of psychopathy are measured using tools like the Self-Report of Psychopathy (SRP) scale, which asks interviewees whether they agree or disagree with statements such as 'Most people are wimps' or 'People cry way too much at funerals'.[13] The SRP, which relies on psychopaths to self-report the truth, has obvious limitations. But tests like this - and the broader Dirty Dozen - enable psychologists to see how the Dark Triad relates to personality, and thinking styles, more generally.

As we learned in Chapter 4: 'Have your parents fucked you up?' (page 24), our personalities are often described using the Big Five model. As a reminder, these are: extraversion (how social you are), agreeableness (how friendly and compassionate), conscientiousness (your sense of duty), emotional stability (your level of depression and anxiety) and openness to experience (your curiosity about new things). And research shows that psychopathy is negatively linked to both agreeableness and conscientiousness, meaning people high in the trait are less likely to think about the well-being of others and their sense of duty, and more likely to be dishonest and insincere.[14] This may help people who score highly in psychopathy to think more clearly about their own, selfish motives, but in doing so it's possible they may fail to see the bigger picture. Coupled with their willingness to think bullishly, and take high-stakes gambles, it may also help their march up the career ladder, with some estimates suggesting that 4–12 per cent of CEOs have psychopathic traits.[15]

But such callous and bullying ways of thinking often lead to them, eventually, being found out. As Furnham told us:

'Psychologists make a distinction between "leadership effectiveness" and "emergence". In a big organisation, some people seem to float to the top. They seem to "emerge" as potential leaders. But dark-side traits predict emergence, not effectiveness.'

In other words, while psychopaths may demonstrate the ruthlessness and decisiveness that are seen as desirable qualities in some professions, those same traits may actually make them less effective at making thoughtful, evidence-based – and inclusive – decisions.[16] And this can damage their career and life prospects down the road. Indeed, apart from there being no direct link between the Dark Triad and mental ability, they're often too rash and undisciplined to fulfil the role of the 'evil mastermind'.[17]

* * *

Moving on from psychopathy, let's take a look at the second Dark Triad trait. In Greek mythology, Narcissus was a handsome hunter, who vainly fell in love with his own reflection and doubtless would have plastered pictures of it all over Instagram if only there had been such a platform back then. In fact, he was so enamoured that he remained gazing at the pool it shimmered from until he dropped dead. Narcissists are his heirs – and may feel particularly at home in the social media age, where they can curate their own image and harvest 'likes'.[18] Vain and egotistical, those high in the trait have an overinflated view of their own attributes and seek the admiration of others, whether justified or not.[19] The Narcissistic Personality Inventory (NPI) captures features of the trait such as superiority, entitlement, vanity, exploitativeness and exhibitionism. High levels of narcissism are also linked to lower levels of agreeableness, increased levels of extraversion (they love to be on show, after all), but, more surprisingly, also to higher levels of creativity.[20] They may not be as inclined to violence as psychopaths, but they do have a tendency to lash out when their ego is punctured. Again, such a focus on themselves rather than others can limit their understanding of the world, and their ability to think flexibly, due to them being somewhat blinded by their own self-absorption.

Finally, we have Machiavellians, this time named after a real historical figure. Niccolò Machiavelli was an Italian diplomat and philosopher renowned for his book *The Prince*, which outlines the unscrupulous methods the powerful can employ to stay on top. People high in this trait may be cautious and deliberate as they seek to fulfil their selfish goals and are often less impulsive than psychopaths.[21] But they also think largely about themselves and use duplicitous, malicious, cynical and immoral tactics.[22]

Some researchers recently have suggested adding sadism, to make a Dark Tetrad, although others argue it is too similar to psychopathy.[23]

Sadists, after all, get enjoyment from others' pain and often gravitate towards extreme situations – although sadistic bullies are relatively common in offices and school playgrounds, too. Among undergraduate students, 6 per cent confess to having sadistic traits – and most of us, as with psychopathy, narcissism and Machiavellianism, likely sit somewhere on the spectrum.[24]

We all have a dark side, then, and the traits we like to stereotypically label as 'evil' may cloud our thinking just as much as believing in the existence of 'evil' itself. So, what can we do to temper our more sinister facets? Psychopathy and narcissism may simply be part of our personalities, meaning you can't really 'cure' them. But it may be possible to change personality traits – such as agreeableness – by small amounts. For those with clinical conditions, meanwhile, talking therapies and medication can help. SSRIs (selective serotonin reuptake inhibitor drugs), for example, may reduce violence and are often given in prisons, as psychologist Coral Dando explained to us in an interview.

But while the world is full of horrors, psychopaths and narcissists certainly aren't exclusively to blame. How can science explain that? Throughout history, perfectly 'ordinary' people have acted and thought in horrific ways – often because they have identified with a narrative about another group being 'evil'. People aren't unthinking zombies, but our thoughts and beliefs can be influenced by powerful biases and storytelling, particularly if the narrative resonates with our sense of identity. Stories about 'evil' are a potent and dangerous example of this and act to 'dehumanise' another group, which philosophy professor and author of *Less Than Human* David Livingstone Smith has argued 'paves the way for the very worst things that human beings do to one another'.[25]

In the early 1960s, political philosopher Hannah Arendt famously reported on the trial of German Nazi leader Adolf Eichmann, one of the Holocaust's main architects. Arendt saw in Eichmann an ambitious but ordinary and mediocre bureaucrat, rather than a pathologically malevolent mastermind, highlighting what she calls in the last three words of her book, *Eichmann in Jerusalem*, the 'banality of evil'. Her portrait of Eichmann actually contains plenty of nuance, but it drove the idea that we are *all* capable of horrific acts and that we may commit them because we want to fit in, 'follow orders' or get ahead in a particular environment – without thinking clearly about the consequences.

Arendt's observations reflected ideas that were gaining ground in psychological research, too. At the same time as Eichmann's trial, Yale psychologist Stanley Milgram was conducting some of the twentieth century's best-known – and controversial – studies. His 'obedience' studies required participants (as 'teachers') to obey an 'experimenter' wearing a lab coat and deliver what they thought were ever-increasing electric shocks to someone they believed to be another volunteer (they were actually one of Milgram's associates) every time they failed a word task.[26] If the 'teachers' hesitated, the 'experimenter' would urge them to continue. Disturbingly, 65 per cent of the 'teachers' administered shocks to the maximum 450 volts, a level that evidently would cause severe harm to the 'learner'. All participants continued to 300 volts. The results appeared to suggest that ordinary people will *unthinkingly* torture another human being, simply because they're told to.

The ethics and methodology behind Milgram's studies have been widely criticised. But subsequent research – including re-examinations of Milgram's studies – suggests the truth may be even more disturbing.[27] Some psychologists have argued that people – including 'ordinary' Germans under the Nazi regime – don't just thoughtlessly inflict harm because they are instructed to do so, but do so willingly, even enthusiastically, because they identify with a cause, group or purpose. As Stephen Reicher, professor in the School of Psychology and Neuroscience at the University of St Andrews, and colleagues have noted: 'What is truly "fearsome, word and thought defying" (to echo Arendt) is emphatically not that killers are unaware that what they are doing is wrong. Rather, it is that they *really believe* that what they are doing is right.'[28]

Which is why stories about 'evil' can be so dangerous. Believing we are battling against an 'evil', inhuman other can motivate us to act in violent ways that we may think are entirely justified. Indeed, Reicher has suggested that such 'us' and 'them' stories – coupled with compelling leadership – may make us more vulnerable to accepting tyrannies such as Nazi Germany's abhorrent regime.[29]

In Nazi Germany, for example, ordinary people existed in a closed system with a moral narrative that was utterly warped but many came to identify with. It may seem absurd, but many Nazis believed that *they* were the victims of injustice and 'evil' forces and were, in the words of Roy F. Baumeister, author of *Evil: Inside Human Violence and Cruelty*, 'setting things right'.[30] They saw themselves as victims of defeat in the First World War. Victims of the punitive sanctions that followed. Victims of meteoric US progress. Victims of an imagined Jewish conspiracy. As such, they felt compelled to act against these 'evils' and go about the 'virtuous' work of building their utopian Thousand-Year Reich.[31]

As Dr Tom Clark, who researches the sociology of evil at Sheffield University, says: 'When you demonise something, you valorise something else. Evil reflects as much what we want as what we don't.'[32] In other words, calling another group 'evil' helps us to think about ourselves as 'good'. History offers countless examples of this. Following the 9/11 attacks, for example, US president George W. Bush, announced the existence of an 'Axis of Evil'. It comprised Iran, North Korea and Iraq, the latter of which the US-led coalition invaded the following year. This wasn't just about highlighting a threat, but also justifying a war of questionable legality to the American electorate and wider world. But anyone can be targeted in this way. Women, minorities and immigrants, for example, are more likely to be branded 'evil' by the dominant group, making them fair game for discrimination, mistreatment and worse.

But branding things evil doesn't only justify discrimination and violence, it entrenches biases about other people and detracts us from considering many of the world's more disturbing realities – and why people do the things they do. Ultimately, it limits our ability to think clearly and freely for ourselves and can often blind us to what is right in front of us.

So, what can we do about it? Certainly, we should treat the word 'evil' as a red flag – and think more clearly about how it may be used to shape our identities. When used in a newspaper headline, or a political speech, ask whether its use is justified and consider what the motives behind it are. Is the word being attached to a whole group because of the actions of one individual? Because they're a minority? Because they're 'different'? Remember that certain groups are more likely to be called 'evil' than others – particularly if a dominant or majority group wants to justify discriminating against them. Ultimately, it's a way of dehumanising someone, so also be vigilant of other words that serve the same purpose by suggesting people are monstrous or animal-like – labels such as 'vermin', 'rats', 'hordes' and 'swarms' are equally dangerous.

British philosophy professor Michael Hand also argues that children should be taught that people are capable of both good and bad, and that we should judge actions, not individuals.[33] We can all learn from that. No one is all good or all evil; it's what we do, and why, that matters. Essentially, we don't live in a world of automaton heroes and villains, but of human beings – who make their own choices. And by seeking to better understand – rather than always dismissing as purely 'evil' – the people and behaviours that make us uncomfortable or fearful, we can improve our chances of making more informed, independent choices in the future. It may even make us less likely to commit 'evil' deeds ourselves.

17

Are you happy?

When Massachusetts-based freelance artist Harvey Ball put pen to 'sun-shiny yellow' paper in 1963 to design a morale-boosting image for workers at the State Mutual Life Assurance Company, he surely couldn't have imagined the mind-blowing significance of what he was about to create.[1] There wasn't much to it: two scribbled oval eyes and a slightly skew-whiff smile. But then its genius was perhaps its simplicity. In just ten minutes – and for a retrospectively paltry $45 paycheque – he'd sketched one of the most instantly recognisable and widely reproduced graphics ever.

The smiley face.

That instantly recognisable yellow emblem began circulating through the insurance company's offices on badges. But it was soon powering a multi-million-dollar industry. In Europe, French jour-nalist Franklin Loufrani trademarked his own 'Smiley' in 1971, which flagged positive stories in newspapers before growing into a global brand.[2] Smileys adorned T-shirts, symbolised the acid house music scene and starred in the London 2012 Olympics opening ceremony. The graphic also inspired many of the emojis that populate our elec-tronic messages today.

So what was it about this simple little image that captured the world's imagination? As children in the late 1970s and 1980s, we grew up on Roger Hargreaves's Mr Men books. Mr Bump, Mr Tickle, Mr Loud – all made a huge impression. But it was Mr Happy – who perhaps unsur-prisingly took the form of a walking, talking yellow smiley – that stuck in our young minds. And the reason for that was that he embodies the idea that achieving happiness is simple and sustainable. That we can *all* live in Happyland. Indeed, perhaps the main reason the smiley has spread so effortlessly around the world is that, even as adults, we all want to believe the same thing: that there's a universal recipe for lasting happiness that can be followed and enjoyed by all. It's a compelling notion and we could all do with more smiling faces in our lives. It's also an idea that has spawned a multi-billion-dollar economy, with a menagerie of self-help books, social media influencers and motivational speakers offering shortcuts for weathering troubling times – be it mindfulness or waking up at a certain time – and coming through them smiling. [3]

But could our relentless pursuit of happiness actually be making us miserable? [4] And could happiness, despite its more obvious benefits, also have a less understood 'dark side' that negatively affects our ability to think clearly? [5]

These are questions that Rafa Euba, a consultant psychiatrist who has worked with thousands of mental health patients over his twenty-year career, frequently asks himself. And his startling conclusion (which became the title of his recent book) is that 'you are not meant to be happy' – at least not all of the time. Euba is no doom-monger. He has a loving relationship with his wife, is content with life as a medical professional and enjoys high levels of well-being, occasionally lubricated by a glass of fine Portuguese wine. Nevertheless, he is aware that his own moments of true 'happiness' are relatively infrequent, frustratingly fleeting and can't just be summoned based on a set of guidelines. As a doctor of the mind, whose job it is to help people think better, he also sees first-hand the pressure many people feel to be happy and the sense of failure they experience when they're not. The pursuit of happiness, it seems, places huge demands on us and the way we think about ourselves and others.

The first problem is that happiness isn't just one thing – it is an abstract and notoriously fuzzy concept, experienced by different people in different ways at different times. While research shows that Americans associate happiness with personal achievement, for example, Japanese people link it more with social harmony. [6] Philosophers and scientists have been agonising over a universal definition of 'happiness' for millennia – and Nobel Prize-winning psychologist Daniel Kahneman perhaps best sums up their progress so far in his book *Thinking, Fast and Slow*: 'The word *happiness* does not have a simple meaning and should not be used as if it does.'[7]

Kahneman argues, for example, that we have two sides to us, each of which have different motivations and think about and judge happiness in different ways. Our 'experiencing self' feels a form of fleeting, spontaneous happiness in the moment, such as on a sunny summer's evening in a pub beer garden with friends. Our 'remembering self', meanwhile, is more concerned with an alternative form of happiness, perhaps best described as 'life satisfaction'.[8] This form of happiness derives from feeling content with life when it's remembered as a whole, having met career goals and social expectations, for example. The problem is that what makes the 'experiencing self' happy in the moment is often at odds with what makes the 'remembering self' feel satisfied – and vice versa.[9] If we spent an entire summer shunning all obligations and drinking with friends, for example, we might experience plenty of 'happy' moments, but we'd be unlikely to feel 'satisfied' afterwards. And that's before we even get to the hangover. Similarly, working hard, getting that promotion and buying a bigger house might make us 'satisfied' when we look back at our achievements, but it may come at the expense of socialising, spending time doing what we enjoy and being 'happy' in the here and now. After years of research, Kahneman has argued that most people don't actually want to be happy in the present; they want to be satisfied with their life when they remember it.[10] And that, of course, can lead us to some muddled thinking about how we live life and what we want to get out of it.

Of course, most of us will describe ourselves as 'happy' when pleasant, positive emotions outweigh the unpleasant, negative ones.[11] Our experiences, circumstances and personalities also contribute to our perceived levels of satisfaction and well-being, with high levels of extraversion and low levels of neuroticism, for example, being perhaps two of the most important personality traits of the contented mind. People with high levels of extraversion are also more likely to experience positive emotions and feel fulfilled by hedonistic pleasures, such as a nice meal, a boozy party or a roller-coaster ride, while introverts are more likely to feel fulfilled by pursuits they find meaningful. But Kahneman's observations reveal how elusive a neat definition of happiness can be and suggest how thinking about happiness as a single, simple thing can leave us confused and conflicted.

Second, we simply aren't hardwired to be happy all of the time. As Euba explained to us, 'We imagine happiness as an abstract idea, but it doesn't actually exist in our nature or reside in our biological self. It is not in our blueprint.' While there are clear brain areas that govern functions such as sight, hearing, rational thought, language and even pleasure, the biological centre for what we'd consider to be pure happiness – especially the lasting, unadulterated kind we're encouraged to chase – is harder to pinpoint. And while the neurotransmitters serotonin and dopamine are, respectively, linked to mood and reward, their functions are far too varied and complex for them exclusively to be described as 'happy chemicals'. Happiness can't be definitively located in the brain nor can it be created with a scalpel or (lastingly) with a pill. After all, while antidepressants and other medications are used to treat a range of psychiatric conditions, they are not designed to make people 'happy' but rather to help alleviate the conditions' more unpleasant symptoms.[12]

Instead, your brain, remarkable as it is, has been honed by evolution over millions of years not to make you permanently and ecstatically happy, but rather to keep you alive. And this has profound implications for the way we think.

Research shows that people generally tend to be in a mildly positive mood – at least in the absence of other extreme emotional events.[13] There is also plenty of robust research showing how moderate levels of happiness can broaden our attention and make us more cognitively flexible and better at forging social bonds and pursuing key goals.[14] Happiness also contributes to better health, improved life outcomes – and feels great.[15] No wonder we all seek it. In recent years, the relatively new discipline of positive psychology has further explored ways of improving the well-being of both individuals and society by focusing on positive traits, emotions, relationships and institutions.

But while there are undoubted benefits to happiness and positivity, evolution has also favoured certain negative patterns of thought that, though unpleasant, improve our odds of survival, something which nature invariably prioritises over a smile.[16] The reality is that your brain contains some state-of-the-art hardware for negative thinking. One culprit is the amygdala, a pair of nut-sized structures at the base of the brain. It's an ancient, primal feature that appears to stay ever alert to potential hazards and drives our responses to them, such as feelings of fear and anger. These emotions are hardly tickets to happiness, but they do serve a purpose. Anxiety makes us more vigilant, while depression may have persisted to help us elicit social support, reduce our willingness to take risks and even help us to think better and solve complex problems.[17] While there's an evolutionary advantage to experiencing positive emotions, which can, for example, help people bond and take chances that could lead to better opportunities, if we all existed in a perpetual state of bliss, we'd likely never strive for anything else.

As Euba knows all too well, depression and anxiety can present as dreadful, debilitating conditions that require treatment. But we all experience negative thoughts and emotions, such as fear, social discomfort or restlessness, to a greater or lesser degree – and we do so because our brains have evolved to sometimes favour certain patterns of defensive thinking over happiness. They are part of who we are as human beings. 'It's important that we recognise this as we live in a culture now where it is believed that if we are not happy then we must be doing something wrong,' Euba told us. 'And that if we only do this or that, or follow some guidelines, or think in a certain way, then we should be able to be happy. This is wrong.'

Pursuing happiness in prescriptive, often simplistic ways, then, may have the reverse of the desired effect by putting us under pressure, making us depressed and anxious. Research supports the idea that while happiness is a key ingredient of our well-being, leading to better health and improved social outcomes, pursuing it too relentlessly can 'backfire'.[18] Two studies by social psychologist Iris Mauss, for example, suggest that 'valuing happiness could be self-defeating because the more people value happiness, the more likely they will feel disappointed'.[19] That doesn't mean that we should strive to be *unhappy*, of course. Nor that we should entirely abandon our attempts to be happy. But we shouldn't expect to feel content all the time – sometimes we should just be content to be discontent . . . Discontentment, after all, can lead us to think about, and aim for, better things.

In a detailed review of the research, Mauss, June Gruber and Maya Tamir have also highlighted how happiness itself can sometimes negatively impact our thinking.[20] They suggest, for example, that there may be such a thing as being 'too happy'. While moderate levels of happiness make us more creative, intense positive emotions do not. Instead, at excessive levels, they may make us more rigid in our behaviour and thinking – compromising our ability to solve complex problems. And this appears to have an impact on our fortunes. There is evidence, for example, that while the happiest people are more successful at forging close relationships, people with lower levels of happiness are more politically involved and enjoy improved earning and educational prospects.[21] Excessive happiness may also make us more likely to act in a disinhibited way and take dangerous risks, such as engaging in unsafe sex. So, while negative modes of thinking play a role in keeping us vigilant and safe, supercharged positive emotions can do the opposite. In fact, an excessive absence of *negative* emotions (such as fear and anxiety) is implicated in psychopaths' willingness to behave antisocially and harm others.

Mauss, Gruber and Tamir also found that happiness can negatively impact our thinking when we experience it at the wrong time. Emotions often serve a purpose; they are 'adaptive'. While fear prepares us to protect ourselves, for example, happiness is often experienced as a reward – for completing a task or achieving a goal, for example. But happiness can also put us in a 'job done' mindset, making us worse at performing in competitive tasks, and less able to convincingly argue a point of view and detect potential dangers.[22] It can also make us more likely to rely on stereotypes, leading participants of one study to more readily judge members of a stereotyped group as being guilty of a crime.[23] In a secure environment, then, happiness is great. But it can also compromise our ability to think clearly in more uncertain situations. After all, our negative emotions are often entirely justified and the way they can shape our thinking – by driving us to consider new solutions or avoid making the same old mistakes – can be hugely beneficial.

Being too happy can also change the way others think about us. One study, for example, found that 'very happy individuals' were considered to be more naive than those perceived to be 'moderately happy'.[24] Perhaps unsurprisingly, they were also more likely to be taken advantage of. Indeed, next time you're bouncing off the walls with joy, ask yourself whether your mood might be making you gullible, too.

We all want to be happy – and its benefits are wide-ranging and well known. But we should also be realistic about the ways both happiness, and the pursuit of it, can influence our thinking. Happiness is not a single, simple thing that can be derived from a manual, so we shouldn't be surprised or disheartened when it eludes our efforts to grasp it.[25] Nor should we believe that negative emotions are a failure – they, too, are part of who we are and often exist to improve our thinking in difficult situations. Indeed, while happiness feels wonderful, it can sometimes compromise our ability to think clearly in harder times. While we may want to exist in Happyland, we actually live on planet Earth. And for that, we need all our wits about us.

18

Should you see a doctor?

In May 1997, Tony Blair's New Labour swept to a landslide victory in the UK general election. High up the new government's agenda was to build on a recent ceasefire and bring a lasting peace to Northern Ireland, where decades of sectarian violence had cost thousands of lives. Tasked with this job was the new Secretary of State for Northern Ireland, Dr Marjorie 'Mo' Mowlam.

Mowlam was a clever, charismatic and increasingly popular political operator known for her gregarious, uninhibited style. Some even tipped her as a future prime minister. But as she entered the fray in Northern Ireland and began her game of brinkmanship with the province's various political and paramilitary factions, she was also concealing an explosive secret.[1] Just months earlier, her doctor, Mark Glaser, had diagnosed her with a massive and inoperable malignant brain tumour. She would likely have just three years to live.

Not only did Mowlam hide the truth from Blair and the public – claiming the condition was benign and treatable – Dr Glaser also believes that the tumour's scale and position, stretching across both frontal lobes, would have had a profound influence on her thinking. Typically, a tumour of this kind would cause a dramatic loss of inhibition and lead to illogical and obsessive behaviour, all features Glaser saw evidence of in Mowlam. But there was a flipside, too. Glaser also believes that the tumour – and the way it affected Mowlam's personality and thinking – may have played a part in laying the foundations for the 1998 Good Friday Agreement, which largely ended the conflict. 'There is no question that the tumour was unfortunate,' he says. 'But that negotiation was also aided by her behaviour.'

We met Glaser, a professor at Imperial College London and still a leading cancer consultant, in the Reform Club on London's Pall Mall. The building's grand, historic surrounds are aptly reminiscent of Hillsborough Castle, the official residence of the Northern Ireland Secretary where Glaser would regularly meet with Mowlam to discuss her condition and the political situation, often in the gardens as she believed the rooms were bugged.

'I wouldn't like to be so presumptive to say we were close friends,' said Glaser. 'But we were a team and she checked nearly every action with me, which I am prepared to now speak about. For instance, when Prince Charles visited Belfast, she was unwell and felt like she needed to vomit, so she rang me in the middle of the visit. I said, "Mo, go to the river, stand there, take deep breaths." I would advise her on how to keep going and not be found out or collapse in front of Prince Charles . . . There was a sort of entanglement.'

Glaser became entangled with Mowlam, who died aged fifty-five in 2005, not just because he was her doctor, but also because he was the only person – other than her husband – who knew the full truth about her condition. And she made it clear to Glaser that she trusted him with her secret and that she wanted it to remain that way. Which left him in a deeply awkward position. Northern Ireland was a tinderbox at the time. Unionist and nationalist paramilitaries were still heavily armed and many of the politicians representing the two sides were notoriously stubborn and po-faced. A wrong move by Mowlam could all too easily have fanned the flames.

Given Mowlam's diagnosis, Glaser said that 'it was surprising she could function at all'. Consequently, he had to deftly balance patient confidentiality and loyalty to Mowlam with the significance of her role in such a sensitive situation, a responsibility that weighed heavily on him. But while Glaser carefully monitored Mowlam's condition over the course of regular visits, her eccentric, disinhibited style seemed to cut through the political impasse in Northern Ireland, enabling her to find a common ground with both sides and lay the groundwork for a lasting way forward. Many considered her brilliant, but outlandish. She flashed her (orange) knickers at a gobsmacked David Trimble, who would soon become First Minister of Northern Ireland. She was famously tactile. She turned the air blue with her language, once telling Democratic Unionist Party leader Ian Paisley to fuck off.[2] But her manner also broke the region's notoriously thick ice.

'It was aided by her disinhibition, and the disinhibition somehow was symbiotic with her warm personality and ability to relate to both sides,' said Glaser. 'The brain tumour accentuated the disinhibition, and her disinhibition was extraordinary . . . But the disinhibition also allowed her to be trusted by both sides to a great degree, because they were all shocked by the style of negotiation . . . I think if one had gone in as very, very cautious, careful people, one wouldn't have got there.'

But while Glaser – who is also now a trustee of the Brain Tumour Research Campaign – believed the tumour's impact on Mowlam's thinking may have helped bring peace to Northern Ireland, he also thought it might have been affecting her personality and behaviour long before she took her ministerial position.[3] Indeed, the sheer size of the tumour suggests it could have been developing for a decade or more. 'One can postulate that her behaviour, the political persona prior to her diagnosis, was this tumour growing,' he told us. 'In her case, I would say it had been there longer than ten years, judging by the history, the size, the pathology.'

Years later, Peter Hain, who served as Northern Ireland Secretary between 2005 and 2007, paid tribute to Mowlam's efforts by saying, 'She was the catalyst that allowed politics to move forward, which led to the signing of the Good Friday Agreement in April 1998. She cut through conventions and made difficult decisions that gave momentum to political progress.'[4] But despite the pivotal role she played in the peace process, Mowlam was replaced as Northern Ireland Secretary in 1999. While she survived until 2005, her life after politics was troubled and according to Glaser – who continued to support her – she became ever more aware of the influence the tumour was having on her mind. On one occasion, she even asked Glaser: 'What is the tumour, and what is me?'

Mowlam's poignant question sits at the very heart of this book. It shows how we can never entirely separate our thinking from the multitude of external and internal factors that influence, shape and manipulate it, sometimes for worse, sometimes for better. Although we can't possibly control all these factors, a deeper understanding of them can clearly benefit us. While some well-known physical conditions that affect our thinking, such as Alzheimer's, can't currently be treated, others, such as many brain tumours and strokes, can. Some psychiatrists argue that early detection of cognitive decline caused by incurable conditions like dementia may be counterproductive, leading to unnecessary distress. But everyone reacts to a diagnosis differently and we certainly should be vigilant of the warning signs of conditions that could benefit from early treatment.

One large recent study, for example, found that people who had a stroke were suffering from noticeably decreased cognition and daily functioning up to a decade before the event, compared to those who didn't have a stroke.[5] This is likely because patients begin suffering from brain damage, caused by cerebral small vessel disease, neurodegeneration and inflammation, long before they have an actual stroke. But the research, which followed 14,712 participants between 1990 and 2016, also suggests that spotting these early changes in people's thinking could lead to better preventative interventions, potentially saving some of the 38,000 lives strokes claim annually in the UK alone.

149

While the study found that women, people with few academic qualifications and those with the APOE gene, which is also linked with Alzheimer's disease, were most at risk, we are all vulnerable to slow and subtle changes to our brains.[6] And there are scientific ways of mapping any decline. The researchers, for example, used tools including the Mini Mental State Examination (MMSE) to spot memory problems and the Stroop task to measure mental processing speed. But they also assessed how effectively the participants managed everyday tasks, such as eating, dressing and managing their money. We are all aware how severely a stroke can damage our thinking after it has happened, but by being more aware of the cause's impacts beforehand, we may be able to better protect ourselves from having one in the future.

Glaser, whose distinguished career stretches back decades, has regularly witnessed the extraordinary – and sometimes dangerous – effects such conditions can have on people's thinking. One of his former patients was a senior English judge with a frontal-temporal brain tumour, which would have caused similar symptoms to Mowlam's. He once told Glaser that he'd have to miss his next appointment because he was presiding over a murder case. But even though the case had yet to be tried, the judge explained that the accused was definitely guilty and that he would sentence him to the maximum prison term. And when Glaser asked why he was jumping to this conclusion before the trial, the judge's response was as brief as it was shocking – 'Because he's Black.'

'Now I'm sure that wasn't him,' said Glaser. 'I was really concerned and I made some enquiries, but I could not tell the clerk of the court because of patient confidentiality . . . And I wondered how many times this is happening.' Of course, it's impossible to prove, but Glaser now believes that the judge's racism had been triggered by – or at least significantly exacerbated by – his tumour. 'I spoke to his wife,' he recalled, 'and she said that he used to be such a kind man, but over the years that he'd kept on losing his temper.' In another case, one of Glaser's patients out of the blue wrote his wife and children the 'most vicious, disgusting pornographic letter'. The wife visited Glaser in tears, saying, 'This can't be my husband.'

Glaser could recall numerous cases of his male patients leading extraordinarily disinhibited secret lives – often involving numerous mistresses – which only came out after their deaths or during the illness. In fact, he believes that changes in the brain, including those caused by undiagnosed tumours, may explain why some middle-aged men go through especially dramatic mid-life crises, exhibiting profound changes in personality and behaviour. 'I believe some of these changes can be explained by physical changes in the brain, rather than anything environmental, genetic or psychological. And I also believe these structural changes often go undetected because the patient subsequently dies of something else . . . and people don't have routine MRI scans of the brain . . . I think that brain tumours are much more common than we believe.'

Glaser is the first to admit that he can't prove his theory, but it does add a further dimension to the recent stroke study and the theory that subtle structural changes in the brain can affect our thinking and behaviour long before many conditions are diagnosed. It is widely believed that brain tumours, for example, begin growing between three and twenty years before presentation and that, as Glaser told us, 'is a big span in a person's life to change'. For growths in the temporal, frontal or parietal lobes, a sudden onset of irascibility or impatience may be early warning signs. But whether it's a stroke or a tumour, 'nothing just happens. It's a gradual build-up' – and personality and behavioural changes may occur incrementally as the brain's structure subtly alters. As Glaser explained to us, genetics and biochemistry play a central role in many brain conditions, from Alzheimer's to cancer, but science should also explore in depth the way the brain's changing structure over time can influence the way we think.

In the meantime, we can reduce our risk of suffering from cancer, stroke or dementia by living more healthily, not smoking, eating better, staying active, both mentally and physically, maintaining a rich social life and avoiding and treating high blood pressure, cholesterol and blood sugar. But we should also stay alert to sudden changes in our personality and behaviour. Increasing disinhibition may, at least in part, have helped Mowlam to leave her mark on history, but we should all be aware that similar changes in the way we think may also be an early warning sign of something more dangerous.

19

Is your gut thinking for you?

On an otherwise ordinary summer's morning in 1822, Alexis St Martin was minding his own business at a remote trading post when a musket accidentally discharged beside him – and changed his life forever.[1] The young Canadian, who made a dollar selling fur and other goods in the North American wilderness, was on Mackinac Island, in the modern-day US state of Michigan, and was steeled to the perils of the frontier. But the weapon fired a shot into him from almost point-blank range, slicing through the left side of his torso and igniting his shirt as he dropped, seemingly dead.

But while his life was saved by William Beaumont[*] – an army surgeon who was stationed nearby – a stranger, more gruesome fate awaited. The blast had cut through St Martin's side, breaking several ribs, severing muscle and part of one lung, and leaving him with a hole in his stomach, a fistula that would never properly close. Not that Beaumont seemed too concerned. In a move that would leave modern ethics committees calling frantically for security, Beaumont instead employed St Martin as a human guinea pig, using the persistent fistula as a window through which he could explore, over the next decade or so, the digestive tract's inner workings.

The pair's chilling collaboration did, however, produce some novel and extraordinary findings, which contributed to Beaumont's later reputation as the 'Father of Gastric Physiology'. Not least among the results was Beaumont's observation that St Martin's digestion

---

[*] Remarkably, St Martin lived until 1880, when he died at the ripe old age of seventy-eight.

was influenced by emotions, such as anger.[2] Indeed, it was this finding that first sparked the idea that the brain and the gut are closely entwined – and, much later, that this 'axis' is a two-way street that not only allows the brain to control the gut, but also, remarkably, the gut to control the brain.

Two centuries on, our understanding of the human gut is becoming ever more sophisticated. We now know, for example, that it is far more than just a clever piece of anatomical plumbing; it is also home to trillions of microorganisms – the gut microbiota. And these tiny lifeforms have a direct line to our brains and may also be manipulating the way we think.

Research into this potentially dazzling relationship between our thoughts and behaviour and the microorganisms that have colonised us is still in its relative infancy. But over the last two decades, experts like John Cryan, a professor of anatomy and neuroscience at University College Cork, have begun to draw back the curtain on this 'second brain' in our guts and its implications for medicine, neuroscience, psychology and who we are more generally.[3]

What is clear is that our partnership with the microorganisms that call us home is ancient and far-reaching. The microbes, after all, were here first and there has never been a time when our brains existed without microbial influence of one kind or another. Indeed, our ancestors had a rich and diverse microbiota long before they became human and our microorganisms now outnumber our own cells by a ratio of 1.3:1. Well over half of the cells in our body are not human.[4] Yikes! Indeed, as Cryan himself has colourfully explained in a TEDx talk on the subject, 'When you go to the bathroom and shed some of these microbes, just remember: you are becoming *more* human.'[5]

This microbial parliament in our bowels isn't fixed throughout life; it is constantly in flux. Our microbiota includes thousands of species, many of them bacterial, and its make-up is affected by a huge range of factors from our genes, our environment and what we eat to our emotional state.[6] A glut of some, or a shortage of others, may make us ill, while many play a vital role as 'little factories' that manufacture the chemicals we all need to survive, think and feel, from sugars to serotonin, a hormone linked to our sense of well-being.

Cryan's research goes a step further though. While aspects of who we are and how we live our lives affect the make-up of the microbiota in our guts, he argues that the relationship also works in reverse and that some play a key, early role in shaping the brain itself by breaking down the complex sugars in breast milk to form vital chemicals that contribute to its development in babies. Meanwhile, research suggests that myelin, which forms the fatty sheaths around nerve fibres, is also regulated by the microbiota, with potential implications for the treatment of conditions such as autism, multiple sclerosis, anxiety and schizophrenia, which are often associated with a significant change in gut-based microorganisms.[7]

And the relationship between gut and brain goes further still: these organisms may be influencing how we think in a direct way, too.

The question is: how? Research shows that there may be numerous ways by which our microbiota can communicate with our brains, including through hormones. But they may also 'hijack' the vagus nerve to send signals that manipulate our thinking and behaviour.[8] The vagus nerve connects the brain with the main internal organs, such as the heart, lungs and digestive system. Apart from telling us when we're hungry and full, this connection, which sends signals in both directions, may help to explain why we talk about 'gut feelings' or experience 'butterflies' when we're nervous or excited.[9] There is evidence that certain strains of bacteria in the gut do communicate with the brain in this way.[10] *Lactobacillus rhamnosus JB1*, for example, has been shown to have a beneficial effect on depressive- and anxiety-related behaviour in mice. But these effects are removed when the vagus nerve is blocked, suggesting that these bacteria are indeed hijacking the connection.[11]

Whether via the vagus nerve or other pathways, some researchers believe that the microbiota may be able to influence a wide variety of brain regions. But a particular area of interest is the amygdala, an almond-sized structure linked to powerful emotions, such as fear and anxiety, and our 'flight or fight' response to potential threats.[12] Research shows, for example, that 'germ-free' rats – which have been kept in a sterile environment and therefore lack a microbiota – have a heightened anxiety response to stress.[13] Altering the make-up of the microbiota in animals can also induce depressive-like behaviours.[14] And in humans, a study of forty women revealed that individuals responded differently to unpleasant images depending on the make-up of their microbiota.[15]

We are all aware how low mood, anxiety and how we respond to stress can affect the way we think; they may muddle our thoughts and cause us to act in rash, destructive ways. But while research in this area remains in its infancy, it seems increasingly clear that the microorganisms in our gut could be playing the role of hidden puppeteers, pulling our strings behind the scenes, through the amygdala and other brain regions. A better understanding of this axis between the brain and our gut microbiota may help us to overcome the negative effects – and support the positive ones – think more clearly and even treat more serious conditions, such as clinical depression and anxiety.

On top of affecting our responses to fear and anxiety, our microbiota may also be influencing our appetites, with Cryan explaining that we aren't only what *we* eat, but also what our microbes eat. After all, just as some of us prefer cheeseburgers to curly kale, our microorganisms also crave different nutrients. And they may even be able to influence our thinking to ensure they get what they want – so next time you feel guilty about craving chocolate, you may want to give yourself a break; it could be your microorganisms giving you the nudge in the first place. Fruit flies deprived of protein, for example, will generally opt for yeast over sugar. But this preference can be changed by altering the microorganisms in the flies' guts, leading them to opt for sugar as well.[16] What if *your* microbiota is doing the same thing, causing you to select the unhealthy option to satisfy its own cravings? Researchers increasingly believe this may be happening and argue that better eating habits may support beneficial organisms that in turn aid our efforts to think more positively and healthily about our dietary choices.

Perhaps even more intriguing and mysterious, however, is research that suggests how our microbiota may manipulate our social behaviour as well as our food cravings.[17] Humans and the organisms within them have evolved together in a close symbiotic relationship and our choices affect them, just as they affect us. Experts argue, for example, that widespread social interaction – including kissing – enables microbial species to jump between hosts, boosting diversity and benefiting our odds of survival as well as theirs.[18] Certainly, studies of animals, such as baboons, in the wild show that individuals in the same social group have strikingly similar microbiota, even if they are not related.[19] Indeed, perhaps we should think of ourselves as 'holobionts' – not just individuals, but whole 'ecosystems' that include the countless other organisms we host.[20]

There is also evidence showing how the influence of these 'friends with social benefits', as Cryan describes them, plays out in real-world behaviour. Research shows, for example, that germ-free rats and mice (i.e. those without a microbiota) are less interested in interacting with others and appear less able to remember social partners.[21] Tellingly, this reduced social behaviour can also be reversed by dosing the animals with particular strains of bacteria, including *Bifidobacterium* and *Lactobacillus*. Meanwhile, changes in the microbiota are correlated with altered shoaling behaviour in zebrafish – with anti-biotics limiting shoaling and probiotics increasing it.[22]

This could also have implications for humans – and how we socialise and think about others. 'Much more work is needed,' says Cryan, 'but this could be especially important post-COVID, for example, because we have messed up our social structures through lockdowns and we've changed our microbiota through cleanliness and changes in diet. Which begs the question: what has all this done to our overall signalling and social behaviour?'

So what can we do about it? Definitive answers can be hard to come by in this intriguing but so far under-researched field. But the evidence suggests that maintaining a healthy and diverse microbiota is critical for both our physical and mental well-being. Indeed, it seems a depleted microbiota may lead to negative outcomes, such as increased fear and anxiety and deficits in social behaviour, while the 'right' bacteria may help sharpen our thinking and even protect our ageing brains. For example, in a recent study, old mice that received a transplant of bacteria from the guts of young mice became better at solving a maze, pointing to improvements in their ability to remember and learn. [23]

Perhaps the easiest way to keep our microbiota healthy is through diet. Cryan, for example, still credits his long-lived grandmother, and her dedication to good food, as the original inspiration behind his research. And now he knows that 'good food' means – at least for our microbiota – a Mediterranean-style diet rich in omega-3s (found in walnuts, flax seeds and many fish, for example) and polyphenols (found in red wine, dark chocolate and red onions). Fermented and pickled foods, such as kimchi or sauerkraut, also contribute to a healthy and diverse population of microorganisms. As does exercise.

Unfortunately, modern life – and the related increase in processed and fatty fast foods – has waged a war on our microbiota, with research showing that many of the microbes our ancestors had have since gone extinct. Any link between this and the broad decrease in mental health is purely speculative – for now. But given the well-evidenced benefits of a healthy diet on our microbiota and bodies more generally, it makes sense to eat well to help bolster our minds and thinking, too.

We should also be aware that the relationship between our brains and our microbiota is an axis that runs both ways. While the organisms inside us apparently can influence how we think, the way we think may also affect them. A high-stress lifestyle, for example, can have a detrimental effect on our gut and its inhabitants, which anyone with stress-related gut issues will be very familiar with. So finding ways to relax and think more positively may also help to support a mutually beneficial feedback loop.

We're still a long way off supercharging our thinking through faecal transplants or 'crapsules' that could replace an unhealthy microbiota with a sparkling and optimal new one – although their use to treat a wide variety of health conditions may soon be a widespread reality. [24] And while the evidence so far is intriguing, much of it relates to animals and has yet to be replicated in humans. This is a novel and pioneering field. Nevertheless, things have come a very long way since the harrowing days of Beaumont's experiments on St Martin – and a window has gradually begun to open that may yet reveal an extraordinary new frontier. A frontier where our thinking isn't just shaped by us, but by the trillions of tiny organisms that have made us home and wired themselves into our innermost workings.

20

Are you hangry?

Writing a book about thinking involves a lot of, well, thinking. This is something both your authors have always loved – in fact, throughout our lives, we've each been accused of thinking too much and told to 'lighten up' or 'go with the flow'. But while writing this book, there were days when thinking became difficult and muddled. Perhaps we were more biased than usual, or our logic was more flawed. Sometimes we simply felt less motivated.

The benefit of having a co-author is that one of you can spot when the other is having a slow day. Though sometimes, such as during a long car journey through the Scottish Highlands when we had a heated and poorly defined debate (well, argument) about whether it is 'better' to be an optimist or a pessimist, neither of us was thinking clearly. Analysing these 'bad days' in retrospect, however, we noticed a clear pattern: they were very often preceded by a bad night's sleep, a stressful or emotional event, or a missed meal.

As discussed in many other places in this book, there are a lot of flaws in thinking that are consistent: learned behaviour, entrenched biases, or a tendency to be more of an optimist or pessimist. However, sometimes, the root cause is something else entirely. Sometimes, we might simply be hangry. And things like this can cause us to become temporarily and seemingly randomly muddled in our thinking. In the book *Noise*, Daniel Kahneman, Oliver Sibony and Cass Sunstein explore how professional judgement – for example, doctors' diagnoses of the same symptoms or judges' sentences for the same crimes – can vary dramatically, even though they shouldn't. This 'noise' is caused by fluctuations in thinking that aren't systematic in the way biases are. In fact, while cognition and personality can offer some protection against noise, it seems that 'lower-level processes', such as hunger, tiredness and stress, can be contributing factors. The brain is, after all, an organ, and needs the right amount of nutrition and rest to run at full capacity.

Anders Sandberg, a research fellow at the Future of Humanity Institute at the University of Oxford, who has studied thinking and cognitive biases, believes these lower-order factors are, in fact, the biggest obstacles to thinking clearly. 'When I'm tired, I notice that my ability to reach logical conclusions gets weaker, because the line of thought kind of peters out,' he explained in an interview with us. 'So I'm going to go for shorter lines of thought, simpler arguments, than when I have a lot of energy.'

This effect, which we have all experienced, has been explored in countless studies. For example, it is clear that we struggle with concentration, and attention in general, when we are tired.[1] Attention is an important prerequisite for thinking, particularly if it is abstract or complex, and a drop in it can have real-life consequences. Physicians, for example, are more likely to prescribe opioids at the end of the day, when they are tired, than they are in the morning.[2] But tiredness can make us all discombobulated during the most basic tasks, such as following a simple recipe or driving safely.

Perhaps even more worrying is that we tend to lose some of our cognitive flexibility, the ability to change perspective and adapt to the environment, when we are tired – a hugely important factor when it comes to thinking well.[3] Memory is another area strongly affected by a lack of sleep. This includes both working memory (our ability to remember several items for short periods of time, such as a mental shopping list), and long-term memory (such as our ability to remember what we learned in school).[4]

When we sleep, our memories are 'consolidated', a neural process in which our recent experiences, stored as memory traces in the hippocampus, are transformed into long-term memory in networks in the cortex (the outer layer of the brain, linked with many complex abilities such as reasoning, emotions and language). So if we don't sleep, we may struggle to form long-term memories, which are essential for learning and therefore essential for thinking. Young children, for example, learn new words from storybooks more easily if they have a nap straight after hearing the story.[5]

Sleep deprivation and fatigue can also deplete our levels of self-control, making us worse at suppressing prejudice and more likely to rely on shortcuts our brains like to take; such as stereotypes.[6] Researchers have even suggested that fatigue may increase racial bias in moments when police officers must decide whether to shoot – having life and death consequences.[7] That said, some researchers have challenged the idea that self-control is limited in this way, and have failed to replicate certain findings in the area.[8]

A brain imaging study suggested that the cognitive deficits associated with tiredness are largely down to deactivation of the thalamus, involved in sensory perception, and the prefrontal cortex, which is implicated in complex cognitive tasks, though researchers are still debating what the exact neural mechanisms are.[9] Either way, even relatively minor sleep deprivation can cause similar cognitive deficits to those experienced when drunk. When people haven't slept for seventeen to nineteen hours, for example, their performance on certain cognitive tests is equal to, or even worse than, those who have a blood alcohol concentration of 0.05 per cent, the drink-drive limit in many countries.[10] And after several consecutive days without sleep, many people's thinking will collapse altogether, triggering symptoms of psychosis such as hallucinations, delusions and paranoia.

The negative effects of tiredness, however, may be stronger for some people than others, and those differences between individuals are to a large extent genetic. Older people and women, for example, seem more resilient to the effects of tiredness.[11] If you know yourself to be a person who suffers considerably from a lack of sleep, it makes sense to prioritise it.

Alongside lack of sleep, hunger is another commonly experienced obstacle to thinking clearly. Not only can daydreams about sponge cakes and cheeseburgers become utterly distracting when we're trying to concentrate on a boring work task; many of us can get downright hangry. When we are feeling irritable, we are more likely to lash out or think carelessly when faced with complex or contro-versial problems than to calmly think through them.[12]

One famous study even revealed how judges on an Israeli parole board were more lenient at the beginning of the day or just after their lunch break, when they weren't hungry, than they were just before lunch, or towards the end of the day, when pangs of hunger are more likely to return.[13] The authors argued that the judges' harsher rulings could have been explained by them lacking the energy to make bold, difficult decisions, and instead favouring the status quo. Others have suggested the effect may have had more to do with how the cases were scheduled, but even the most evenly tempered among us will admit to hunger shortening our fuse and making us more unreason-able and irrational.

Hunger seems to affect our time perception too. One study showed that hunger makes us more 'present biased', driving us to opt for immediate gratification rather than future rewards.[14] Of course, this makes sense if the reward is food – most of us would prefer an immediate snack when we're starving to a two-hour wait for some-thing better. But curiously, this urge for immediate gratification seems to apply more broadly, leading us to make poorer decisions in general when we're starved. The researchers found that when people were offered a reward, £20 in cash or twenty song downloads, right away or one that would double in size in future, they were generally able to hold off for ninety or forty days, respectively, to get the bigger reward. But if they were hungry, they were only prepared to wait for forty or twelve days, respectively. Hunger seems to make us impatient and potentially impulsive, rather than thoughtful and measured.

As many people noticed during the various COVID-19 lockdowns, a lack of physical exercise can also make our minds sluggish. Taking a break by going for a walk outside can make us feel energised and sharp, providing some much-needed oxygen and increased blood supply to the brain. Indeed, studies have shown that a sedentary lifestyle is associated with poorer cognition in domains ranging from memory to executive function and processing speed.[15]

People who are physically fit, as measured by walking as quickly as they can for two minutes, are also more likely to have a well-preserved structure of the white matter in the brain, which is made up of nerve fibres and involved in communication between brain cells. Such information transfer across the brain is important to thinking well, and abnormalities in white matter has been found to precede Alzheimer's disease.[16]

In addition, exercise can help the brain form new neural connections and even aid cell growth. So it is perhaps no surprise that people who are physically fit on average score better on a range of cognitive tests than those who are unfit, including on processing speed, cognitive flexibility and fluid intelligence.[17]

But if you're not a regular runner, don't despair – even a single exercise session has an overall small positive effect on cognition, and may therefore come in handy before an exam, for example.[18] When it comes to executive function – which includes attention, working memory, problem solving and cognitive flexibility – it seems moderate aerobic exercise has the biggest effect, while intensive exercise may be better for information processing. A single bout of exercise has also been shown to boost mood, something which deeply affects thinking.

Overcoming these cognitive obstacles may seem easy: simply eat better, sleep more and exercise a bit. But we can also avoid the pitfalls these states of being present by making concerted efforts to avoid important decisions on an empty stomach, or pulling an all-nighter just before sitting an exam.

Of course, there are times when these things are simply not an option. Most parents struggle to get enough shut-eye, and many people are forced to work several jobs at the cost of a good night's sleep to make ends meet. If that's you, you may want to try napping, which could help you feel more alert, and possibly even have a positive effect on cognitive function.[19] You'd be in good company – Winston Churchill, Albert Einstein, and Leonardo Da Vinci all adopted this technique.[20]

And let's face it: many of us are just plain lazy, something which Sandberg doesn't think is all that bad. 'It's been said that you need smart, lazy people. They are going to spend some time coming up with the simplest, quickest ways of doing something,' he argues. 'Dumb and energetic people are downright dangerous because they go off with great force in some random direction and then put all their effort into doing the wrong thing.'

Sandberg is a keen 'transhumanist' – a movement celebrating technological progress and aiming to make humans better, including with their thinking. He has tried a number of different methods to make himself 'smarter', or at least less vulnerable to 'noise'. But not every method suits him. 'I used to have an office right on top of a gym and I never set my foot in there, even though, in many of my standard presentations, I have this slide showing the good effects on mental performance of aerobic exercise,' he recalls. 'I would rather take a pill for that because going to the gym takes time. It's tiresome and you get sweaty.'

Sandberg has done research into 'cognitive enhancement' – ways to essentially hack our cognition. Some techniques are relatively straightforward. If you are tired, for example, caffeine, glucose and nicotine have all been shown to boost cognition temporarily – making us more attentive and energetic, and increasing reaction times.[21] According to a recent review by Sandberg and others, omega-3 fatty acids and herbal medicines such as *Bacopa monnieri* (commonly known as waterhyssop) have also been found to have some cognitive enhancing effects, while meditation can boost attention and cognitive flexibility.[22] And if you don't have time to go running, oxygen therapy can enhance memory.

For high-stakes tasks, Sandberg and other transhumanists even occasionally opt for 'smart drugs', pharmaceuticals that can increase cognition temporarily without making us high or changing our personality, including modafinil and stimulants such as Adderall and methylphenidate. Barbara Sahakian, a neuropsychologist at the University of Cambridge, has studied the effects of such drugs and believes they could make us better at thinking – especially modafinil, which unlike stimulants, doesn't seem to come with crippling side effects or be addictive.[23] 'You become better at planning and problem solving, and that should have knock-on effects,' she explained to us, adding that it also helps with more emotional aspects such as motivation. 'If your working memory improves then obviously you have more space to consider things at the same time and work through them.'

She has even shown that smart drugs can make sleep-deprived doctors and people with schizophrenia more cognitively flexible, which may be true for the rest of us too.[24] That said, the pharmaceuticals are still not available legally in many countries, and the safety of taking them long-term hasn't been sufficiently studied, she warned. Most people buy the drugs online, which can be risky as you can't be sure what you are getting. What's more, people with high cognitive ability who are working at their optimal level, perhaps having had a good night's sleep, don't seem to benefit very much from these stimulants. Some, such as methylphenidate, can even make their thinking worse. And while modafinil seems to be able to focus our minds, it can make us slower.[25] This may help prevent us from being impulsive, but could be a disadvantage if we run out of time playing chess against a clock.[26] So while smart drugs may be helpful in certain situations for certain people, they are not a reliable shortcut to thinking more clearly in the long run.

Transhumanists don't stop at smart drugs, however. Many are increasingly interested in gene therapy and gene editing to boost cognition, including Liz Parrish who we meet in Chapter 23: 'Are you getting old?' (page 184). Meanwhile, Elon Musk and others are keen to find ways to connect the human mind to computers.

Keeping in mind that a lot of these options simply aren't accessible for the vast majority of us, at least you can rest safe in the knowledge that a good night's sleep, exercise and a healthy diet that keeps our blood sugar level even is the best and safest approach to protect against daily dips in thinking and decision-making ability. That said, we live in times when nutrition and exercise have become a religion for some – a proxy for a smarter, healthier and longer life. And it's true that these things are excellent for our health and cognition, counteracting some of the noise caused by sleep deprivation, hunger and sitting. But in reality, no amount of green shakes or marathons will miraculously make us profound thinkers. Many people are more willing to endure physical discomfort more than mental discomfort – but ultimately you do need the latter if you want to improve your thinking. Challenging our minds – finding flaws in our thinking, becoming aware of our biases and learning difficult concepts throughout life – is uncomfortable. But, like a hard workout session, it also has huge benefits, and lucky for you, if you're reading this book, you've already taken a step.

21

Are you high?

Imagine a mountain. It is vast, beautiful and covered in virgin snow. Now picture yourself skiing down it. At first, you are alone, and the snow is untouched. There's nothing to guide you and there are no tracks to follow. You feel free to chart your own line. But as you descend towards the valley below, you encounter the tracks of other skiers – and these ruts get bigger and bigger as more and more people start following them and they become more established. At first, you can still ski around the ruts, but before long there are so many, and they are so deep, that you can't help but become trapped in them. And rather than plotting your own route, these trails are now just leading you to the bottom. You're quite literally stuck in a rut.

It's a familiar scenario if you've ever spent a week skiing. But this isn't a detail from our last winter holiday; rather it's the colourful picture painted by Professor David Nutt, a leading neuropsychopharmacologist (a mouthful of a job description that essentially means someone who studies how drugs affect the mind and influence behaviour) at Imperial College London. David Nutt conjures up this image to describe how the human brain can become imprisoned by certain ways of thinking. Ultimately, the hardware in our heads is expansive and flexible, a supercomputer of unparalleled scale that can make spectacularly complex decisions. But it also serves a simple biological goal: survival. Underneath all our complexities, our brains are tasked with ensuring we eat, drink and live long enough to produce the next generation.

And this can make it fallible.

Although the brain is intellectually supercharged, it must also ensure that it runs as economically as possible, lest it overuses precious energy resources. In fact, the human brain is many times more energy efficient than any computer. And one way it achieves this remarkable efficiency is by making inferences. Rather than endlessly updating and re-doing their calculations about the world around us, our brains often rely on assumptions and shortcuts. This reduces the amount of processing power our brains need, but it also means that we can easily get locked into inflexible beliefs and ways of thinking. Fair enough – we can't expect our blobs of grey and white matter to endlessly remodel the world in real time. The mind is extraordinary enough. 'But suppose,' proposes Nutt, 'it gets it wrong.' Indeed, Nutt believes that this is how the brain can get trapped in certain states, from depression and paranoia to addiction. Based on our education, the society we live in and past, often childhood, experiences, our beliefs, behaviours and thinking – some of them erroneous or destructive – can become rigid and habitual. And we may find ourselves skiing in those imaginary ruts, unable to think freely or clearly.

Which is where certain drugs may offer a solution.

Some drugs, of course, can cause severe addiction. Used incorrectly, they can also cause serious harm and kill (not least alcohol and tobacco). Others, however, may offer profound insights into how we might overcome the brain's tendency to become trapped in harmful states of mind. In fact, certain psychedelic drugs such as LSD and magic mushrooms (psilocybin), when used responsibly and in the right environment, can be used to effectively treat a range of psychological conditions including addiction, depression and end-of-life anxiety. 'To use the skiing analogy,' says Nutt, 'psychedelics just break up all the ruts and turn it into a virgin snow field again. You can then ski where you want. You can go wherever you need to go . . . The last freedom we have is to think differently.'

* * *

170

Broadly speaking, drugs can be divided into 'uppers', 'downers' and 'mind expanders'. Some are illegal and considered taboo in many cultures; others are not. But all, to a greater or lesser degree, make us 'high' and all, to a greater or lesser degree, change the way we think. This is why mind-altering substances have been used by humans for longer than even history can recall.

Uppers, such as cocaine, amphetamines and caffeine, tend to make us think faster and can prolong our attention. But at higher doses, many can also cause paranoia and violence (the latter frequently triggered by the former). Cocaine, for example, has a reputation for transforming users into twitchy, narcissistic chatterboxes. However, it has its origins in the coca leaf, helpfully chewed or brewed into a tea for centuries by indigenous Andean communities as a stimulant and treatment for altitude sickness, and as nature's very own 'caffeine pill' alternative. Like any drug, cocaine targets particular features of the brain, in this case the neurotransmitters dopamine (which is linked to feelings of pleasure) and noradrenaline (part of the 'flight or fight' mechanism, which prepares you for action in stressful situations).[1] For a while, cocaine – like many other uppers, such as amphetamines – can sharpen our thoughts, improve our mood and make us more energetic. But it can also lead to addiction and structural changes in the brain, which themselves can negatively affect our ability to deal with stress, make sound decisions and think clearly.[2]

Downers (or depressants) such as alcohol and heroin, reduce brain activity, which can provide users with a welcome (if brief and later regrettable) vacation from the stresses and responsibilities of everyday life. Our old favourite, alcohol, for example, impedes electrical communication between neurons all across the brain, essentially sinking us into a state of blissful ignorance. While booze reduces most cognitive functions, however, there is evidence that it may enhance creativity.[3] Heroin and similar opiates, meanwhile, have a more focused target in the brain: dedicated opiate receptors that play a key role in pleasure, reward and pain perception. But unlike the body's naturally occurring opiates (enkephalins), these drugs turbo-charge the response, burying the mind – and all the irksome worries of reality – beneath a blanket of all-consuming anaesthesia. While opium, morphine and heroin have long been associated with creative thinkers, from poet Samuel Taylor Coleridge and *Confessions of an English Opium-Eater* writer Thomas De Quincey to singer-song-writer Amy Winehouse, downers can easily take us too far down.[4] In high doses, they can switch off not only parts of the brain responsible for thinking but also vital functions, such as breathing. No wonder, then, that downers kill far more people than uppers, not least synthetic opioids often prescribed as painkillers such as fentanyl (which is fifty to one hundred times more potent than morphine) and oxy-codone (often sold under the brand name OxyContin), which have contributed to a longstanding opioid 'crisis' in many countries.[5] In 2019, nearly 50,000 people were killed by overdoses involving opi-oids in the US alone.[6] Like many uppers, downers such as heroin and alcohol may also lead to serious addiction, one of the most obvious obstacles to independent thinking.

Of course, many of these uppers, downers and derivations thereof have been, or are still being, used for medicinal purposes, including as prescribed painkillers. Some are also being used to treat psychiatric disorders, including MDMA and ketamine.[7] Also known as Special K, Wonk or Donkey Dust when sold illegally as a party drug, ketamine is a powerful tranquiliser that has been shown to have anti-depressive properties.[8]

Ultimately, however, it's the mind expanders that most radically change the way we think. So, let's return to our imaginary magic skiing mountain. Research into how psychedelics, such as LSD and psilocy-bin, could benefit the way we think peaked in the 1950s and 60s, when Aldous Huxley wrote about his own experiences on mescaline, a psy-chedelic found in the peyote cactus. Some of the experiments at the time were downright bizarre – on one occasion, an elephant named Tusko was injected with 297mg of LSD (hundreds of times the human dose) in an Oklahoma zoo and swiftly collapsed and died – arguably because of the anti-psychotics and barbiturates given in an attempt to revive him.[9] But other, more scientific, studies began to offer valuable insights, with many psychologists and psychiatrists at the time believing that psychedelics could provide useful treatments for mood disorders and act as an aid in psychotherapy.[10] They were also found to be relatively safe, when used correctly in a medical setting, and carried no risk of dependence. Despite these early successes, however, the work was soon curtailed as governments banned the drugs, fearful they might be driving the anti-Vietnam war movement, radicalising the next generation – and encouraging them to ask too many uncomfortable questions about the status quo. Psychedelic research entered a dark age.[11]

Over the last two decades or so, however, research into psychedelics has been resurrected and studies by Nutt and others have uncovered some intriguing findings.[12] Much of the research has focused on psilocybin – which induces a shorter trip (four to five hours) than LSD (eight to twelve hours) and is less likely to trigger frightening, negative experiences – which is administered to volunteers under strict clinical conditions. Psilocybin has been shown to improve depression in sufferers for weeks and even months after the trial, making it one of the most powerful therapeutics for treatment-resistant depression, while fMRI scans have shown it boosts connectivity between different brain regions.[13] Its use has also been linked to people with depression feeling more connected to others and the world around them and accepting, rather than avoiding, their emotions.[14] Psilocybin is also a promising treatment for end-of-life anxiety (perhaps because it makes people feel more connected to the wider universe) and addiction to alcohol and tobacco.[15] Future studies will investigate how psilocybin could help treat anorexia and obsessive compulsive disorder (OCD).[16]

The research is still in its infancy, seen as controversial by some, and the current legal status of psychedelics remains an obstacle for those conducting it. But many believe the drugs, which are far less likely to trigger addiction than the vast majority of uppers and downers, could provide powerful new psychiatric treatments – if only we have the imagination to scientifically explore their properties in more detail.

But how *can* psychedelics so powerfully change the way we think? The human brain contains around 100 billion computing neurons and each of these is like a mini computer. Some process raw sensory information from our eyes, ears and other senses. Others bring all of that data together to transform it into a stable model of the world and our place within it, and it is these neurons which are heavily laden with receptors for psychedelics. 'These neurons control what you do and think and see,' says Nutt. 'And when you disrupt them with psychedelics, then the brain starts to do its own thing.' The consequence is that your brain's standard model of reality begins to unravel. Solids may turn liquid and universal laws, such as gravity, may become unstable. In fact, the sparkling Christmas-light hallucinations so familiar to users of psychedelics are actually a rare glimpse of the raw data your brain is receiving from the world before it has been properly processed.

But drugs such as LSD and psilocybin don't just disrupt our model of the physical world. They also break down the brain circuits that control our rigid and habitual ways of thinking. Indeed, a recent study by Parker Singleton at Cornell University and others examining brain scans of people on LSD and a placebo found that the drug enabled the brain to move more easily between different states, becoming more occupied with sensory-driven activities and less focused on higher-level processing.[17] This is partly why Nutt and others believe that the drugs may successfully treat depression, addiction and anorexia.[18]

These psychological conditions tend to be driven by repetitive, entrenched negative thoughts, and psychedelics temporarily allow sufferers to break out of narrow 'ruts' of thinking, gain fresh insights about their condition and imagine new solutions. To ski freely across the mountain of their mind again. Imagine having the power to quieten the parts of your brain that could be holding you back, to dissolve the walls within your mind and allow you to – if only temporarily – experience reality afresh without the weight of the rules that normally dictate the way you see the world. Crucially, the way psychedelics work on the brain means that users are also more likely to remember their experience than those getting high on many other drugs.

But could they also be used to address other entrenched negative biases, such as racism and sexism? Nutt is sceptical, but remains hopeful that people with the right attitude could learn from the experience if administered correctly. 'People used to ask if I could "cure" Trump,' says Nutt, 'but I'd have no drug that powerful! It is a fundamental question, however. The people that go into our studies and the people that take psychedelics recreationally usually do it for some kind of self-awareness. And I think people that don't want to change will be able to resist the drug.' Ultimately, then, psychedelics, like many other interventions, seem to work best when people are both aware that they want to change something about their thinking *and* are willing and open to change.

There's still a long way to go before psychedelics are used more widely to treat disorders of the mind. Nutt has argued for a regulated market for some psychedelics, particularly psilocybin – which was banned in the UK in 2005 but has recently been decriminalised in parts of the US – but don't hold your breath for behind-the-counter

LSD at your local pharmacy. That's a policy potato that is likely too hot to handle, for the foreseeable future at least. The research, however, will continue to offer fascinating insights into innovative new therapies – and the spectacular and still mysterious workings of our mind and how we think. 'The brain may focus on the simple things like drinking, eating and sex, but it's got so much more capacity than that,' says Nutt. 'Psychedelics can bring some of it out.'

22

Are you an addict?

Jackie Malton was a highly successful police officer when she discovered the destructive power of her 'Fuck It Button'. An openly
gay woman in the straight and male Metropolitan Police of the late
twentieth century, she busted stereotypes, became a Detective Chief
Inspector, worked on some of London's biggest armed robbery and
murder cases – and inspired the character of DCI Jane Tennison
(played by Helen Mirren) in the acclaimed TV drama *Prime Suspect*.
But while Malton powered through the ranks, apparently shrugging
off the brutal crimes she investigated, the job's relentless pressures,
the casual misogyny – and the sex toys male colleagues gave her
when there was a secret Santa at Christmas – she was also becoming
an addict.[1]

On one level, alcohol was a way of coping with the trauma of
her police work and investigations such as the New Cross house
fire, which killed thirteen young Black people in January 1981. As
a self-confessed overfeeler – at a time when expressing feelings was
taboo in the police – Malton suppressed hers. She'd press the Fuck
It Button and order another round. Booze was the culmination of a
case solved, a criminal caught, a hard day's work completed. It also
served a deeper purpose. Malton's police appraisals identified her
as a flexible and creative thinker, a psychological profile confirmed
when she recently took a Hogan personality test. But this put her at
odds with the rigid modes of thinking in the police at the time. 'I
tried to change things, but the Metropolitan Police was very fixed
in its ways then and there was an institutional reluctance to self-ex-
amine,' she says. 'It was like trying to turn the *Titanic*. I wanted to

belong, but this made me feel like I didn't. So I used drink to change the way I felt.' She was left feeling even more isolated when she blew the whistle on a corrupt fellow officer who was subsequently suspended.[2] Shortly afterwards, her colleagues got up and left as she entered the staff canteen.

As she privately battled these demons, alcohol enabled Malton to feel 'less fearful, less vulnerable, more together'. Until it didn't. Gradually, her drinking just added to the shame she already felt about her sexuality. She'd promise that she'd leave the bar early, that she'd only have two or three drinks – but it never turned out that way. She'd say, 'Fuck it,' and carry on drinking anyway. One day, whisky found its way into her morning tea.[3] When it came to alcohol, it had become clear that she was no longer choosing when to press the Fuck It Button – her addiction was making the decision for her. Malton was a courageous, flexible and forensic thinker who overcame prejudice to become one of the Metropolitan Police's greatest detective minds. But addiction had hijacked her thinking regardless.

We all have a Fuck It Button. Another chocolate? Fuck it. A glass of wine for the road? Fuck it. A sneaky cigarette at the end of a night out? Fuck it. Like many of the habits discussed in Chapter 12: 'Are you a creature of habit?' (page 96), a nightly glass of wine or a puff on a ciggie can easily become part of our daily routine. But there's a point where too many 'Fuck its' constitute a full-blown addiction. Ian Hamilton, an associate professor of addiction at the University of York, knows this all too well. His father was a (recovered) alcoholic and he has worked with countless addicts in the community. One of his patients was a female intravenous drug user. Because of her habit, her children had been placed in care, she'd had one leg amputated and she was now in danger of losing the other. A significant part of the problem was that she was injecting herself in the groin. But despite understanding the facts and the scale of her addiction, she was unable even to change how she took the drug, let alone stop it altogether. 'The key word is "salience"', says Hamilton. 'The worst affected addict becomes unable to think about anything other than how they're going to source the drug, pay for the drug, use the drug.' But that doesn't mean addiction is only about the drug. 'A lot of it happens prior to even an introduction or the exposure to the drug.'

In the 1980s, Nancy Reagan – wife of the then US President, Ronald Reagan – popularised the 'Just Say No' anti-drug campaign. This helped promote the idea that drug addiction is a binary yes/no choice directed by our own free will. The reality, however, is far more complex. Hamilton's patient, like most serious addicts, had seemingly become incapable of making rational, considered choices regarding her habit. Indeed, addiction is a compulsive behaviour that prioritises a substance over the facts, over family, over friends, over the user's own life. Supporting research shows that much addictive behaviour may not be conscious at all, but instead triggered by primitive parts of the brain – such as the nucleus accumbens, which plays a role in the brain's reward circuit – that we have no real control over.[4] Addiction can quite literally make the decision for us. As this book shows, numerous internal and external factors influence and manipulate our thinking, but it seems addiction capitalises on the human brain's many fallibilities to a quite extraordinary degree – and profoundly impacts our ability to think for ourselves.

Many factors put us on the path to addiction. Our genes certainly play a part, with studies estimating that alcoholism, for example, is between 40 and 60 per cent heritable.[5] It is also deeply linked to mental health. In the UK, 40 per cent of tobacco is consumed by people with mental health issues, while over 75 per cent of addicts also present a psychiatric condition, such as depression, anxiety or post-traumatic stress disorder (PTSD).[6]

But while much research, particularly in the US, focuses on addiction as a biological process, our environment is also a factor, as Malton and countless others have discovered. In 1971, as the US began withdrawing 200,000 troops from the war in Vietnam, President Richard Nixon began to fret that a large part of the country was about to hit the Fuck It Button. His panic attack had been triggered by two congressman, who had returned from a visit to Vietnam claiming that 10–15 per cent of US troops there were heroin addicts.[7]

To address this, a researcher named Lee Robins was tasked with investigating how servicemen were using heroin, both in Vietnam and after they returned Stateside – and her resulting study contained some intriguing findings about addiction.[8]

She found that there had been a radical change in behaviour once the soldiers returned to the US. Only 10 per cent reported using narcotics once back in America and only 7 per cent of *that* 10 per cent (1 per cent of the total) said they had been addicted *after* their return. What had happened was entirely unexpected: most of the addicted Vietnam veterans either quit narcotics of their own accord just before leaving or remained drug-free after a brief detox once their use had been discovered.

There are numerous reasons why this may have been the case, including heroin being less available and more expensive and its use being more stigmatised in the US than in Vietnam. But some addiction specialists, including Hamilton, believe that the study also points to the environmental nature of addiction. The men had used and become addicted to heroin in an uncertain, alien and often stressful war zone where its use wasn't only acceptable, but may have led to a sense of belonging with others in the same situation. But the veterans also had far less need for it when they returned home to friends, family and a more secure environment.

In most cases, addiction is profoundly difficult to overcome. Research shows that around 90 per cent of drug addicts will relapse at some point following treatment – although many will show improvements long term.[9] This is partly because addiction so effectively hijacks our thinking, quite literally rewiring our brains to the degree that the physical changes are visible in scans. For example, scans show that binge drinkers of alcohol use different parts of their brains to non-binge drinkers when completing a number recognition task.[10] It appears that new parts of the brain may be recruited to make the calculations to compensate for reduced capacity elsewhere. But while recovery often takes years, it is possible. And this is cause for optimism – not just for recovering addicts, but for anyone hoping to think more clearly. After all, if we can eventually overcome this most deeply ingrained form of compulsive thinking and regain control of our Fuck It Button, surely we can do more to address many of the other biases highlighted in this book.

Jackie Malton joined Alcoholics Anonymous in 1992, left the Metropolitan Police five years later and went on to earn a master's degree in Addiction Psychology. She hasn't had a drink since and now works voluntarily with male criminals who are dealing with their own addiction issues in prison. And as she discovered, the first step to overcoming addiction – as it is with beating many other biased and compulsive thoughts – is acknowledging the problem and the hold the substance, or the belief, has over our thinking. Not that this is easy. Through his own work with addicts, Hamilton has found that many hazardous drinkers don't view themselves as having a problem because they don't see themselves as being a stereotypical alcoholic: of needing a drink first thing in the morning, of drinking every day. They fool themselves into believing it's someone else's problem. For Malton, it was no use someone else highlighting her alcoholism; she had to become self-aware, think for herself and own it. To overcome compulsive thinking, then, we first have to stop kidding ourselves.

Changing for the better takes time. 'It's no good just doing the same thing and expecting a different result,' says Malton. 'You have to create new habits, new neural pathways, new connections.' Treatment programmes, particularly those that are individualised and broad-based, can help enormously, but, as Robins's Vietnam study suggests, we should also consider the environmental side of addiction.[11] Stress and the availability of a substance are factors, but so is our social situation. As Malton discovered, it's a struggle to control your drinking when you're isolated or in an environment where heavy boozing is the norm and you feel like an outsider. Instead, like the Vietnam veterans perhaps, we are better able to maintain control of our thinking when we are at 'home' and surrounded by positive relationships that aren't co-dependent. When we feel like we 'belong'.

And so, addiction can teach us some broader lessons about compulsive thinking more generally. That anyone can be susceptible. That it can be painfully difficult to overcome, but we can succeed. That we must identify and acknowledge our own harmful, biased thinking, from addiction to sexism and racism, if we are to address it. That we should be aware of the role our environment and our relationships play in reinforcing – and mitigating – our behaviour, a factor supported by research that shows multicultural regions, for example, tend to be less racist than more homogenous ones.[12] And that while this process can be long and hard, it can also be hugely rewarding and beneficial.

'Has my experience of addiction made me a better thinker? Definitely,' says Malton.

'It was a process of education and recovery and made me more open about myself. We are all made up of dark and light. In recovery, you have to be really open about the dark side of who you are . . . And that's the point. We don't want to look at that shadow side of us because it's not quite so nice, but you have to put your shadow self on the table and look at it and just say, "What are my biases?" And then you can start to uncover the treasure in your trash.'

Whether we are confronting an addiction, or some of the other forms of compulsive thinking covered in this book, we should all try and follow Malton's example and face our darker biases head on. We are all vulnerable to them, but we can also all do something about them – and learn to think more freely as a result.

23

Are you getting old?

It was a 'harrowing few months', recalls Elizabeth Parrish, CEO of the Seattle-based biotech company Bioviva, which is working on treatments to slow down the ageing process. In September 2015, she made the controversial decision to get injected with two experimental – and illegal in the US – gene therapies. One was myostatin, a drug investigated for its potential to reverse muscle loss. The other was a 'telomerase' gene therapy, which has been used to extend lifespan in mice.[1] Her goal was to see if she could slow down her ageing – and potentially also help combat the impact the advancing years have on our ability to think clearly, a process she likens to 'a book burning'.

It was no doubt risky – several people have died after receiving gene therapies in the past, albeit with other drugs. And as Bioviva hadn't done sufficient pre-clinical research to get the experiment approved by the US Food and Drug Administration, Parrish, then forty-four, had to travel to Colombia to receive it. The anxiety set in as she returned home. 'Every time I didn't feel very good, if I felt tired or achy, I was very concerned,' she told us in an interview, adding that she nevertheless didn't regret it. 'The premise of the company was that the founders would try the technology and see if it worked,' she explained. 'The reality is that forty-one million people will die this year. If this technology could save them, how could you not try it?'

When a cell gets damaged, or old, or simply needs replacing, the DNA inside it will divide and replicate, creating two new cells with identical DNA. However, this can't go on indefinitely; unlimited growth is what makes cancer so invasive and dangerous. And so, as a protection feature, our chromosomes (which consist of DNA) have these protective caps on the end of them. Think of them like aglets on a shoelace. These are called 'telomeres'. As most human cells can't copy the telomeres themselves, they get shorter every time a cell divides; the DNA is copied and replicated, but the telomere just gets sliced in half, over and over again. In doing so, it limits the number of times a cell can divide, acting as a sort of biological clock on our cells. Eventually, telomeres get so short that the cell isn't able to divide further, whereupon it enters a toxic state called senescence. Senescence can hamper the function of tissue – causing the rather poorly understood process that we call ageing.

The telomerase gene therapy that Parrish received was designed to lengthen her telomeres, and therefore potentially slow down her own ageing process. Luckily, she didn't experience any adverse effects, and the results, released by Bioviva six months later, seemed promising – at least to her. She discovered that, before she had the treatment, the average telomere length in her white blood cells was roughly that of a sixty- to sixty-five-year-old. But after the treatment, they appeared to have lengthened by 9 per cent – corresponding to the telomeres of a forty-five-year-old. Despite these results, scientists weren't convinced.[2] For one, some argued, it is dangerous to experiment with a biological function that seems to be designed to safeguard us against tumour growth. And though Parrish's anecdotal results seemed to indicate success, we don't actually know yet whether telomere lengthening can indeed slow ageing in humans. Others pointed out that the effect had only been demonstrated in one type of cell, and that it was unknown whether the telomeres in the rest of her body had also lengthened. It was also pointed out that telomere length measurements have notoriously low precision, and that the lengthening Parrish experienced may be insignificant – it was within the error margins of the measurement. Parrish, however, is passionate about her quest to extend the human lifespan, and when you consider what ageing does to your mind and body, it's not surprising.

Everyone ages differently, but there's no denying that grey hair, wrinkles, loss of muscle mass, and increased risk of diseases including stroke, heart attacks, cancer and dementia are part of the package deal. Beyond that, even in the absence of diseases, the brain shrinks and its cortices thin. Individual brain cells shrink too, while the connections between them weaken and the formation of new ones diminishes. All this can have knock-on effects, making us slower at processing information, worse at remembering and potentially less attentive, for example in noisy environments – all influencing how we think.[3] But while people often believe that such decline begins in early adulthood, a recent study involving more than a million people has revealed that the slowing of mental speed doesn't actually start until the age of sixty.[4] As we age, we may also lose some of our cognitive flexibility, potentially making it more difficult to think in new ways and fight ingrained biases.[5] This is consistent with research into how personality changes with age, suggesting we become less open to experience after the age of sixty, albeit more emotionally stable and conscientious. Younger people often accuse older generations of being prejudiced when it comes to issues such as race and gender. And while attitudes vary from person to person, studies have shown that older people are, on average, more likely to rely on stereotypes and be socially inappropriate than younger people.[6] The researchers argue that this may be linked to diminished functioning of the frontal lobes, which normally help us inhibit our behaviour.[7]

Parrish highlights another explanation, called terror management strategy. This line of research suggests that when we are forced to think about our death, which younger people can more easily avoid, we become anxious and feel threatened. This can make us more close-minded, punitive,[8] nationalistic,[9] religious[10] and prejudiced.[11] We hold on to our 'in group' – other people who look and behave like us – and become suspicious of new things and people who are different. That said, there have been failures to replicate some of these studies and, on average, old adults actually seem to have slightly less explicit death anxiety than younger or middle-aged people.[12]

But there are other explanations. Ingmar Skoog, a professor of psychiatry at Gothenburg University in Sweden, runs a unique and long-running study, called the Gothenburg H70 Birth Cohort Study, which shows that our generation may matter more than our age when it comes to thinking and attitudes.[13] The study, launched in 1971 with 392 participants born in 1901 and 1902, compares the physical and cognitive health, attitudes and behaviour of seventy-year-olds born in different decades. Rather than our shrinking brains or a fear of death making us more conservative and bigoted with age, it could simply be a reflection of the society we grew up in. According to Skoog, around 40 per cent of Swedish people who were born in 1944 – and are now in their seventies – actually vote for the left-wing Social Democrats party, compared with just 20 per cent of younger people.[14] Interestingly, more than 40 per cent of people voted for that party when this generation was young. By comparison, seventy-year-olds in the UK remember, and perhaps nostalgically long for, the society they grew up in – when their country was a colonial superpower and proud winners of the Second World War. Skoog believes that declining openness among older people may also be down to changing social circumstances. When we retire, we don't tend to meet as many new people as we did when we were working – which might mean our thinking isn't challenged as much.

Ultimately, though, everyone's situation is different and some people become more open and less prejudiced as they age. We know that the brain retains an ability to adapt, creating new networks and connections. Interestingly, Skoog's study shows that the cognitive ability of seventy-year-olds today – including processing speed, logical thinking, spatial ability and memory for images – has increased dramatically and almost linearly since the first cohort, with the current cohort scoring nearly twice as high on some tests as the people born in 1901–02.[15] Huge improvements are also seen in physical tests, such as climbing up on a stool or standing on one leg. It even seems like each generation has its own collective personality, with later cohorts of seventy-year-olds being more emotionally stable than previous generations, with the ones born in 1944 also being less conscientious and more assertive, particularly the women. This generation infamously also engages in more risky drinking and has more sex than previous cohorts.

The reasons are complex. People who were born in 1901–02 lived completely different lives. They were far more likely to grow up in poverty and didn't get a two-week holiday allowance until they were fifty. They had low levels of education, had children earlier and ate a poorer diet. And we know that education and socioeconomic status, in particular, are linked to physical and cognitive health and longevity. So people who are young today may have unparalleled physical and mental fitness when they are seventy. And regardless of which generation we belong to, there are things we actually become better at as we age. One is lexical and verbal ability, something that can ultimately improve our thinking. We may be better at understanding and analysing politics, for example, if we understand terms such as 'McCarthyism', 'plutocracy' or 'demagogue'.

In Skoog's opinion, getting slower can also come with benefits: 'While young people may enthusiastically take on new projects or embrace a work reorganisation, older people stop and think. They have seen it so many times before, and realise that an idea can play out differently to what you had imagined.' This is clearly a useful skill – what's the point of being a quick thinker or a good problem solver if you haven't sufficiently pondered which problems are actually worth solving? What's more, the experience and rising levels of emotional stability that come with age can compensate for any reductions in cognitive ability. If we have to make a decision, we may not have to think it through as carefully if we've made a similar decision before. And the fact that we can regulate our emotions better is a massive bonus. Research shows that older people, who are better able to avoid ruminating on past negative experiences, for example, make better financial decisions.[16] They are less likely to hold on to projects that are no longer profitable, a common mistake known as the 'sunk cost bias'.[17]

Though there are a few comforting benefits to ageing, the fact remains that most of us will become worse at reasoning and slower at processing information and will struggle more with our memory as we get older. And we will be much more vulnerable to developing diseases of the mind, which could profoundly alter how we think. So can we do anything to protect our minds as we age? As we have seen, education is closely linked to cognitive abilities in older age. And while genes account for nearly one quarter of the change in thinking skills across our lifetime, our social environment has a huge impact.[18] A sedentary lifestyle, smoking and diabetes have all been linked with cognitive decline. What helps is to build resilience throughout life by staying physically and socially active, as well as intellectually challenging ourselves by learning new things – particularly languages. Some studies have suggested that this may reduce the risk of Alzheimer's disease by 35–40 per cent and may also help you maintain your cognitive flexibility and openness.[19] Conversely, being open to experience is associated with a greater 'cognitive reserve' – a type of resilience to cognitive decline – in old age.[20]

The broader the learning, the better. Solving sudokus makes us better at sudokus, and solving crosswords makes us better at crosswords – neither is a panacea that can make us substantially smarter. Brain training games can help with certain aspects of our cognition. But according to Skoog, we should try to push ourselves beyond such activities, perhaps by reading literature that we struggle to understand or listening to music we don't normally like. We should also maintain our interests, as these tend to stimulate us – even if society has other plans for us. 'Imagine a woman who has always been interested in fashion,' says Skoog. 'When she gets older, people will often start criticising her for not dressing like a seventy-year-old, whatever that is.' Essentially, you don't have to retreat to the edge of society, lock the door and vigilantly look out of the window for threats. You can assert yourself, challenge your thinking and others', and make the most of all that knowledge you've gathered throughout your long life. It may be challenging, but it's safer than experimental gene therapies.

Despite this, research shows that ageing anxiety among the young is common – and that we worry about things ranging from our physical appearance to faltering physical and cognitive health. A 2018 report by the Royal Society for Public Health (RSPH) found that almost a third of the British population believe 'being lonely is just something that happens when people get old', and a quarter of eighteen- to thirty-four-year-olds think it is 'normal to be unhappy and depressed when you are old'.[21] About half also think older people struggle to learn new skills, with 40 per cent of eighteen- to twenty-four-year-olds believing there is 'no way to escape dementia as you age'. A similar proportion of this age group also agree that 'in elections, most older people just vote for their own selfish interests rather than the well-being of the younger generation and society as a whole'. Meanwhile, a quarter of eighteen- to thirty-four-year-olds agree that old people 'can never really be thought of

190

as attractive', and the majority of women say they worry about the effect of ageing on their appearance. These all reveal how common anxieties about ageing are.

So, it isn't just ageing that changes how we think, age anxiety does too – potentially leading to ageism, health obsession, midlife crises or huge amounts of money being spent on plastic surgery or unproven anti-ageing therapies. But not everyone is equally affected. Research reveals that people who have quality contacts with older people, as well as knowledge about the ageing process, are less likely to have ageing anxiety or be ageist than those who don't.[22] It makes sense – when we actually interact with people who are going through something we fear, we may discover that things don't play out the same way in reality as they do in our imagination. Sadly, according to the RSPH, two-thirds of people in the UK don't have friends with an age gap of thirty years or more.

So, whether you fear getting old or are actually approaching your emeritus days, remember: seventy is the new fifty, which is fittingly also the title of Skoog's latest report. And don't forget that while some, particularly in the Western world, view old people as cognitively inferior and bigoted, another stereotype exists too: that old people are incredibly wise. This idea is so powerful that we even apply it to aliens, such as Yoda. It just goes to show that how we age isn't set in stone: there are probably as many ways of 'mature thinking' as there are old people. Which route will you go down? The choice is, to some extent, yours.

24

Are you scared of being different?

Gladys West could easily have chosen the kind of life that society expected of her as a young, Black woman in 1940s America. She could have worked in a service job, perhaps, or taken over her parents' small farm. But growing up in humble conditions in Virginia, where her mother also worked in a tobacco factory, West preferred order, logic and learning to heavy lifting and dirty clothes. 'She wanted to do something different,' explains her daughter Carolyn Oglesby.

After excelling in high school, she won a full scholarship to Virginia State University. But she wasn't particularly confident, and didn't immediately know what to major in. She considered home economics – essentially a training programme for aspiring housewives – and it's easy to see why. This was another socially appropriate 'career' for women in the US at the time, when fewer than 5 per cent had a college degree.[1] But with a little encouragement from her teachers, she eventually made the unusual choice to pursue mathematics – then as now a discipline dominated by men.

And it is lucky for all of us that she did, as her early decision to break social norms – and the brilliant mathematical work she did afterwards – changed the world.

After completing a master's degree in mathematics, she began work at the Naval Proving Ground in Dahlgren, Virginia (now the Naval Surface Warfare Centre). And it was no doubt daunting. She was only the second Black woman ever hired by the institution, and one of just four Black employees – including a man, Ira, who she later married. Although she encountered discrimination, she aimed to work twice as hard as everyone else. 'She just wanted to be the best she could,' explains Oglesby. And it was here that she mathematically modelled the shape of the Earth and developed 'satellite geodesy', helping to create the Global Positioning System (GPS), which so many of us rely on for navigation today.

Remarkably, it wasn't until decades later that West finally got the recognition she deserved as a 'hidden figure' behind the GPS. But in 2018, she was inducted into the United States Air Force Hall of Fame and chosen as one of the BBC's 100 women of the year.

While West doesn't see herself as particularly nonconformist, she undoubtedly defied social expectations – and continues to do so. In 2000, at the age of seventy, for example, she completed a PhD in public administration via a distance-learning programme, despite suffering a stroke during this time.

We all like to think that we make our own decisions and form our own opinions without social norms pulling our strings. But there are few things we care about more than what other people think. We are biased to make choices that certain people approve of, and we constantly compare ourselves with and compete against others. That means we may lose out on the kind of life that would make us thrive and grow, intellectually and emotionally – massively impacting our thinking. Think about your own choices. Were they really just your own? Are you in a job you want, or one you think others approve of? Do you worry about what others will think of your romantic partners? Do you dress for yourself, or to impress certain people? Even West, who did something radically different to those around her – having no role models to inspire her, or peers to compare herself to – needed the support of her teachers and family to finally make the leap and go her own way.

Other people profoundly influence our thinking. Most of us borrow our deepest beliefs and values, including political and religious views, from those we trust and admire. In fact, we often end up identifying so strongly with some people or groups that their views may often feel like our own. Neuroscientific research has shown that similar areas of the brain activate when we think about our 'in-groups' and our own personal identity, which means that the two are inextricably linked in our minds – whether we like it or not.[2]

We are social animals, and being sensitive to what others think helps us cooperate. The various social groups we belong to, be it a social class, a religious group or a sports club, help us to define who we are as individuals – creating a social identity. This helps inform how we think and act. 'It is fairly predictable that people are going to think the way their neighbours think, the way their friends think,' argues Daniel Kahneman. But this can also make us biased, favouring our own 'in-groups' while being judgemental, even prejudiced, of others.[3]

Most of us dread being cast out of our favourite groups. In fact, research suggests it actually hurts to be excluded. One neuroimaging study found that when participants were excluded by others while playing a virtual ball tossing game, areas of the brain that scientists believe are important for registering and regulating pain, activated – and more so in those who found the experience most stressful.[4]

To stay in the group, then, we conform to shared sets of norms, attitudes and behaviour. This is true for specific groups, with their own sets of norms, and society as a whole. If you see yourself as a metropolitan liberal, for example, you may adopt certain group-appropriate behaviours – be it religiously voting a certain way, living in a particular, fashionable neighbourhood, shunning the tabloid press and popcorn cinema, buying a fixed-gear bicycle, or baking your own sourdough bread. In fact, these group-appropriate behaviours may become so widely adopted that they become (potentially damaging) stereotypes themselves. But that doesn't mean we only conform to a single group – we often belong to several, each with their own norms. We may highlight other aspects of ourselves, for example, when we're at work or spending time with our mates at the local sports club.

Modern research on conformity dates back nearly a century to experiments by Muzafer Sherif in the 1930s and Solomon Asch in the early 1950s. Building on Sherif's early work, Asch designed an experiment that is still used today.[5] He invited small groups of people to the lab for what he claimed was a 'psychological experiment in visual perception', and showed them two cards. The task was simple: match a single, vertical line on one card with one of three lines on the other.

Most participants had no problem solving it independently – they failed less than 1 per cent of the time. But Asch wanted to see whether participants would conform to others' views when put in a group. So he put the true research subjects in groups with actors tasked with giving the wrong answer most of the time. Tellingly, the true participants conformed to the false, consensus view, giving incorrect answers 35.8 per cent of the time (instead of 1 per cent) on average. Some didn't conform at all and some gave in to the (erroneous) majority view nearly every time. But 74 per cent conformed on at least one trial (out of eighteen). And when people had just one other person agreeing with them, they were far more likely to stand up for their views.

The experiment has since been repeated many times in various settings – including for moral reasoning.[6] It has also been explored by neuroscientists.[7] One study asked participants to rate the attractiveness of female faces while in an fMRI scanner. After they had done so, they were presented with ratings given by other people, and then had to judge the faces again. Like Asch, the researchers found that ratings changed in line with the majority view.

But the brain scans revealed something else intriguing – when participants' ratings differed from the group's, an area called the rostral cingulate zone, which is involved in processing conflict, lit up.

At the same time, activity in the nucleus accumbens, which is linked to expecting a reward, dropped. The strength of these neural signals could even predict conformity in participants – people with larger differences between the two signals were more likely to conform. Proof, indeed, that many of us find it incredibly rewarding to agree with others, and distressing to challenge them.

Several processes are at work when we conform. 'Social psychologists would distinguish between when you're just learning from what other people are doing, and when you are worried that people will laugh at you if you're different,' Nick Chater, a professor of behavioural science at the University of Warwick, told us. Clearly, learning from others isn't a bad thing – being humble about our own abilities can lead to better decisions. The risk if it goes too far, argues Chater, is that it can be very homogenising. 'You get this kind of explosion in interest in a small number of things,' he said, such as everybody reading the same books, having the same views and listening to the same music. This may trap us in 'echo chambers', which severely limit our thinking. If everyone we know relies on the same sources of information and has similar views, it's hard to challenge our own thinking. Ultimately, varied social and cultural experiences can help break such habits and force us to realise there are other ways to think about the world.

When we conform out of fear of being punished or excluded, the consequences can be even more severe. 'Historically, all sorts of very narrow social practices – prejudice, sexist structures in society, rigid class systems . . . all of these things are powerfully based on this fear of ostracising,' Chater explained. This suggests we sometimes ignore our own thinking because we worry that others will make fun of us. It can also keep us from speaking out against unfairness – it is partly how oppressive cultures, such as the one West grew up in, are maintained.

People sometimes conform to completely arbitrary views.[8] One study found that people change their minds to agree with other people's judgements, even when they're told that a computer glitch had randomly allocated them the views. This can't be explained by either a fear of social ostracism or a desire to learn, which prompts researchers to suggest that people often conform to certain groups' norms simply because they want to belong – and quite literally let the group think for them. Of course, it is unclear to what extent people genuinely change their own views in such situations and to what extent they pretend. And we don't conform completely blindly – we are more likely to follow others when we identify strongly with a group, and when the norms suit us.[9]

Our desire to fit in is so powerful that it is harnessed by governments to shape our behaviour – from getting us to eat more healthily to making us more environmentally friendly. Chater was once involved in the UK Cabinet Office's Behavioural Insights Team – or 'Nudge Unit' – which does just that. One of its early projects was to encourage people to file their annual tax return earlier – by giving individuals feedback on how many people in their local area had already completed theirs. 'People who do unusual things often don't realise how unusual they are,' he explained to us. 'If you are a late tax returner, you probably think everyone is. So, if you are the tax authority, you need to remind people that what they are doing is quite weird.' In other words, people will feel far more uncomfortable filing their return at the last minute once they realise doing so goes against the norm. Research suggests many of us don't like to stand out in this way, and so these 'nudges' can influence behaviour. The impact of an individual nudge isn't particularly dramatic. But even small changes can be useful on the scale of an entire country's population, argues Chater.

Single individuals can influence us, too. When we like, respect or look up to someone, perhaps because they are successful, have a beautiful home or are good-looking, we tend to believe they are superior in other ways, too – such as having deep moral, medical or political knowledge. This tendency, dubbed the 'halo effect', means we may erroneously trust certain individuals more than others and copy their attitudes or behaviour more readily.[10] The process also works in the other direction – making us judge others more harshly because of one or two traits we perceive to be negative, such as being cheap or having cheated on their spouse.[11] Clearly, such preconceived ideas affect how we think, making us view the world in a deeply biased way.

We can mitigate these pitfalls by being more aware of such biases, and questioning whether we like things because we like them, or because someone else likes them. But it turns out we don't just follow other people, we also compete with them. This doesn't mean we like to be different; we want to be similar to others, just slightly better within an often narrow set of parameters. According to social comparison theory, developed by Leon Festinger in 1954, people tend to feel a perpetual desire to move upwards in life.[12] This makes us constantly compare ourselves with others. Such comparisons can deeply impact how we think about ourselves – and others – leading to a competitive case of 'Keeping up with the Joneses'.

When we want to evaluate ourselves, we often compare ourselves with similar people from roughly the same socioeconomic, religious or educational background. But we do tend to compare upwards, against those we think are slightly better than us, whether they are a little wealthier, brighter or more attractive. If we have low self-esteem, however, we may instead compare downwards to boost our self-esteem.

Social comparisons are rarely objective – they're relative, not absolute. If the Joneses across the road have a nice car, for example, we'll often covet an even nicer one. But it won't need to be the *best* car, it will just need to *better* than the Joneses'. This typically applies within groups with a shared set of norms and those norms will also help define what 'better' means. If you and the Joneses are keen environmentalists, for example, you'll likely end up competing by owning the greenest, rather than the fastest, car. Remarkably, research shows that many people would be happy to earn less if that meant they earned more than people they considered competitors, such as their neighbours, for example – an effect dubbed 'positional bias'.[13]

This competitive fixation can make us preoccupied with boosting or maintaining our status by mindlessly buying or achieving certain things, rather than thinking deeply about what *we* need and value. It can even affect our views of fairness and justice, with those making it to the top being particularly wary of losing their positions. One study asked university students to evaluate a new bonus programme that would enable some students to boost their grades, while the rest would see theirs remain the same.[14] While nobody would ultimately lose out, high-status students, the highest achievers, nevertheless perceived the programme as unfair – their relative superiority could be downgraded by others catching up. This may have been compounded by the fact that these students likely defined themselves by their academic achievements. This is similar to high earners who value themselves through their financial success, and find progressive income tax or wealth distribution programmes deeply unfair. Many people may similarly take unkindly to lottery winners moving into the grand house across the street.

So, what can we do to ensure we aren't so influenced by those around us, getting stuck in echo chambers or being prejudiced towards groups that are different? And how can we avoid getting into an exhausting – and potentially expensive – race with the Joneses?

Research shows that encountering many different types of people is key to overcoming prejudice – and people who live in diverse communities tend to have less prejudice towards those who aren't in their in-group.[15] So keeping your social circles wide helps protect against negative preconceptions.

Being open to different viewpoints can also help counteract the bias we can develop from being overly influenced by single individuals or groups. Identify who you rely on most for advice and insight – and why. Is it your old mate who once went to Oxford? Your local book club? Your parents? None of them can know everything about everything, and sometimes it's worth questioning what they say or casting your net a bit wider.

It is often the norms themselves, rather than the fact that we eagerly follow others' lead, that we need to be wary of. While many norms, such as queuing patiently, are benign – preventing chaos and affecting everybody equally – others, such as not reporting your boss sexually harassing a colleague, might not be. It therefore makes sense to ask yourself who benefits from the norms you are following, and whether they harm anyone.

Protesting, however, isn't easy. 'Standing out requires a lot of courage,' explains Ayse Uskul, a professor of social psychology at the University of Kent. 'You might be expected to make justifications for why you are not doing the same things as other people.' People can be judgemental and unpleasant when you make choices that go against the norm – be it showing up to an important business meeting in shorts, declining alcohol at a party or shelving your job and selling everything you own to travel the world. 'People like some sort of control and predictability over their lives,' says Uskul. 'If we have a certain world view and that gets shattered by someone doing something differently, we find it hard to come to terms with that.' Again, having a wide social circle can help protect against such behaviour, and keep us out of narrow echo chambers.

The good news is that it's possible to change norms. One study, based on laboratory experiments in which people were asked to agree on a linguistic norm, showed that it was difficult for a tiny group to influence the majority.[16] But once that minority grew to constitute 25 per cent of the larger group, they were quickly able to establish a new norm. The authors argued that a quarter is a sort of 'tipping point' for social change, although the exact number in real life may vary depending on the situation. Still, it's an encouraging finding: you can change things (hopefully for the better) by convincing just a few people of your view, and encouraging them to do likewise.

Some people are also more naturally nonconformist, a quality linked to high levels of the personality trait 'openness to experience' and low levels of 'agreeableness'.[17] Those who are very agreeable (how friendly and compassionate you are) and extraverted (how social you are), on the other hand, by prioritising getting on with others, may find it more difficult and less rewarding to challenge other people's beliefs. But even the most radical rebels don't tend to be nonconformist about everything – that would be a sort of conformity, too. And they typically share their ideas with a small group of peers who have their own set of norms.

People also differ in how they compare themselves to others, leading to biased thinking. If you always feel superior to those around you, you probably aren't comparing fairly, learning very much about yourself or developing. And if you constantly feel hopelessly inferior, this isn't very constructive either. Instead, use comparisons flexibly to learn difficult and motivating truths about yourself, while also identifying your strengths and privileges – and being grateful for them.

And quit that never-ending race with the Joneses – for the sake of your thinking and your wallet. If you are constantly trying to keep up appearances, you'll develop more and more expensive habits the more money you earn, and risk ending up poorer and less free.

Remember that being different, even an outsider, has its perks, too. It's hard to be creative if you only surround yourself with people who are clones of yourself – the resulting norms will solidify and start to seem insurmountable. While cooperation is certainly one of the cornerstones of humanity's success, so is the ability of certain individuals, such as Gladys West, to break out of their comfort zone, set a course for new horizons and radically change the world.

25

Where are you from?

Which two of the following three things are most closely related and why?

Banana. Panda. Monkey.

Don't worry, there's no correct answer. But the question – and more importantly, your response – reveals the powerful part culture plays in shaping the way we think.[1] A fascinating study which included just this question found that participants from the West were more likely to think that 'monkey' and 'panda' belong together.[2] This is because people in the West tend to think about things in categories – in this case, 'animals'.[3] However, those from East Asian countries, such as China, were more likely to pair 'monkey' with 'banana', because one eats the other. This connection involves a different approach to thinking, which gives greater weight to context and the relationship *between* things, rather than the categories they fall into.

That might just sound like a fun anecdote, so let's try a completely different example that highlights another way culture can influence thinking about a major, real-world event.

When the COVID-19 pandemic first erupted, how quickly and willingly did you adopt face masks?

You may think your answer reflects your own, *individual* choice – albeit one tempered by local rules and laws. But other, intriguing psychological factors are also pulling the strings behind the scenes. As SARS-CoV-2 began to spread around the world in early 2020, evidence suggested that face masks could play a key role in reducing the spread of the virus and the number of people it killed.[4] But while their adoption was swift and widespread in countries like China, South Korea, Thailand and Japan, there was far greater hesitancy in Western nations, such as the UK and US. And this disparity wasn't coincidental – it was cultural.

Research shows that levels of mask use on a regional level could be predicted by how individualistic, or collectivistic, the local culture was – with collectivistic countries and areas far more likely to adopt masks than individualistic ones.[5] Individualistic cultures prioritise individual rights and well-being, and the independent self. Collectivistic cultures, meanwhile, view the self as interdependent and give greater weight to the needs and well-being of the group. In fact, masks were already widely being used in many collectivistic, East Asian countries before the COVID-19 pandemic struck. The researchers argue that in collectivistic cultures, such as many Asian countries, people are more inclined to think about others and wear masks to protect them, while those in individualistic cultures, such as the UK and US, are more likely to think of masks as an inconvenience or intrusion on their individual freedoms and avoid them as a result. Indeed, one survey cited by the researchers revealed that 40 per cent of Americans who didn't wear masks agreed that 'It's my right as an American not to wear a mask', while another 24 per cent said they didn't use them because they were 'uncomfortable'.[6]

Ching-Yu Huang grew up in 'collectivistic' Taiwan before moving around the world and eventually settling in 'individualistic' England, where she is now a social and developmental psychologist at Keele University. During her travels, and through her research, she has vividly experienced the impact culture has on the way people think – from government policy to COVID-19 responses to the criminal justice system. She is also aware of how her own thinking has been shaped by exposure to different cultures. 'Even if you compare me now with the me from five years ago, I'm a completely different person,' she says. 'And after experiencing different cultures, I can definitely see a lot of shattered stereotypes in my head.'

The influence culture has on our thinking and behaviour is a growing field of research. A longstanding problem with psychology has been its vastly disproportionate use of participants from WEIRD (Western, Educated, Industrialized, Rich and Democratic) societies and the assumption that people from these, often North American and Western European, countries reflect humans as a whole (spoiler: they don't).[7] Luckily, researchers are now taking an increasingly cross-cultural perspective (with many comparing the West with East Asia, in particular), exploring how different cultures help mould people's minds.[8] As Huang explains, we are all born with similar mental hardware, but the 'factory settings' we start life with can be altered by the cultures we are exposed to. Just as a software update can affect your home computer's performance, so experiences of a different culture can alter the way we think about ourselves, others and the wider world.

Some of the most wide-ranging research in this area has been conducted by Professor Geert Hofstede, who died in 2020, and his colleagues. Hofstede defined culture as 'the collective programming of the mind distinguishing the members of one group or category of people from others'.[9] The Hofstede Insights Country Comparison tool, developed out of his research, measures culture across six dimensions.[10] These include individualism vs collectivism (essentially, whether people think more in terms of 'me' or 'we'); indulgence vs restraint (whether the society encourages people to pursue, or suppress, their immediate desires); long-term vs short-term orientation (whether a society prefers traditions or a more pragmatic, future-focused way of thinking); and power distance (the degree to which a society accepts established hierarchies).

And it reveals some interesting differences in thinking across countries.[11] Broadly speaking, for example, those from the US and

UK are far more individualistic, and less willing to accept authority than those from China or South Korea. Those from China and South Korea, meanwhile, are more likely to be long-term oriented and thrifty and to invest. They also tend to be less indulgent and more likely to be restrained by social norms than those in the US and UK.*

Models such as Hofstede's are, of course, generalisations. We are all different and our thinking and behaviour at an individual level isn't set in stone by the culture we live and grow up in. It is widely accepted that North Americans and Western Europeans are more likely to think about themselves as separate, autonomous individuals,[12] rather than part of a bigger system, interdependent on others – as is more often the case in Asia,[13] Latin America, Africa and some southern European regions.[14] In the latter, people are more likely to describe themselves in terms of their social role. Yet there are plenty of individualistic Chinese people and community-minded Brits. Similarly, huge numbers of Americans will think 'monkeys' are more closely related to 'bananas' than 'pandas'. Nevertheless, research shows that we, generally, are deeply influenced by the social norms we are exposed to, which can start shaping our minds from early childhood and drive our thinking in certain directions.

Huang's own research, for example, reveals how even young children from different cultures think differently about authority.[15] There are basically two, very different types of compliance. 'Committed compliance' is when you are asked to do something and you do it happily and wholeheartedly. In contrast, 'situational compliance' is when you follow instructions, but do so reluctantly. Huang

---

* Scores out of 100 for the following dimensions: Individualism: US (91), UK (89), China (20), South Korea (18); Power Distance: China (80), South Korea (60), US (40), UK (35); Long-term Orientation: South Korea (100), China (87), UK (51), US (26); Indulgence: UK (69), US (68), South Korea (29), China (24).

took three groups of five- to seven-year-olds – from Taiwan; non-immigrant, white English; and Chinese immigrants in the UK – and compared their responses to a parent's authority. While there were no differences in committed compliance among the groups, the Taiwanese children showed far more situational compliance than the other two.

According to Huang, this suggests that children in Taiwan – where *guai* (being well behaved) and *tin hua* (being obedient, listening to adults' words) are regularly used to laud children – are more encultured to be compliant, even when it involves doing things they object to. But it also shows that children of Chinese immigrants have the same, more individualistic attitudes towards authority as English children. 'It reveals that culture really makes a big difference,' says Huang. 'In an environment that encourages individuality, Chinese children are less likely to let their parents' culture override it.'

And this has clear implications for how we think as we move into adulthood. If we're brought up in a culture that encourages us to be more compliant, even when we disagree with the instructions we're given, we may fit more readily and happily into an established hierarchy and accept our place within it, thinking less about our own needs and what we might do differently. This may, however, limit our ability to think creatively, outside the consensus. In a culture where compliance is seen as less important, meanwhile, we may feel empowered to think more freely, but struggle more to adapt to life within systems and institutions that prioritise collective, rather than individual, well-being.

These cultural differences may become deeply entrenched – to the degree that they're even visible in brain scans. One study used fMRI scanning to explore differences in brain responses between Western (English, American, Canadian and Australian) and Chinese participants when asked to judge whether a series of adjectives were appropriate for describing themselves, their mother or another individual.[16] In the Western subjects, a part of the brain called the medial prefrontal cortex (MPFC) was activated when they thought about themselves, but not others, leading the researchers to conclude that 'for Westerners, MPFC is specific to the self'. But this contrasted with the brain responses of the Chinese subjects. In them, MPFC activity was increased when thinking about themselves *and* their mothers, suggesting less separation between the two – a cultural difference that is also reflected at a neural level. While Western thinking tends to err towards an *independent* self, then, Chinese thinking appears to be more motivated by an *interdependent* self. And the brain appears to respond differently as a result.

Other research has explored how these cultural differences in thinking styles are reflected in, and influence, how we view and think about the world. In keeping with the cultural variations between independent and interdependent, and individualistic and collectivistic, thinking, one study found that when asked to describe underwater scenes, Japanese participants focused more on context and the relationship between objects, while Americans paid more attention to describing the objects themselves.[17] Another study, meanwhile, found that when participants were asked to take a photograph using a camera with a basic zoom lens, the East Asians tended to make the subject of the portrait smaller and more a part of the wider picture.[18] The Western participants, by contrast, were more likely to zoom in, placing the figure front and centre, with less emphasis on the wider environment. In fact, the researchers noted that this is reflected in art more generally. Historically, they found, East Asian landscape paintings often feature a higher horizon than their Western equivalents, enabling the artist to include more detail and context in a scene. In essence, then, East Asian culture generally encourages a more holistic way of thinking than in the West, prioritising the 'big picture' rather than individual people and things.

Cultural differences in thinking also play out on a spiritual level, a phenomenon explored by Professor Tanya Luhrmann, an anthropologist at Stanford University. She and her colleagues recently investigated how people from the US, Ghana, Vanuatu, China and Thailand reported their sensory experiences of gods and spirits.[19] The study found that, culturally, individuals from Ghana, Vanuatu and rural China viewed their minds as more 'porous' – essentially that their thinking was more connected with and susceptible to interventions from the outside world – than those in the US and urban China, where the mind is seen as less 'sieve-like' and more separate from external influences. She also found that people who had this more 'porous' mindset were more likely to report vivid spiritual experiences, such as feeling the presence of a god or the supernatural. On the other hand, even practising evangelical Christians in the less porous US spoke of having a 'bounded mind', which God had to 'break through' to reveal himself.[20]

'This is about whether, as a society, we see ourselves as all separate individuals or somehow entwined,' says Luhrmann.

In fact, in other research, Luhrmann has also noted how people with psychosis from different cultures experience auditory hallucinations.[21] Interviewing individuals in Ghana (Accra), the USA (California) and India (Chennai), Luhrmann and her colleagues found that the Americans tended to experience the hallucinations as a 'bombardment' of negative and unwelcome noise caused by a diagnosed condition. In India, on the other hand, many heard the voices of family members, who often chastised them, but also offered guidance. While in Ghana, the majority said they were spoken to by a divine being and were more likely to report the voices as being positive.

Luhrmann believes these differences have a cultural basis. In the less porous, more independent US, disembodied voices are perhaps more likely to be seen as an intrusion or assault than in more porous, less secular Ghana, where there is a cultural tradition of connectivity with the wider world. In India, meanwhile, the increased likelihood of the voices being those of parents, siblings or in-laws may be explained by the more central role family plays in individuals' lives there.

And so culture appears to powerfully influence how we think in numerous ways. But these effects aren't fixed in perpetuity. 'There is a lot of flexibility, too,' says Huang. 'These days, people travel around and visit other countries. And when they get exposed to other cultural norms, and other ways of thinking and behaving, they can modify their thinking and how they make their decisions. The beauty of cultural influence is that it is not set-in stone. We get moulded by it as children, but we can remould ourselves, too, if we are exposed to other ways of thinking. People change and learn throughout life.'

Indeed, we should make a concerted effort to avoid cultural arrogance, and the belief that our way of doing things is better than the alternatives, and talk, listen and (when possible) travel widely. Even reading books, viewing art or listening to music from other cultures – and really thinking about how and why they portray things differently – can broaden our horizons. It's about being open to experience.

Many in the West, for example, may benefit from experiencing a more holistic, interdependent way of thinking. This may not only help you to see the bigger picture when confronted with the problems and puzzles of daily life, but may also reduce the amount of pressure you put on yourself to achieve personal goals and ambitions as well as the disappointment that can come from failing to achieve them. As research has shown, financial status and career advancement may lead to a degree of life satisfaction, but chasing them can also be stressful and emotionally exhausting. Instead, sustainable well-being often stems from our interpersonal relationships and time spent with friends and family. Thinking of yourself as part of a broader, interconnected world can help put things in perspective and enable us to better adapt to the needs of others – including the planet we live on. Indeed, there are also clearly benefits to us all showing a little more *simpático*, an arguably interdependent quality important in Hispanic cultures, that encourages us to think about and share the feelings of others.[22]

As Huang discovered during her travels, collectivist cultures can also learn from more individualistic ones. As she says: 'Individuals in collectivistic cultures tend to feel more powerless to change things; to stand up for their rights or to speak out against the government.' Thinking in a more individualistic way, then, may help you to ensure that you're not taken for granted, that your rights are protected, and that you have a degree of freedom to think creatively, challenge the status quo and question hierarchies and dogma. Ultimately, to express *yourself*.

But as cultures increasingly mingle in our globalised world, it's also important that we all have a better understanding of one another. Huang, for example, investigates how culture and related parenting styles can affect how children behave, communicate and remember things – and the implications for teaching and the justice system.[23] For example, if Western teachers and investigators aren't aware that Chinese children may be more likely to describe and remember context than individual people and objects, give brief responses to questions, be more compliant around adults and potentially less willing to report abuse, damaging misunderstandings may result.

The key is to acknowledge that there is no universal human mindset and that culture can shape the way we think in numerous and various ways. By being open to experience and exposing ourselves to as many different cultures as possible, we will be well-placed to benefit from the best of *all* worlds – and think as broadly, dynamically and clearly as possible.

26

Do you lose your
mind in a 'mob'?

It began like any other spring day in the inner Bristol suburb of St Pauls. But 2 April 1980 was about to light up. A little after 3 p.m., two plain-clothes police officers entered the Black and White Café.[1] The café had been stripped of its licence the year before and the police were responding to reports of illegal drinking and drug-taking. More police entered the café soon afterwards, two men were arrested and hundreds of cases of beer were confiscated. But as a nearby school emptied into the warm afternoon, and people who had been inside the café left, news of the raid quickly spread. Before long, a crowd had assembled outside the Black and White.

The raid took place during a period of turbulent race relations and mistrust in the police. Unemployment was high, stop-and-search laws were being used disproportionately against Black youths and housing was in a risible state. Initially, however, the mood was calm. But around 4.30 p.m., this changed. What triggered the initial violence remains unclear. But as Stephen Reicher, a professor of social psychology at the University of St Andrews, reported in his study of the events: 'All the accounts contained as a central theme an unjustified and unprovoked police attack on the Black and White – seen by many as the focus for St Pauls' inhabitants.'[2] Many of the eyewitness accounts also contained allegations of police racism, although the police claimed they were simply trying to restore order.

Either way, the police were soon being pelted with bricks and bottles and several were injured. But while the unrest came in fits

212

and starts, punctuated by periods of relative calm, by early evening there were running street battles. Police cars were overturned and burned, missiles were thrown and some police were forced to use milk crates and dustbin lids as shields. By 7.30 p.m., the police had retreated and the 'Battle of Bristol' soon came to an end. In total, more than thirty people, including twenty-two police officers, were injured – and around 140 arrests were made (although all sixteen eventually charged with rioting were acquitted).[3]

There was nothing particularly exceptional about the size or destructiveness of the St Pauls' 'riot' (locals often refer to it as an 'uprising').[4] Collective crowd action on a far larger scale – and driven by groups from across the political divide, from Black Lives Matter and Extinction Rebellion to pro- and anti-EU groups, anti-vaxxers and the alt-right – is rarely out of the headlines and in January 2021 led to the storming and temporary takeover of the US Capitol by supporters of Donald Trump.[5] Indeed, the sheer number of protests and riots over the last decade or so has led some to brand it the 'Age of Dissent'.[6] In 2011, 'The Protestor' was even named *Time* magazine's person of the year.[7] Reicher's study of St Pauls, however, began to change how crowd behaviour is understood, suggesting it is far more 'sophisticated and creative' than is widely believed – with profound implications for how we think in crowds and how others, such as governments and police, should consider their response to them.

There are many models of crowd behaviour, but the idea of the 'mad mob' is the most popular and persistent. This essentially is the notion that we become 'mindless' in a crowd, casting off our reason and sense of self to become something more primitive and animal-like.[8] That we stop thinking clearly. It was popularised by thinkers like Gustave Le Bon in his 1895 book *The Crowd: A Study of the Popular Mind* and gained traction in the nineteenth century when industrialisation led to sprawling cities, cascading social problems and, perhaps unsurprisingly, an uptick in social unrest.

213

But, as Clifford Stott, a professor of social psychology at Keele University, argues, this was a time when the establishment had no interest in understanding the root causes of unrest; it just wanted to snuff it out.[9] The idea that people become uncivilised, unreasonable and barbaric en masse fitted neatly into this – it was a justification for dismissing and cracking down on protests against the status quo. Indeed, it frequently still is.

The casual observer of a riot may think that the idea of the 'mad mob' seems reasonable; that it is virtually impossible to think clearly in a crowd. When shoppers engage in violent high-street scrums as the Black Friday sales begin, truckers block the streets of major Canadian cities, people deface, tear down and throw into rivers historic statues, or – in the distant past – hunt, hound and burn 'witches', it's all too easy to dismiss their behaviour in the same terms: as the unthinking and chaotic violence of people who have disengaged their rational minds. Indeed, when widespread protest and violence erupted in the UK after the 2011 shooting by police of Mark Duggan in London, politicians, newspapers, police commanders and others referred to 'mindless' and 'irrational' people engaging in 'anarchy', 'mayhem' and 'mob rule' – words that have been attached to countless 'riots' since.[10] But Reicher's research on St Pauls, supported by numerous investigations into other 'riots' since, from the 1990 Trafalgar Square poll tax demonstration to the 2011 riots following the Duggan shooting, suggests that crowds are far from 'mindless' and that the thinking within them is complex, sophisticated and changeable.[11]

So, what does influence how we think in a crowd?

First, we should acknowledge that we're social beings. We're not walled off from the world and people around us, thinking only 'for ourselves', but instead are endlessly adjusting our thinking and behaviour to adapt to the situations we find ourselves in. We're not fixed, but endlessly responsive to external influences. Indeed, according to this line of research – which often takes place in the field, rather than the peaceful confines of the lab, and involves interviews with participants and analysis of video, audio and other sources of information gathered at the event – our *social* identities are a central part of who we are.

Take the violence in Bristol, for example. While it may have looked like the work of a 'mad mob' to a casual observer, Reicher reveals that people's behaviour wasn't indiscriminate, random or chaotic. Instead, it was limited by clear social boundaries.[12] And these boundaries, which were shaped by people's shared sense of social identity, defined the crowd's actions, who and what was targeted, and the geographical limits of the unrest. In St Pauls, people strongly identified with their community, with a shared sense that they were being economically left behind and exploited by outsiders, and suspicion of the police.[13] And this shared identity helps explain the events that followed. The 'riot' didn't spread beyond the neighbourhood; only the police, banks, outsider-owned businesses and the benefits office were attacked or damaged (while many locals were left to go about their business in the usual way); and when the police finally left, the crowd peacefully helped usher traffic through the streets. As local resident Ray Mighty said later in a BBC report: 'There was a sense of unity, it was time to fight the enemy.'[14]

These themes – particularly how social identity shapes our thinking and behaviour in a crowd – have been replicated over and again. During the 1990 poll tax riot, for example, Stott's research – which again drew on video footage and interviews with police officers and protestors – shows that the vast majority of the crowd initially was united in its 'good-humoured' and 'non-violent' opposition to then Conservative prime minister Margaret Thatcher and the new poll tax.[15] This explains why they gathered and sat down outside the prime minister's Downing Street residence and thought the small minority of violent protestors were an unrepresentative 'out group'. But Stott – who now advises law enforcement on how to deal with

crowds – argues that this identity changed when the police inter-
vened with force. At this point, the crowd – formerly bound by their
'peaceful' opposition to the poll tax – became united by a collective
opposition to the police and their use of 'illegitimate' physical tactics. And it was this shift in identity that caused the protestors to
rethink their motivations and behaviour, leading to the subsequent
riot. They didn't turn to violence *mindlessly*, but because they were
responding to a changed social situation. Ironically, Stott argues that
it was the police's thinking at the time – that crowds are inherently
disorderly and that they had to intervene to regain control of the
'mad mob' – that actually played a key role in sparking the riot.

Believing that people can simply lose their minds in a crowd
overlooks the enormously powerful influence that our beliefs – and
how we share them with others – can have on our thinking. It also
prevents us from understanding why people may turn to violence
when they do. Take the recent spate of statue topplings, for example. Critics, echoing mad mob theory, have widely criticised those
involved for engaging in wanton vandalism. But those behind the
felling of monuments to historic figures, such as the seventeenth-
century British slave trader Edward Colston, knew exactly what they
were doing – and why. Colston's statue in Bristol, for example, was
torn down and thrown in the river during 2020 anti-racism protests
triggered by the murder of George Floyd by US police.[16] In this light,
the Colston monument wasn't just the random target of indiscriminate violence – it was a symbol of the very injustices that had led to
Floyd's killing. Indeed, one protestor even knelt on the statue's neck,
echoing the method of Floyd's murder. As one of the protestors later
suggested, they weren't mindlessly smashing things up, they were
'rectifying' history.[17] And that involves thought.

The same lessons apply across the political divide. It's easy – reassuring even – to think that those who stormed the US Capitol in
January 2021 did so in a mindless and sheep-like pique of rage or that

they were just 'following orders'. But the truth is more complex, as Reicher has argued.[18] Instead, the crowd was motivated by sincerely held beliefs and a powerful social identity – as 'US patriots' battling to save the soul of America from a 'treacherous' establishment. This may seem bonkers to many on the opposing side. But the protestors, legitimised and represented by the 'anti-establishment' Trump who spoke beforehand, didn't just want to smash down walls and kick down doors. They, too, wanted to rectify history and Make America Great Again. They, too, thought they were doing good work.

To critics of any given crowd action, this may be an inconvenient truth. But thinking about mass unrest in this way – rather than just dismissing it as the kneejerk response of a mad mob – will enable us to better understand the thinking, beliefs and behaviour of others – and, ultimately, ourselves.

It can even point to how rival groups might find common ground. Another study by Stott, Reicher and others investigated the riots that broke out across England in 2011.[19] In London, for example, participants began to convene on Wood Green High Road in the northeast of the capital. This meant that youths from different parts of the city – with well-established and violent 'postcode rivalries' – found themselves face to face. But while many of those interviewed by researchers afterwards initially feared being attacked by rival groups, it seems these differences were largely replaced by a 'sense of common identity', even 'camaraderie', motivated by their shared experience of, and opposition to, the police. Many of these youths were no longer thinking about the threat posed by other groups, but about what they had in common. As one, quoted in the study, put it: 'Because, like, maybe they were thinking if we just do it as groups it's not going to work. If we all come as one, it will make us bigger and stronger . . . So it's like, stand up for your community.' While another, also quoted in the study, said:

'Half the people who did the riots weren't even from our area. They come to help us. I mean if it was a gang wise, why are people from like Hackney coming down to Tottenham to help us? If it was to do with gangs wouldn't we be trying to hurt them? They'd be trying to hurt us. It wasn't like that. They all come down to Tottenham to try to help us.'[20]

And this also had an effect on many participants' emotions, 'away from merely anger towards joy, pride and celebration'.[21] Indeed, by making an effort to meet, listen to and better understand others, we will be better placed to discover the shared beliefs and social identities that can bring us together rather than keep us apart.

So what does all this tell us about our ability to think clearly more generally?

First, we don't simply lose our minds in a crowd. While the theory of the 'mad mob' only predicts chaos, crowd behaviour is significantly more sophisticated than that and is, according to many social psychologists, widely motivated by people's sense of social identity – which, in turn, changes depending on the situation they are in. This has profound implications for governments, police and society more generally – and how they think about protest and civil unrest, for example. By assuming people become irrational and mindless in a group, they may disregard or misunderstand the crowd's true motivations – and what lies behind them – and disproportionately respond in ways that aim to restore order, but actually end up inflaming the situation.

Second, we are social beings, not simply individuals isolated on our own mental islands. According to social psychologists, the self is multiple and complex, incorporating a whole host of identities that may relate to your race, gender, class, politics, profession or parental status. Each may influence you to think and behave in a different way, and each may come to the surface depending on the social context you're in. In a crowd, this may shift your focus from discontent with a new tax to opposition to the police. But it can play out at home, too. In your own house, your thinking may be primarily motivated by your identity within your family group. You may be more generous than you are with others, more willing to compromise, more conscientious and protective. At least until someone brings politics up at the dinner table. At that point – if you feel particularly strongly about Brexit, socialism or Trump, for example – your political identity may surge to the surface and all bets are off. If your loved one is on the other side of the political divide, God help them, they could be in for a domestic riot.

These social identities are often related to group affiliation. And feeling like we're part of a group can boost self-esteem.[22] We all want to feel like we belong, after all. But group affiliation can negatively affect our ability to think clearly, too. Identifying with a group too strongly and unthinkingly can lead us to conform to its norms, reinforcing echo chambers and bolstering biases and stereotypes, particularly about people outside the group. It's impossible that *all* police are bad, for example. But if we're in the middle of a group that's collective identity is in opposition to the police, we may be more inclined to think that they are. And if the situation is particularly inflamed, emotions like anger can make us think and behave in ways we wouldn't normally condone – potentially driving us to violence. In extreme cases, such as in Nazi Germany, a powerful sense of belonging to one group, especially when defined in opposition to another 'out' group and motivated by powerful leadership, can lead to the very worst atrocities.[23]

The human mind is endlessly nuanced and fascinating. We're not just machines, but a sum of endless working parts, many of which relate to our role as social beings. To think more clearly, we could all benefit from better understanding the various social identities we have – and how they intersect.

After all, we are all prone to favour our own group, often at the expense of others. As 'identity politics' is becoming ever more important, with many different groups arguing with each other, this knowledge may help us find common ground, just like the 'postcode rivals' during the 2011 riots. It could also help us identify what our differences are in a more rational, and less emotive, way, which could make it easier to talk about them.

While it may be easier to blame a certain group of people for the difficulties facing our own group, it is often a wider system that is the problem – creating disadvantages for many groups in different ways. And as long as people with different social identities keep quarrelling and blaming each other for their hardship, those systems might quietly grow ever stronger.

27

Are you a sucker for advertising?

How do you get more women to smoke?

That was the big question being asked by tobacco companies in the early twentieth century. Back then, lighting up was viewed as taboo among women, particularly in public. But the US tobacco industry saw this both as a massive waste – and an opportunity; an untapped 'gold mine' of sales growth. It was time for Big Tobacco to change the way people thought – at least about smoking. And to do this, they turned to a man named Edward Bernays.

Bernays had an impressive track record. A nephew of Sigmund Freud, the founder of psychoanalysis, Bernays was in the business of changing people's minds – and a firm believer in the power of propaganda (or 'public relations', as he preferred to call it) to shift and manipulate people's opinions.[1] Working with an array of clients, from politicians and governments to large corporations, Bernays enjoyed a long and illustrious career. But his methods were not without controversy – not least his solution to the female smoker question.

Tasked with normalising smoking among women, Bernays tapped into the growing wave of feminism sweeping America at the time, promoting the idea that cigarettes were 'torches of freedom' that placed women on an equal footing with men and marked their emancipation from hackneyed old taboos. His *pièce de résistance* was to employ a troop of women – who, he said, should be 'good looking' but should 'not look too model-y' – to march in the 1929 New York City Easter Parade and flagrantly puff away as they did so.[2] Feminist Ruth Hale also encouraged women to attend the march, sporting their 'torches of freedom', and Bernays ensured cameras were ready to snap the action in the right light and spread the message through the nation's press.

And – unfortunately for the health of millions – it worked. Bernays' taboo-busting and 'empowering' campaign was reported in newspapers, became the subject of countless water-cooler conversations and was followed by a significant uptake in the number of female smokers. While women smoked just 5 per cent of cigarettes sold in 1923, this rose to 12 per cent in 1929 and to 18 per cent by 1935.[3] Of course, Bernays' campaign wasn't solely responsible for this uptick in female smokers, but a clever piece of advertising had helped shatter entrenched ways of thinking and encouraged tens of thousands to take up a new, and highly addictive, habit.

But are you vulnerable to similar manipulations? According to Agnes Nairn, professor of marketing at the University of Bristol, you likely believe that you are not. 'No one thinks that they're influenced by advertising,' she says. 'But we do think that everyone else is. It's curious, but true.' In fact, ironically, our belief that advertising can't change our thinking may actually make it easier for it to do just that.

The power of advertising is tricky to quantify scientifically, an age-old problem captured in early marketing guru John Wanamaker's frequently recycled gripe: 'Half the money I spend on advertising is wasted; the trouble is I don't know which half.'[4] If I advertise to you on Monday, for example, how can I know whether you bought my product on Tuesday because of the ad or because you were 'going to buy it anyway'?[5] And if I advertise at Christmas because I know my product shifts at that time of year, was the resulting sales boom really a consequence of the campaign – or just the usual, seasonal dash to shops? Certainly, many experts argue both that advertising is often less influential than is widely believed and that a lot of companies waste a whole lot of money on doing it wrong.[6] One 2021 study into the effectiveness of 288 brands' television advertising, for example, found that 80 per cent of them had a negative return on investment (ROI) – hardly something to trumpet to your shareholders.[7]

But that doesn't mean we can just switch off and stop worrying about it. In 2019, a staggering quarter of a trillion dollars was spent on advertising in the US alone, and the industry deploys vast armies of experts, data and technology to shift our thinking in its clients' favour.[8] It's also safe to assume that the secret tricks and techniques behind successful advertising campaigns will be closely guarded by those who deploy them. So while it may sometimes be hard to know how or when, Nairn is very far from alone when she says that 'advertising works'.

So how can advertisers get inside our head and alter the way we think? It's certainly a tricky business and you can't just tell people to buy something and expect them to open their wallets on demand. It's clearly easier to persuade us to buy a luxury car if we're already looking for one, or a pot of paint if we're currently redecorating our house. Indeed, in these cases, advertisers will simply need to nudge us in the direction of their product, rather than change our minds completely. But they often also want us to buy things we didn't know we needed, something that requires a greater level of persuasion.

To be successful, advertisers must take into account the fact that we are all complex and different, work out how best to bypass, or exploit, our pre-existing memories, biases, cultural preferences and beliefs – and consider how different parts of our brain will respond to, or filter out, their message.[9] They must also evade our 'cognitive defences' – our ability to recognise an advert for what it is and to think rationally and carefully about its message.[10] Ultimately, it's a kind of arms race, with people becoming increasingly aware of, and immune to, certain types of advertising, and advertisers seeking new ways to exploit novel technologies, unlock our minds and influence our thinking.

To do this, advertisers use a wide range of strategies, from the mundane and 'explicit' – simply explaining rationally, for example, why Product X is better than the competition – to more sophisticated and 'implicit' tactics, aimed at triggering a positive, often automatic, emotional response to something.[11] Unlike the obvious and easily identified 'hard sell', product placement, celebrity endorsement, shareable memes and funny videos, for example, are harder to spot as advertising.[12] They may also be highly shareable on social media, targeted at those most likely to find the message appealing through the use of sophisticated data mining and algorithms, and connect potential customers with what's being sold in a far more subtle way. Children are particularly vulnerable to these 'covert' or 'stealthy' kinds of marketing,[13] partly because their cognitive defences are less established – but we can all succumb.

'Crudely speaking, we process advertising in two different ways,' says Nairn. 'You have cognitive processing and emotional processing, and they happen in different bits of the brain. Rational [explicit] messaging is processed in the prefrontal cortex and the emotional [implicit] stuff in the limbic system, which has been around for a lot longer and is much more powerful . . . Advertising tends to work first and best when it's implicitly processed, when it's working on an emotional level and not on a rational level. And brands know that.'

In other words, advertisers may appeal to our rational minds by explaining that their product is cheaper or better than the competition. We will weigh this argument up consciously, and make an informed judgement on its merits. But, from an advertiser's perspective, this often isn't the best way into our minds as it allows us to engage our cognitive defences and think critically about what we're being told. Instead, then, advertisers may appeal directly to our emotional minds by making us feel happy, connected or better about ourselves and then linking their product with that positive emotion.

You're probably already aware that at the end of the nineteenth century, a scientist named Ivan Pavlov discovered that dogs didn't just salivate when they were given food, but could also be made to do so when exposed to other stimuli – such as the person who fed them or a bell – that they had come to *associate* with food. This was a powerful example of a type of learning called 'classical conditioning', whereby an automatic response (in this case, salivation) is linked with a particular, learned trigger that didn't evoke the response before the conditioning (a bell or the feeders' approach).[14] And this can work on human subjects, too. Indeed, if advertisers can create a link in our minds between their product and something positive, we're more likely to respond by buying it.

Take Coca-Cola and Christmas, for example. It's a myth that Coca-Cola rebranded Santa Claus so that he started dressing in its corporate colours – he'd been spotted in red-and-white robes long before that.[15] But in the early 1930s, the company began deploying a longstanding series of promotional images by illustrator Haddon Sundblom that popularised the image of the broad-bearded, plump and jolly Father Christmas that we imagine squeezing down the chimney and into our living rooms today. Before this, Santa had taken many forms: he'd been earnest-looking and lanky, sometimes clad in green, sometimes in a bishop's cloak, even a bit spooky. But Sundblom's Santa, who the artist occasionally modelled on himself, became *the* modern blueprint for St Nicholas.[16] This enabled Coca-Cola to establish a subconscious, emotional link in millions of minds between the festive season – a time of joy, connectedness and plenty – and its sugary soft drink. Indeed, next time you reach for a Coke around Christmas, ask yourself whether that red-and-white can – with all its associations with seasonal cheer – is playing a very clever, Pavlovian trick on you.

Countless companies sell their products on this emotional level, bypassing our rational brain and making a beeline for our limbic system instead. We're all aware, for example, how an infectious tune can stick in our mind and evoke a deep emotional response. And advertisers exploit this. When played repeatedly, for example, an advert can cause us to associate a brand with a catchy song, leaving us with a deep-rooted, feel-good earworm that a product can piggyback on. We don't need to know *why* Product X is better than the competition, we just need to have a positive association with it in our mind when we go shopping – and music can help place it there. Characters and catchphrases, when seen or heard over and again, can serve the same purpose, working as Trojan horses that allow advertising to bypass our more rational cognitive defences.

Many brands also use humour to evoke a positive emotional response to their product or service. Indeed, if we find something funny, we will also want to share it with friends, amplifying – and ultimately endorsing – the advertiser's message free of charge. 'Some gambling firms are absolutely superb at this,' says Nairn, who has explored this area of advertising in her research.[17] She recalls how an advert poking fun at the English swept a WhatsApp group she was on with friends. 'They just thought it was really amusing because we were all Scottish,' she says. But as a marketing expert, Nairn was aware that the content had an ulterior motive that was hidden behind the humour: its primary purpose was to make more people gamble. 'I said to my friends, "This is all very hilarious until you look at the bottom – this is a gambling advert, guys. This is actually not very funny,"' she explains. 'It probably sounded like it was Agnes ranting again – but they were all actually shocked.'

Adverts can also help to reinforce our behaviour and beliefs *after* we have paid for a product or service. If we've just splashed out a fortune on a new phone, dress or car, for example, seeing numerous adverts for it afterwards can make us think more positively about our purchase, entrenching our loyalty to a brand and potentially making us a habitual consumer of its products. Buyer's remorse be damned.

Celebrity – and, increasingly, influencer – endorsement can also play a powerful role in shaping how we think about products and services – at least if used correctly. Well-known names have long been used to sell products – Queen Victoria was used to boost sales of Cadbury's Cocoa, for example – but the rise of social media has supercharged the potential impact, allowing it to ripple across Twitter, Instagram, Facebook or TikTok at a mindboggling pace.[18]

This works by allowing a brand to piggyback on our positive feelings for a celebrity or influencer through association. 'Celebrity endorsement works a bit like Pavlov and his dogs,' says Nairn. 'So if you have a product endorsed by Kim Kardashian and you love Kim Kardashian, you'll make a positive association between Kim Kardashian and the product. Over time, the association is reinforced so that eventually, when you take Kim Kardashian away, you still love the product because it is already imbued with Kim Kardashian.'

But the association does have to fit.[19] If you want to sell a tractor, for example, Kim Kardashian may not be the ideal match. Nor may a hotshot gaming YouTuber be the best person to endorse an outdoor clothing brand. And brands can easily be damaged if they are associated with an endorser who falls out of fashion, is involved in a scandal or suddenly starts behaving in a way that is at odds with the brand's values. Indeed, while endorsement – particularly by friends and family – can help change the way we think about something, the endorsement is far more effective if we believe it to be authentic and the person doing the endorsing to be trustworthy.

Nevertheless, if we find ourselves buying a watch because we have seen it on an A-list wrist, we should ask ourselves: why? Is it because the endorser is an expert on the reliability of expensive Swiss timepieces, or just because we loved a character they played in the movies or their last YouTube video? Is it simply because they are attractive?

(Remember that we can be biased to trust attractive people more than unattractive people.)

We should also consider the endorser's motive: is it because they really love the design, or simply because they were paid to wear it? Ultimately, if we want to think clearly about our choices, we need to ensure we're not being duped into letting someone else decide for us and to do that, we need to think critically about the context of our decisions, and the things that influence us.

So what else can we do to protect our minds from manipulation by advertisers? Well, rest assured that we're not robots that advertisers can reprogram at will. On the downside, however, stealthy advertising is on the rise and it's becoming increasingly difficult to spot when you're being played in more covert ways.[20] This is an arms race, remember.

Ultimately, paying attention to the content we consume, its source and its motives is key. This enables us to engage our rational mind and its cognitive defences and censor the more highly charged emotional messages from our limbic system. Unfortunately, this is often easier said than done, particularly if our thoughts are already occupied with other things, such as relationship woes, financial concerns or the fallout of a shitty day at work. In one fascinating experiment, participants were asked to memorise either a two- or a seven-digit number, which they'd have to recall in another room.[21] Between the rooms, they also had to choose between two snacks – a fruit salad and a piece of chocolate cake – with the results showing that those asked to remember the longer, harder-to-remember number (which occupied more mental bandwidth) were more likely to opt impulsively for the cake. Practically, the researchers argued, this suggested that 'any factor that reduces the availability of processing resources in the shopping environment is likely to increase impulse buying by consumers.' In other words, we may be more vulnerable to advertising – particularly the kind that encourages us to act impulsively – if our minds are wandering elsewhere (or we're trying to remember a new phone number).

We should also avoid thinking that advertising only works on *other* people and that we are always smart enough to shrug it off. Yes, most of us notice when we are being advertised to explicitly, but we're much less likely to spot and pay attention to content that aims to push a product or service on a deeper, more emotional level.[22] And that enables it to bypass our critical, rational mind. So next time you find yourself automatically humming a tune after an ad break, or mindlessly sharing a funny video online, it might be helpful to play the detective. Where did it come from originally? And what purpose does it serve? After all, you could be reinforcing a brand's hold on your mind, or promoting online gambling, without even knowing it.

If you see something being endorsed by a celebrity, influencer – or someone closer to you – you should also ask whether the endorsement is authentic and trustworthy. After all, promotional content that is clearly labelled as such is much less effective, as it flags to the consumer the true motive behind it and engages a more rational response. The internet has made it far easier for advertisers to spread content that manipulates our thinking in their products' favour. But it has also made it far simpler for us to seek out objective reviews and do our own, detailed research. By taking the time to uncover our own answers, we will also engage our more rational faculties and find it easier to avoid rash, impulsive thinking.

You're not a soft target – and nor do any of us have the time to question deeply and rationally every advert we walk by, scroll past, hear on the radio or watch on television. Nevertheless, a vast and sophisticated industry has our minds in its sights. So, if we want to think more clearly about the products and services we spend our money on, we should accept that we're all vulnerable – and pay attention to the messages, explicit and implicit, they bombard us with.

28

Is digital technology rewiring your mind?

Let's start with a short story:

It's scary how many people I know who just don't realise how the internet is changing what's real and what's not. I mean, I like the internet. I've even made decent money off it. And I was on the ground floor of virtual reality, and we were all like, 'We're going to spend all our time in this. It's going to be amazing!'

And it was. I spent my days hanging out in virtual worlds, and my wife was constantly trying to get me to take her to dinner in the real world. Then the bots started coming. Not your average AIs, but full on, 'I've been designed to learn, speak, and think like a human being . . .'

And that's when everything changed.

Sure, they were good at their jobs. They could handle email, program games, answer questions, and even write whole news stories. But you know what else they can do? They can turn a virtual world into a real one. So, we start hanging out in virtual worlds, and our friends start saying things like, 'I want to hang out too!' . . . And suddenly, our friends are spending less and less time in the real world.

And, of course, this becomes a problem. When my wife is sitting all alone on a virtual beach, all she's doing is thinking, 'When is he going to invite me to dinner?'

Then, one day, some clever programmers build a bot that answers this question. And the bots start telling us, 'Okay, honey, I'm gonna invite you to dinner right now,' and, 'You know, honey, the steaks that

I like are on sale . . . And my wife says, 'Yes, honey,' and ratings go up, and money's made.

And people start thinking, 'If bots can do this, maybe they can program their own dinner.' And, before you know it, we've got bots that cook dinner for us.

And we're happy.

Until the bots start saying something else.

And everything changes.

Suddenly, the bots start telling us, 'Okay, honey, it's time for your meds . . .'

The reason this brief fable is so remarkable is that it wasn't written by one of us, or indeed any human – but by an AI. Jurassic, trained and developed by AI21 Labs, is a sophisticated language model similar to the one behind ChatGPT. All we did was prompt it to write on the subject of 'Why I worry about the internet, by an AI' and provided it with the first word: 'It'.[1] Jurassic did the rest. But aside from the canny dark humour (and the slightly old-fashioned, seemingly male voice of its protagonist), the AI's story also reflects our hopes – and fears – about where the internet and other digital technologies are taking us.

Rich virtual worlds, such as Mark Zuckerberg's Metaverse, and AIs that can write stories, debate their own ethics, answer questions and beat us at chess and Go are already a reality – and will only become more immersive and sophisticated over time.[2] Companies like Elon Musk's Neuralink, meanwhile, are developing brain implants that may one day link our minds to computers, potentially supercharging our thinking and certainly triggering a whole array of ethical questions.[3] Such developments may give many of us – and a few AIs – the jitters. But the digital technologies we use every day, and often take for granted, are already tapping into our minds and controlling our thoughts and behaviour.

Consider this, for example.

Using whatever means available, answer the following question as quickly as possible: *What is the capital city of Comoros?**

If you didn't already know the answer – and you had an internet connection – chances are you googled it. And that's not cheating. Google, after all, is a vast – and on our smartphones, highly portable – source of information that we could never hope to remember. Indeed, this simple exercise is just one example of how digital technology can *enhance* our cognitive abilities, filling the gaping holes in our knowledge and freeing up valuable mental bandwidth that we can use to think about something else. So far, so good.

In fact, those still pining for a time before Google et al. should heed the story of Galliano di Mugello, an Italian village where famously bad mobile reception means that everything from making a simple phone call to accessing Twitter, Wikipedia, Facebook and Instagram cat videos is pretty much impossible. And far from seeing their internet-free world as a utopia, it has been reported by the *Guardian* that many of the village's 1,300 residents consider it an 'absolute nuisance'.[4] Indeed, most of us would consider the internet and other digital technology to be an inescapable, and invaluable, bolt-on to our daily lives and, indeed, our brains.

But there is also a price to pay. As anyone who has lost hours down the rabbit hole of TikTok or Instagram Reels, or spent the day live-tweeting their every move, will appreciate, digital technologies place huge demands on our attention. And attention is a resource that, as we have seen elsewhere, we need to think clearly. Indeed, one in four of us report being online 'most of the time' and it is no secret

---

* Answer: Moroni. Courtesy of Google, you also likely now know that: 'The Comoros is a volcanic archipelago off Africa's east coast, in the warm Indian Ocean waters of the Mozambique Channel. The nation state's largest island, Grande Comore (Ngazidja), is ringed by beaches and old lava from active Mt Karthala volcano.'

that digital technologies are frequently designed to keep us engaged for as long as possible – not least because the more time we spend on Facebook, Instagram, YouTube or Twitter, the more valuable data these platforms can extract from us.[5]

In a strikingly honest interview with Axios, Facebook's first president, Sean Parker, for example, revealed that a key question behind it was: 'How do we consume as much of your time and conscious attention as possible?'[6] Google does this by providing free email, telling us what the capital of Comoros is, or allowing us to map the fastest route to work. Facebook, meanwhile, achieves this through features such as the 'like' button, which seems innocent enough but actually is the equivalent of flypaper for our attention. As Parker explained, likes and comments on our posts give us a 'little dopamine hit' every time we are notified of them. 'It's a social-validation feedback loop . . . you're exploiting a vulnerability in human psychology.'[7] Ultimately, they tap into our deep human need to seem smart, engaged, popular – to *belong* – and may use these vulnerabilities to hold our attention and control our thinking.[8]

While social media use has been implicated in triggering addictive behaviours in some people, many experts are reluctant to consider it a true addiction – and most of us will be able to regulate our use and enjoy the information and connectivity it provides.[9] But while recent research shows that frequent digital technology use can benefit brain function – with some games, for example, improving things like memory and multitasking skills, particularly in ageing brains – it can also negatively impact our ability to think clearly.[10] Numerous studies, for example, have linked excessive screen time with reduced attention and even symptoms of attention deficit hyperactivity disorder (ADHD). Digital technology use has also been implicated in impaired emotional and social intelligence, disrupted sleep and even social isolation. One study, for example, found that US nineteen- to thirty-two-year-olds using social media for more than two hours a

day were twice as likely to feel socially isolated than those who limited their daily use to under half an hour.[11] And we're all aware how
social media is frequently blamed – rightly or wrongly– for reinforcing echo chambers and polarising and radicalising opinion.[12]

Of course, a link between two things doesn't mean one causes the
other; correlation is not causality. Indeed, a link between loneliness
and time spent online could just as well mean that lonely and isolated insomniacs are more likely to log on – and stay in front of their
screens for longer – than those with a busier social life and healthier
bedtime habits. It's certainly not always the digital technology that's
to blame.

Nevertheless, digital technologies can also affect the way we
think about ourselves and others. We often use social media, for
example, to store – and curate – our memories and flaunt our best
possible selves, often at the expense of reality.[13] Filters allow us to
alter the lighting and iron out wrinkles and blemishes. And we're
far more likely to post images of ourselves in spectacular locations,
eating gourmet food and swimming with dolphins, than slumped
on the sofa in dirty pyjamas surrounded by crushed beer cans and
cigarette butts. But is this really us? And are our friends' social media
posts really a fair reflection of their daily lives? Of course not – real
life is way more mundane than that. But if we're scrolling through
Facebook or Instagram at home, bored and alone, this distorted version of reality – full of smiling selfies, endless vacations and upbeat
hashtags – may negatively impact our thinking, leaving us feeling
depressed, isolated and insecure about our bodies.[14] Like there's a
party going on that we never get invited to.

It may even impact how we remember.[15] When we live our lives
thinking about how we can post each memorable moment as a photo
on social media, we are focusing on the visual aspects of our experience. But this may come at the cost of enjoying the moment and
other sensory experiences related to it – such as what something

smelled or tasted like, or how we felt or what we thought. We all lay down false memories, but this may make it even more likely that our recall is limited and one-dimensional, potentially even self-serving and narcissistic.

But digital technologies are also getting inside our heads on a deeper and potentially darker level. Whenever we ask Google a question, 'like' something on Facebook, watch something on TikTok or post on Twitter, we are also giving these technologies, and the companies behind them, valuable data on how we think. And this data may then be used to manipulate our minds in some spectacularly sophisticated ways.

Michal Kosinki is an associate professor at Stanford University and a leading expert in psychology and the digital environment. His research was behind the *Guardian*'s initial exposé of Cambridge Analytica's use of digital technology to target voters and offers fascinating insights into how that technology can identify, predict and influence how we think and behave.[16] Indeed, his research has shown that digital technologies – much like those used by Google, Facebook, YouTube and TikTok – are better judges of human personality than people are. 'They are more powerful at this than anything we have interacted with before – including ourselves,' he says. Gulp!

In one major study, Kosinski and his colleagues asked over 85,000 individuals to fill out a 100-item personality questionnaire based on the 'Five Factor' (or 'Big Five') model.[17] They then investigated whether a computer model (drawing on what the participants' had 'liked' on Facebook) was better at predicting the participants' personalities (as determined by the questionnaire) than the individuals' real-life Facebook friends. And it was. In fact, provided with just 100 Facebook 'likes', the computer was a better judge of personality than the average human, while with 150 'likes' it could outperform a family member.[18] With 227 'likes', it was, in the words of the researchers, 'comparable with an average spouse, the best of human judges'. It was also better at predicting some life outcomes, such as substance use, than the humans were.

And it's certainly not just data from Facebook 'likes' that allow digital technologies to get inside our heads. They do so in myriad ways. In another 2021 experiment that used a sample of over a million selfies, for example, facial recognition technology correctly predicted the subjects' liberal or conservative political leanings 72 per cent of the time.[19] (For the record, humans only manage this with 55 per cent accuracy.) All in all, then, Facebook & Co. probably 'know you better than your mum'.[20]

But how is a computer able to predict people's personality, politics, behaviour and life outcomes more accurately than we can? 'We all know ourselves to some extent,' Kosinski says, 'but we are very far from knowing ourselves perfectly. We are sometimes surprised by our behaviour. We sometimes cannot predict our behaviour. We sometimes cannot control our behaviour. In fact, we often explain our behaviour *after* we have done something . . . We are also very selective in what we remember . . . and on top of this, we are all subject to a host of biases, which prevent us from seeing the reality . . . But by looking at gigabytes of data, recorded from millions of people, the patterns become completely clear and apparent to a computer.' Indeed, as computers become more powerful and we leave an ever-bigger digital footprint online, the technologies will only get better at reading our minds.

So the technology clearly exists for companies, particularly those behind social networks, to record and predict our thinking and behaviour. But does that mean it can also be used to *influence* how we think and act? Yes, says Kosinski. 'If there is technology that involves knowing you very well and tracking and predicting your behaviour, then this technology can be used to change your behaviour.'

A basic example of this is how music or video streaming services such as Spotify, Netflix or YouTube feed their users new recommendations. Algorithms observe what you listen to or watch, predict your tastes based on your choices, feed in data on what people like you consume where and when, and then suggest content you may not otherwise have been aware of. And this can be a good thing, broadening our tastes and experiences. Algorithms like this can also help us to find love on dating sites, pick the holiday we want or supercharge our search for a new job.[21] By exposing us to different people and opinions, the technology can also educate us, open our minds and change our thinking in novel and positive ways.

But, as Kosinski says, 'The exact same technology can also be used to find ways to convince you to smoke cigarettes or hate your neighbour or vote for a particular politician.'

In another study, Kosinski and colleagues investigated how digital technology's ability to accurately predict people's psychological characteristics from things such as Tweets and Facebook likes could be used to alter our thinking and behaviour on a massive scale.[22] Politicians may use this kind of 'persuasive mass communication' to encourage us to vote (political marketeers are often more interested in encouraging us to go to the polls, or stay at home, on election day than changing our individual political affiliations). Companies, meanwhile, will deploy it to nudge us into buying their products. And in both cases, it has the greatest impact when the style and content of the message is matched to our individual psychological characteristics.

In a series of experiments that reached 3.7 million people, the researchers used individuals' digital footprints – specifically, what they'd 'liked' on Facebook – to determine how highly they scored in two key personality traits: extraversion[*] and openness-to-experience.[†] They then targeted the individuals on Facebook with adverts

---

[*] The extent to which people seek and enjoy company, excitement and stimulation.
[†] The extent to which people prefer novelty over convention.

specifically tailored to their personality profiles. One campaign, for a beauty retailer, for example, was customised to people's level of extraversion. People scoring highly in the trait were targeted with ads containing pictures of people dancing in public and messages like 'Dance like no-one is watching, but they totally are', while the ads aimed at more introverted individuals included images of people grooming themselves in private and messages like 'Beauty doesn't have to shout'. And the results were striking. As the researchers noted: 'Appeals that were matched to people's extraversion or openness-to-experience level resulted in up to 40 per cent more clicks and up to 50 per cent more purchases than their mismatching or unpersonalised counterparts.'[23]

Ultimately, then, digital technologies, drawing on the data we allow them to harvest, can be used to our benefit or disadvantage, largely depending on how they are used, who is using them and how the results are defined. Either way, they certainly can be used to track, predict and influence our thinking.

We are still some way off living in the Matrix or the full-time virtual dystopia imagined by Jurassic-1 at the start of this chapter. But we certainly shouldn't let our guard down. So what can we do to improve our ability to think clearly and freely in our increasingly digital world?

First, to borrow a piece of advice from *The Hitchhiker's Guide to the Galaxy*: Don't Panic. Digital technology comes with its risks, but it can also improve our ability to think clearly by connecting us with different points of view, vast amounts of information and countless services that can save us time and free up valuable mental bandwidth. The key is to use it consciously and carefully as a way to broaden, rather than limit, our mental horizons.

'*Meaningfully* connect with more people,' says Kosinski. 'Don't leave Facebook; try to engage in a discussion on Facebook. Don't shut down your smartphone; use it to connect with friends and family and don't give up on them. Always remember that this idiot spreading stupid stories on Twitter existed before Twitter – you just never heard them, because they were just hidden in a bar somewhere. And it's good that they're now all over the internet because people can see how ridiculous it is. There'll be one person who'll believe in it, but many people who will now make an extra effort to help the world move away from such ideas . . .'

But equally, be aware how digital technologies may hog your attention – and what they do with that attention. Ultimately, most social media sites, for example, are free – because you pay with your attention and data. Check your privacy settings, consciously monitor how long you are spending online and consider whether the disadvantages are beginning to outweigh the benefits. If they are – and you may be particularly at risk if you are lonely or insecure – set yourself limits, by deleting those social media apps from your phone so you can only use them on a computer.[24] Indeed, there are plenty of digital technologies, such as Freedom, that enable you to reclaim your attention by blocking distracting apps and websites when you're trying to focus on something else.[25]

Also think carefully about the purpose of and motives behind the content you consume. Digital technologies may be politically and ideologically neutral – although they can be infected with human biases, including racism and sexism, in their programming – but they are deployed by people who aren't.[26] As Kosinski warns, 'When you use WhatsApp and Facebook and so on, people just forget that this data is being recorded and analysed.' But your digital footprint provides politicians and companies with powerful insights into how you think and behave and the ability to tailor their messages so they appeal most powerfully to you. This can be positive – ensuring that you hear about policies or products relevant to you – but it also opens the door to potential manipulation, particularly if we respond to the messaging on a purely unconscious, emotional level. Being aware of and attentive to this is often the best defence, so slow down a little and take the time to consider, *consciously*, what you are doing and consuming online and why. As Simon McCarthy-Jones, associate professor in Clinical Psychology and Neuropsychology at Trinity College Dublin, has written, 'Creating speed bumps in our thinking could help improve decision making. Clicking unthinkingly on content or adverts from corporations doesn't allow us to exercise freedom of thought. We do not have time to work out if our desires are our own or those of a puppet master.'[27]

Lastly, remember that those dazzling photos you're scrolling through on social media aren't evidence that everyone is more beautiful or having a better time than you – they're just another form of personalised advertising, to be taken with a pinch of salt. The beach they visited may look great, but take heart from the fact that they probably did step on a sea urchin – they just didn't post about it.

Digital technologies aren't going anywhere and their power, reach – and influence on our thinking – will only grow. But that doesn't mean we are doomed to be their mindless playthings. As they take on an ever-greater role in our lives, we should make a *conscious* effort to harness the benefits and be aware of the potential pitfalls. That way, we may well be able to enhance, rather than surrender, our ability to think broadly, flexibly and clearly.

29

How powerful is your 'sixth sense'?

Let's begin with the easy bit. Take a moment to think about what you can sense right now. If you're reading this, your eyes are likely focused on the words as they scroll across the page. Perhaps you can smell the hot cup of coffee on the table beside you and still taste the last, slightly bitter sip you took. Can you hear birdsong, or the rumble of traffic, outside? And how does the chair feel beneath you? Can you sense your weight pressing against the cushion and the long-lost television remote hidden beneath it?

Collectively, our five, 'exteroceptive' senses – sight, hearing, smell, taste and touch – provide us with the raw data that our brains then use to model the outside world.[1] But now go a little deeper and try to feel what is going on *inside* you. Focus and you may now be able to sense the beating of your heart, the gentle ebb and flow of your breathing, the tension in your muscles, the subtle workings of your gut. Most people are surprisingly poor at feeling their heartbeat at rest, but perhaps as you pay more attention to it, you can sense yours strengthen or quicken?[2] And perhaps that is now coupled with a subtle flush of excitement or even anxiety. Your ability to detect and read these inner signals is called 'interoception': a mysterious, often overlooked but increasingly researched inner sense that not only helps keep our biology in harmonious working order – a process known as 'homeostasis' – but may also be driving our emotions, intuitions and behaviour, shaping our mental health and the very way we think.[3] Writing in *New Scientist*, Caroline Williams, author of *Move! The new science of body over mind*, describes it as a 'bit like our sixth sense'.[4]

Our brains and bodies are not two distinct islands, but instead are intricately entwined. Through a mindboggling 'internet' of connections, our organs, as well as an array of other bodily systems, communicate with the brain to control everything from appetite, temperature and blood pressure to our response to danger. As we saw in Chapter 19: 'Is your gut thinking for you?' (page 153), even the microorganisms within us play their part. Indeed, every time our heart beats, our brain responds, as Sarah Garfinkel, a professor of cognitive neuroscience at UCL, has explained in a compelling TEDx talk.[5] It's as if the two are moving together in a lifelong dance between lovers. Much of this two-way communication goes on behind the scenes, out of sight of our conscious minds. But there is also spill-over – when we're alerted to potential threat by a racing pulse or a knot in our stomach, for example, or we feel hot and flushed around a new crush. And whether or not we are aware of these signals, their impact on our brains – and thinking – can be profound. Indeed, many researchers believe that dysfunctions in interoception could play a key role in conditions like anxiety, depression, anorexia or autism spectrum conditions.[6] Interoception may even provide the building blocks from which we construct our sense of self.

The ideas behind interoception date back decades. At the end of the nineteenth century, for example, an American psychologist and philosopher named William James proposed that many emotions, such as fear, don't just originate in the brain but are a consequence of physiological processes. In his 1884 essay 'What Is an Emotion?' he argued that if we encounter a bear, for example, our heart doesn't start racing because we are afraid.[7] Instead, we should think of it the other way round. The nervous system responds to the potential threat by flooding us with adrenaline, increasing our heart rate and preparing us to fight or fly – and the mind then interprets the signature of these particular physiological responses as fear.[8] In essence, then, the body doesn't just respond to the mind, it can actually drive how we think and feel.

Two decades later, the English neurophysiologist Charles Sherrington coined the term 'interoceptive' and developed the notion of senses that relay information about our bodies' inner workings in his 1906 book *The Integrative Action of the Nervous System*.[9] But while research into interoception continued throughout the twentieth century, it has exploded in quantity over the last two decades, offering tantalising new insights into its mechanisms and impacts on our thinking. Which is not to say that science has all the answers – at least, not yet. This is pioneering research, exploring the complex worlds that lurk within us. 'It's like exploring *inner* space,' psychiatrist Dr Sahib Khalsa, at the Laureate Institute for Brain Research in Tulsa, Oklahoma, explained to us.

But the pieces of the puzzle are starting, slowly, to slot together. In 2016, Khalsa staged the first Interoception Summit in the US, bringing together leading researchers to deepen our understanding of the phenomenon and how it manipulates our minds.[10] And afterwards, Khalsa and colleagues formally defined interoception as: 'the process by which the nervous system senses, interprets, and integrates signals originating from within the body, providing a moment-by-moment mapping of the body's internal landscape across conscious and unconscious levels'.[11] This is the definition most researchers now agree on.

But how does interoception affect our ability to think clearly? As Khalsa explained, 'Knowing what's happening in your body is important for knowing what to do next.' When all is well, our bodies are in balance and there's nothing threatening around, there isn't much need to know what is going on inside us. But what if our heart suddenly starts racing, for example? We may actually need to run away from a bear. We may think we are having a heart attack and rush to the ER.

We may be experiencing a panic attack. We may just have drunk too much coffee, or be responding to a barely perceptible threat, such as a spider-shaped shadow in our peripheral vision. Our ability to detect and interpret bodily signals like this, how attentive we are to them, and whether we see them as threatening or benevolent can radically affect how we respond, with implications for our thinking and mental health.

'Sometimes there's something meaningful happening in your body that you need to react to. But sometimes it's just innocuous,' said Khalsa. 'And being able to filter the true alarms from the false alarms is something people with anxiety disorders, with depression, for example, can find very difficult. If there's a miscalibration between the internal sense and one's environment, if you can't come up with a reasonable explanation for what you're feeling, you can understand how people's thinking and behaviours get shaped . . . It's not difficult for people experiencing this kind of sensory ambiguity to lose sight of their logic and end up in a panic.'

Certainly, some of us are more interoceptive (that is, more attuned to signals from inside our bodies) than others. Individual sensitivity to these internal sensations is often measured using the heart – its beat, after all, is often the clearest and most noticeable bodily signal.[12] At UCL, Garfinkel investigates how signals from the body, particularly the heart, shape how we think and feel. She believes the heart has a particularly close and eerie connection with our minds – and the effects can even be seen across a single heartbeat.[13] One study by Garfinkel, for example, found that people think fearful images are more intense – and their amygdalae (which govern emotional responses, such as fear) are more active – when their heart muscles contract (systole) than when they relax (diastole).[14] This perhaps reveals how our emotions and thinking can be shaped by bodily changes, such as a racing heart amplifying our experience of fear. Our hearts may also connect our minds with the minds of others. Research conducted by Ivana Konvalinka and colleagues at a Spanish fire-walking ritual, of all things, discovered that the heart rate of those striding across the scorching-hot coals became synchronised with spectators who were related to them, such as spouses, potentially causing them to think – or at least, feel – similarly.[15]

Back in the lab, interoception tests determine how accurately participants can sense that their heartbeat is in synch (or not) with a periodic sound, for example. But researchers don't just assess how interoceptive people are; they also examine – often through questionnaires, for example – how aware they are of their interoceptive abilities. Some people will score highly on interoceptive accuracy, but be completely unaware how in tune with their bodies they actually are. We may also be more or less attentive to the signals and interpret and respond to them in different ways, with some (such as those with anxiety) seeing a raised heartbeat or a fluttering stomach as threatening while others will see them as more benign or ambiguous.[16] Playing a leading role in all this seems to be the insular cortex, a brain structure that is thought to be associated with consciousness and emotion, and parts of which are more active – and have more grey matter – in people high in interoception.[17] But it isn't alone. An array of other brain areas also seem to be involved, including the amygdala and the hippocampus (which plays a key role in memory).[18]

Either way, these signals appear to be closely related to our emotions. Dr Briony Banks at Lancaster University, for example, has investigated the degree to which people experience different types of concepts with different senses. She found that people tend to associate 'concrete' words and concepts (such as 'apple', 'cat' and 'chair') with different combinations of the five exteroceptive senses.[19] If you hear the word 'apple', for example, you may think of its sharp taste; its fresh, citrusy smell; the sound of its crunch; the waxy feel of it in your hand; a shiny green globe. Collectively, these sensations help establish our knowledge and thoughts about apples. But we tend to think about 'abstract' concepts (such as emotions, time and religion) differently. And this is particularly true of emotions. In fact, as Banks's research shows, we are far more likely to associate emotions like anger, happiness, fear, joy and sadness with interoceptive sensations – as something experienced through the inner workings of our body. Interoception, then, seems to play a central role in how we think about and experience our emotions.

Research also shows that people who score highly in interoception are often better at feeling bodily states, experience heightened emotions and can more easily manage them.[20] But there are also suggestions that those with anxiety disorders have an exaggerated response to bodily signals, perhaps focusing too much on, and thinking too deeply about, what is going on inside them, potentially causing them to overlook the realities of the outside world. Those low in interoception, meanwhile, appear less able to understand their feelings – and this has been implicated in depression, a condition that can lead to monochrome thinking, uncoloured by the full palette of vivid emotions.[21]

It seems these processes can affect our thinking in numerous other ways, too. Take intuition. As we have seen elsewhere in this book, we don't always have enough information to make rational decisions using logic alone. Instead, we often rely on intuition – a kind of instinctive guesswork. In the 1990s, Antonio Damasio – the famed neuroscientist, philosopher and author of *Descartes' Error: Emotion, Reason and the Human Brain* – suggested that decision-making and intuition are driven by emotional cues that originate in the body – and later intriguing research by University of Cambridge clinical psychologist Dr Tim Dalgleish and colleagues set about testing this.[22]

The researchers asked ninety-two participants to play a complex card game for money. The game required the participants to select cards from four decks, two of which were profitable and two of which would lead them to lose money over time. The game was organised in such a way, however, that the participants couldn't use logic to determine whether or not a deck was profitable. Instead, they had to rely on intuition to 'learn' the rules and come out on top. Meanwhile, the participants' subtle bodily changes, such as shifts in their heart rate and electrical changes in their skin, were monitored before they made each decision. Remarkably, the results showed that those subtle bodily changes – and how the participants' perceived them through interoception – really did influence their intuitive decision-making, suggesting that sometimes the brain can, quite literally, 'follow the heart', even when we're not conscious of it.

As Garfinkel explains, 'The body changes before the mind realises it and people with good interoception can tap into that signal and use it as an extra channel of information.' Indeed, her own real-world research, on traders working for a City of London hedge fund, found that those who were best at perceiving their own heartbeats (a common measure of interoceptive ability) tended to be more profitable and have longer careers.[23] The study didn't show causation, but it's another intriguing insight into how our biology may influence our ability to manage risk, rely on our intuitions and think clearly in high-stakes environments.

But increased interoception doesn't necessarily lead to success in card games or a glittering career in finance. It may also lead us to think in disturbing or demoralising ways. If you're highly interoceptive, but misread your bodily signals – by thinking you're having a heart attack every time your pulse surges or believing every flip of your stomach is an omen of impending disaster – you can become stuck in a destructive feedback loop, whereby physical cues trigger negative thoughts, which exacerbate the bodily sensations. Indeed, it's rarely good to focus *too* hard on what's going on inside you – as any hypochondriac will tell you. As Khalsa told us: 'If I gave you a pair of glasses that gave you better than twenty-twenty vision, you might find yourself noticing all of the details, such as just focusing on the fly on the wall twenty feet away instead of seeing the bigger picture.' Similarly, diminished interoception can cause us to misunderstand, or miss entirely, the physical messages our bodies are sending us. Basically, it's about balance. 'You want to be able to attend to the signal and be precise about it,' says Garfinkel. 'You need control over what you're paying attention to.' Only then can you think clearly.

In fact, researchers increasingly believe that a lack of balance in this area may be behind a wide range of mental health conditions – and that interventions, based on our growing understanding of interoception, may help to remedy them. Khalsa, for example, has been exploring new ways of treating anxiety and anorexia nervosa. In one study with colleagues, he explored the potential benefits of ninety minutes of floatation therapy – during which you float in a tank with minimal external sensory inputs – on people with high levels of anxiety.[24] And the results were promising. Participants experienced reduced anxiety, muscle tension and blood pressure and an improved feeling of serenity and well-being. Interestingly, many also experienced enhanced awareness of their breathing and heartbeat – essentially becoming more interoceptive.

At first glance, these findings appear paradoxical – as we discovered earlier in the chapter, anxiety is often linked with enhanced interoceptive awareness. Tellingly, however, many of the participants, who normally associated a heightened awareness of their breathing and heartbeat with anxiety, described the sensations in the tank as 'pleasant'. Indeed, it seems the therapy may have allowed the participants to reset their minds, breaking the damaging association between bodily sensations and anxiety and establishing a new, more positive one between those same sensations and relaxation. Either way, the research furthered the link between anxiety and interoception. In fact, Khalsa is now exploring how floatation therapy could be used to treat anorexia nervosa, an often deadly eating disorder that is also associated with distorted interoception, such as intrusive feelings of chest tightness and palpitations and unpleasant sensations in the gut.[25] Promisingly, an early-phase clinical trial showed that floatation therapy reduced anxiety and improved body satisfaction in a small group of participants.

With Professor Hugo Critchley, chair of psychiatry at the University of Sussex, and others, Garfinkel also recently investigated through a randomised controlled trial whether training that improves intero-ceptive awareness can reduce anxiety in autistic adults.[26] Autistic people are far more likely than the general population to experience anxiety and may struggle to understand emotions. They may also have reduced interoceptive accuracy.[27] But the training programme, which combined heartbeat tests, feedback on how they performed and light exercise (to raise the participants' heartbeats and make them more noticeable) yielded some impressive results. The par-ticipants' reported that anxiety scores fell and 31 per cent of those who received the training met the criteria for 'recovery'. Essentially, it appears the participants became more precise in their awareness of their bodily signals, such as a racing heart, and better at attributing them to normal fluctuations in their body.[28] Consequently, they may have found they could intervene sooner (by taking deep breaths, for example) before the anxiety became unmanageable.

Few of us will have access to these early scientific interventions – at least for now. But by becoming more aware of how our bodies respond in particular situations, we can all improve our chances of thinking clearly, whether we're in a real crisis or just an imagined one.

The first step is simply to acknowledge how these bodily sig-nals can shape our thinking and emotions – and then be attentive (but not *too* attentive) to them. Your heart is changing its rhythm all the time, so if you suddenly find yourself fixating on it speeding up, stop, focus and ask yourself: why? You may well be anxious, but don't panic or catastrophise. As Garfinkel says: 'You don't want to think, "My heart is beating fast, I'm going to have a heart attack," but rather, "My heart rate is elevated, but that's fine, it will return to baseline again."' By noticing signals like these early, we can take positive steps before our thinking spirals out of control.

To a degree, we can also train ourselves to be more interoceptive. Again, the heart is often the best place to start. Some people are sim-ply more interoceptive than others, but you can make yourself more aware of your own heartbeat – and what it might be telling you – by raising it. 'If I got you to do fifty star jumps, you'll definitely be feeling your heart,' says Garfinkel. 'So, when we train people, we take advantage of that. We get them to do exercise to elevate the signals and then we get them to focus on them so, as they fade, they get to stay attuned to them. That way, you get used to accessing the signals even when they're not elevated.' As reported in the *Guardian*, exercise won't just make it less likely that your heart will speed up and beat out of control during periods of stress, it will also ensure you're more used to – and better able to manage – the sensation when it does, reducing the likelihood that you'll misattribute it to something more alarming.[29]

And if the gym or running around the park isn't for you, perhaps book a slot in a floatation tank. By removing the external 'noise' transmitted to your brain by your eyes, ears and other senses, floating like this enables you to focus more intently on what's happening within, whether that's your heartbeat, breathing or sensations from your gut. Meditation, mindfulness – or just sitting still in a quiet, dark room – may offer similar benefits, helping us to break the feedback loop of intensifying anxious thoughts and bodily sensations that can lead our thinking to overheat or melt down completely.[30]

Science still has a very long way to go in its exploration of this mysterious inner space. But thanks to the work of Garfinkel, Khalsa and others, what it is discovering is a vast and highly complex universe of physical processes that are influencing our minds in some extraordinary ways. To think clearly, we shouldn't just consider what's happening in our brains, but listen carefully to what's going on in our bodies, too. As Damasio, one of the world's leading neuroscientists, told us: 'Our thoughts and our feelings and emotions are not just influenced by our bodies but [are] actually inconceivable without them. All of our mental activity is a consequence of body/brain interactions.'

Epilogue: Do you know yourself?

I think, therefore I am.

So said the seventeenth-century French philosopher René Descartes. The good news is that by reading this book – and thinking about it – you now have some evidence that you exist. And that's got to be reassuring. The trickier bit, however, is knowing who that thinking 'I' really is.

In this book, we haven't set out to crack the mystery of consciousness. Science has many theories but remains a long way from discovering its genesis or explaining how the seven octillion (that's a seven followed by twenty-seven zeros) atoms in our bodies somehow coalesce to make us sentient, thinking beings. Instead, we've gone on a journey into the human mind to investigate how our thinking is shaped, influenced and manipulated by a complex cocktail of external and internal phenomena. And what we've discovered tells us something about who that 'I' is, too.

The truth is that we are not just one person; an isolated automaton who thinks in a single, fixed way. As we've discovered, thanks to a whole host of factors, our thinking evolves and shifts, ebbs and flows – and sometimes goes completely haywire. Some of these factors, like our genes, are hardwired into us; some are more fleeting and can be controlled. Some scream in our ear, demanding all of our attention; others whisper, pulling the strings by subterfuge. Some originate inside our brains and bodies; others are a consequence of the people around us, our social identities, where and how we live, or our memories and experiences. To think better, we need to recognise how malleable, vulnerable to bias and varied our minds can be, and begin to understand the often competing forces that may be shaping our thinking at any given time. We must also acknowledge that different combinations of these factors will impact each of us differently in different situations.

As we warned you at the start of this book, we're not going to bullshit you and claim there is one key ingredient to thinking well. Despite what countless other books will tell you, positivity and optimism come with plenty of pitfalls – not least that they can make you overconfident, blinkered and gullible – and the relentless pursuit of happiness will likely only make you miserable. Nor is a high IQ the foolproof solution it is claimed to be – it doesn't make us immune to bias, prejudice, hanger or mental illness, and it won't automatically make us challenge our own thinking. To make the most of our intelligence, we also need intellectual openness, flexibility and conscientiousness as well as emotional stability and intelligence. And if you believe love will clear your head, think again. We all know how muddled and mindless that can make us.

But what does help is to know yourself – and to better grasp the many factors, outlined in this book, that contribute to making you, you. If you don't know where to start, take some of the psychological tests mentioned in this book. But also talk to the people around you – ask for honest assessments (warning: this may hurt) and reflect deeply on your past behaviour and the thinking that preceded it.

So how have *we* gone about doing this? While writing this book, we have tried to apply its findings and lessons to our own lives. As we said at the outset, we are not just one biased author, but two. And by recognising this, identifying each other's thinking pratfalls and then arguing (well, debating) late into the night, we helped usher one another out of our bubbles, began to dismantle many of our individual thinking traps and learned a huge amount about ourselves. We are still fallible, of course, but perhaps a little less so.

According to personality tests that we took throughout the process, as well as feedback from those around us, your female author is open to experience, which is helpful as it can make us more cognitively flexible and protect against cognitive decline as we age. Less helpful is the fact that she can also be anxious and disorganised. Her lack of organisation has an upside: she is far more focused on abstract ideas and the big picture than the bureaucratic drudgery of filing, diary-keeping and, yes, tidying. But she realised that missing important details, or spending valuable thinking time looking for your endlessly misplaced keys, can also muddle your thinking. She specifically addressed this thinking trap by using a proven psychological intervention that seeks to improve your score on certain personality traits through daily tasks.[1] And it worked – to a degree. By the end of the programme, which she completed at home, her score in the conscientiousness sub-trait organisation had significantly increased.

The tests also identified that she has a moderate pessimism bias, at least part of the time. On the downside, this could make her defeatist and anxious, but it also helps to boost her performance. By thinking about her pessimism as a prompt to 'do better', she harnessed it to increase her motivation. And through exploring the research on pessimism, she also learned the extent to which she blamed herself for any little failure in life, and began to 'give herself a break', show more self-compassion and realise that some things are simply out of our control. But this is all about striking the right balance and avoiding rigid, binary distinctions. Her pessimism also helped her to identify potential pitfalls or problems with the book, and with life more generally. Optimism, after all, can blind you to the things that might go wrong.

Take your male author, for example, who scored more highly in extraversion and optimism. This might sound desirable, but by applying the research findings – with a little help from his ever-vigilant co-author – it became clear that this was having both positive *and* negative effects on his thinking. His flashes of blind positivism, for instance, could make him too certain that deadlines and other commitments would be met. This led to frustration and anxiety when they (perhaps too frequently) weren't. Overconfidence, meanwhile, meant that he could be more reluctant to change course – or his mind – when confronted with a better argument.

By identifying these negative effects, he was able to change his thinking in constructive, new ways and apply the lessons more broadly. As an adventure-sports enthusiast, for example, he realised that his optimism might be putting him in peril, causing him to take unnecessary risks by underestimating the potential dangers. Indeed, in some environments, being a defensive pessimist – or at least a more cautious optimist – and thinking carefully through the dangers and how to mitigate them, might actually save your relationship, career or even your life.

It also caused him to question his own background and privilege – as a white man, who was the first in his family to go to boarding school and university. After all, it's easier to be optimistic and confident when you have been given opportunities and educated to believe in yourself. But the private-school system has also historically failed to reward empathetic thinking, instead encouraging blind individualism, rationality and oppressive stoicism, which he felt had left him disconnected from his emotions. As we've learned in this book, people who are more in touch with their emotions, and can think critically about them, are often less driven by them. So taking more control of his mind by questioning years of such indoctrination – and thinking more openly about his own emotions – has made him better at understanding the world and his privileged place within it. Without actually chasing it, it has also made him happier.

Your female author, on the other hand, who is half Indian, grew up in Sweden in the eighties and nineties when immigration was more limited than now. She encountered prejudice, which sometimes made her feel like an outsider. But some of these moments, she now realises, she may have 'over-remembered' and sometimes used to interpret the world in a more threatening, and less nuanced, way than she could have. But growing up in two different cultures – and learning from both – also helped to open her mind, question stereotypes and broaden her thinking. As a university-educated woman now living in multicultural London, she also began to identify more clearly her own privilege, something she believes has benefited her thinking, too. A lecture about the benefits of future-oriented thinking, for example, may not be of interest to or help someone who is deeply depressed or struggling with poverty – and our own privilege can blind us to this.

We also started questioning and paying more attention to our intuitions. As we've discovered, we frequently don't have enough time or information to make informed, rational decisions, so we rely on our 'gut feelings' instead. Intuitive thinking can be enormously powerful – particularly if you're an expert in the field, have great emotional intelligence, or have experienced a situation many times before. But we need to be aware that these cognitive shortcuts can also make us biased, rash and impulsive. We've each learned to trust our intuitions more in areas in which we have some experience, such as how best to word a sentence, fly a paraglider or come up with a new recipe (not that they're always right, even then). But we've also recognised how important it is to engage slow, analytical thinking in unfamiliar situations, or in those where we may be prejudiced. We should all be particularly aware of the potential traps of lazy, intuitive thinking when dealing with numbers and statistics, when we're afraid or when we encounter new people. If in doubt, stop for a moment and make an active attempt to think carefully.

We also all have habits and routines, but your authors both scored relatively low on the 'Creature of Habit' scale. This has its obvious benefits. It means you are more likely to try new things and think through your decisions, rather than just make them on autopilot. Having a varied life also helps slow down time, at least in retrospect – making our lives feel longer and fuller. Avoiding routine at all cost, though, can be counterproductive. Habits and routines, after all, are advantageous because they save us time and mental bandwidth for important things. We don't constantly have to think about what new things we can wear, eat or do.

Our daily routines can impact our thinking in all sorts of ways. While writing this book, for example, we discovered that two of the biggest obstacles to our thinking clearly were tiredness and 'hanger' – and so setting routines that ensure you get enough sleep and eat well can be hugely beneficial for the mind. We also calculated how long we spent on social media and doom-scrolling the news. (Answer: too long.) We've both tried, but largely failed, to make progress in this area, but always bear in mind that while digital technologies can improve and augment our thinking, too much time comparing our lives with others' on social media can impact our mood and self-esteem.

We've also tried to devote a little more thought to what our bodies are telling us. The largely hidden influence of interoception and the microorganisms inside us can be hard to identify on a daily basis, but good food, exercise and paying a bit more attention to bodily signals (without becoming obsessive or too earnest about it) will all help contribute to clearer thinking. And remember that habits can also become addictions, which can hijack our thinking in the most profound way possible and cause us to prioritise a substance or behaviour over absolutely everything else. Think about that next glass of wine, cigarette or pill – don't just pour, puff or pop it out of habit.

Habits and routines, though, can also help us stick with something long enough to become proficient at it. To write this book, we had to become more habitual – working and eating at set times, often wearing the same clothes, scheduling exercise, shopping and free time. This new routine was hardly inspiring, but it suited the circumstances and helped us to finish the book and learn a lot about ourselves. In future, we'll both be dedicating more time and thought to projects and activities, rather than just mindlessly jumping between things we never finish. But again, it's all about knowing yourself and striking a healthy balance. We also both knew that too much habit would break us and kill our imagination, so we made sure there was just as much routine as we could stomach, mixing that with spur-of-the-moment trips or activities.

One of the biggest themes in this book, which comes up over and again, however, is how habit can dangerously limit our thinking. Eating the same thing for lunch every day is one thing, but having the exact same experiences, talking to the same people in the same culture and relying on the same sources of information are profound threats to thinking clearly. You can never develop and grow your thinking if you never question yourself, and you can't challenge and question yourself if you never experience anything new. Research has shown that people who grow up in diverse areas, for example, are less prejudiced towards those who aren't in their own 'in-group'. It seems to us that diversity can help in other ways, too. Those who speak many languages or grow up with more than one culture may also be less biased in some aspects of their thinking. Ultimately, a broad approach to life is beneficial to thinking in general – you will reap benefits from socialising widely, engaging in a range of different intellectual tasks and taking in a variety of viewpoints.

If there's one lesson you should take away from this book, it's that we all need to be open, pay attention to others, be willing to change our minds and admit that we're wrong sometimes. The alternative is that we become locked into echo chambers, which, taken to an extreme, lead to polarisation and the 'good vs evil', 'us and them' narratives behind so much small-mindedness, bigotry and conflict in the world.

Know yourself, think broadly, think bold – and listen.

Acknowledgements

No book like this is merely the product of its authors. These pages would be pretty much empty were it not for the extraordinary work of the psychologists, neuroscientists and other researchers who devote their lives to scientific inquiry and the exploration of the human mind. We dedicate this book to every one of them – bold, tireless and inspirational thinkers all.

In particular, we are indebted to Barbara Sahakian, Rafael Euba, Magda Osman, Parashkev Nachev and Anders Sandberg, who helped us map out the scope of this book, which otherwise might have remained an impenetrable maze. We are also enormously grateful to all those who spoke with us about their research and allowed us to gaze a little deeper into how we think: Daniel Kahneman, Christian Clot, Elizabeth Loftus, Simon McCarthy-Jones, Adrian Furnham, Gina Rippon, Simon Baron-Cohen, Elizabeth Phelps, Jennifer Wild, Colette Hirsch, Tali Sharot, Julie Norem, Karen Ersche, Wolfram Schultz, Nick Chater, Ayse Uskul, Clifford Stott, Ian Hamilton, Magda Osman, Tom Stafford, Agnes Nairn, Ching-Yu Huang, Gerd Gigerenzer, Anders Sandberg, David Nutt, Mark Glaser, John Cryan, Ingmar Skoog, Yulia Kovas, Barbara Sahakian, Petter Johansson, Rafael Euba, Claude Steele, Viren Swami, Antonio Damasio, Panos Athanasopoulos, Michal Kosinki, Sarah Garfinkel, Sahib Khalsa, Tom Clark, Parker Singleton, Terese Glatz, Briony Parks and Tanya Luhrmann. You make the world an endlessly interesting place.

But this book isn't only about the science; it is also about the stories that help bring it to vivid life. And so we send heartfelt thanks, too, to all the brave people who shared their own personal tales with us, including 'Helen' and 'Alex', Kajsa, Cayle Royce, Jackie Malton,

Henrik Carlson, Terry Waite, Elizabeth Parrish, Jila Mossaed and Carolyn Oglesby.

As ever, our family and friends also played a starring role, not least Göran Frankel, who read and critiqued many parts; Oliver Sherratt, who got one of the earliest glimpses of a chapter, in the cockpit of a plane somewhere over the Atlantic; and Torben Warren and Miles Frankel-Hamid, who had to put up with one of their parents being nose-deep in Google Scholar for months on end (yes, we can go to the beach next week). And we appreciate the boundless moral support from Amala Frankel, Richard Warren, Sue Duncan and Ann and John Carter.

We also owe a huge debt of gratitude to all our colleagues and authors at The Conversation. Its mission – to take academic research to a global audience for the benefit of all – remains a daily inspiration for both of us, and we are proud to play a part in helping to make it a reality. We send particular thanks to Chris Waiting and Stephen Khan for their support and encouragement – and all those who had to suffer our endless progress reports (yes, that's definitely you, Khalil).

And finally, none of this would have happened without the belief, inspiration, support and endless patience of Harriet Poland, Izzy Everington, Tom Atkins, Ollie Martin and Alyssa Ollivier-Tabukashvili at Hodder. Harriet and Izzy take full credit for turning a hopeful email – sent sometime in the middle of a pandemic – into the book you are holding now. As a result, we will never think the same way again – and for that, and everything else you have done, we are forever grateful.

Notes

1. Do you wear a watch?

1 Associated Press in Lombrives, '15 French volunteers leave cave after 40 days without daylight or clocks', *Guardian*, 25 April 2021.

2 Adaptation Institute EN website, https://adaptation-institute.com/; Deep-Time website, https://deeptime.fr.

3 Chess Stetson, Matthew P. Fiesta and David M. Eagleman, 'Does Time Really Slow Down During a Frightening Event?' *PLoS ONE* 2(12).

4 Bob Holmes, 'Why time flies in old age', *New Scientist*, 23 November 1996.

5 Ibid.

6 Christian Yates, 'Why time seems to go by more quickly as we get older', The Conversation, 10 August 2016, https://theconversation.com/why-time-seems-to-go-by-more-quickly-as-we-get-older-63354.

7 Marc Wittmann, *Felt Time: The Psychology of How We Perceive Time* (MIT Press, 2016), p. 83.

8 Ibid., p. 88.

9 Ibid., p. 87.

10 Ibid., p. 86.

11 Stetson et al., 'Does Time Really Slow Down'.

12 Mariya Davydenko and Johanna Peetz, 'Time grows on trees: The effect of nature settings on time perception', *Journal of Environmental Psychology* 54.

13 Leslie Iversen, 'Cannabis and the brain', *Brain*, 126(6).

14 Associated Press, '15 French volunteers leave cave'.

2. Are you stuck in the past?

1 Terry Waite, *Taken on Trust* (Hodder & Stoughton, 1993).

2 Elliott Green, 'How Brexiteers appealed to voters' nostalgia', LSE BPP (blog), 30 August 2016, https://blogs.lse.ac.uk/politicsandpolicy/how-brexiteers-appealed-to-voters-nostalgia/.

3 Michael D. Robinson et al., 'The politics of time: Conservatives differentially reference the past and liberals differentially reference the future', *Journal of Applied Social Psychology* 45(7).

4 Philip G. Zimbardo and John N. Boyd, 'Putting Time in Perspective: A Valid, Reliable Individual-Differences Metric', *Journal of Personality and Social Psychology* 77(6).

5   C. Routledge et al., 'The past makes the present meaningful: Nostalgia as an existential resource', *Journal of Personality and Social Psychology* 101(3).
6   Philip Zimbardo and John Boyd, *The Time Paradox* (Rider Books, 2010), p. 19.
7   Ibid., p. 95.
8   Ronald Purser and Andrew Cooper, 'Mindfulness' "truthiness" problem: Sam Harris, science and the truth about Buddhist tradition', Salon, 6 December 2014, https://www.salon.com/2014/12/06/mindfulness_truthiness_problem_sam_harris_science_and_the_truth_about_buddhist_tradition/.
9   Kate Pickert, 'The Mindful Revolution', *Time*, 3 February 2014; NHS definition of mindfulness: https://www.nhs.uk/conditions/stress-anxiety-depression/mindfulness/.
10 Ronald Purser, 'The mindfulness conspiracy', *Guardian*, 14 June 2019.
11 Miriam Frankel, 'How talking to your future self can improve your health and happiness', *New Scientist*, 22 May 2023.
12 Ruth F. Hunter et al., 'Association between time preference, present-bias and physical activity: implications for designing behavior change interventions', *BMC Public Health* 18; Yang Wang and Frank A. Sloan, 'Present bias and health', *Journal of Risk and Uncertainty* 55.
13 Ran Kivetz and Anat Keinan, 'Repenting Hyperopia: An Analysis of Self-Control Regrets', *Journal of Consumer Research*, 33(2); Wittmann, *Felt Time*, p.14.
14 Marc Wittmann et al., 'Now or later? Striatum and insula activation to immediate versus delayed rewards', *Journal of Neuroscience, Psychology, and Economics* 3(1).
15 Zimbardo and Boyd, *The Time Paradox*, p. 19.
16 Ibid.
17 George Loewenstein, Ted O'Donoghue and Matthew Rabin, 'Projection Bias in Predicting Future Utility', *The Quarterly Journal of Economics*, 118(4).
18 Amelia Dennis, Jane Ogden and Erica G. Hepper, 'Evaluating the impact of a time orientation intervention on well-being during the COVID-19 lockdown: past, present or future?' *The Journal of Positive Psychology* 17(3).

3. Can you trust your memories?

1   Martin A. Conway and Christopher W. Pleydell-Pearce, 'The Construction of Autobiographical Memories in the Self-Memory System', *Psychological Review* 107(2).
2   Giuliana Mazzoni, 'The "real you" is a myth – we constantly create false memories to achieve the identity we want', The Conversation, 19 September 2018, https://theconversation.com/the-real-you-is-a-myth-we-constantly-create-false-memories-to-achieve-the-identity-we-want-103253.
3   Harlene Hayne and Fiona Jack, 'Childhood amnesia', *WIREs Cognitive Science* 2(2).

4   Ira E. Hyman, Troy H. Husband and F. James Billings, 'False Memories of Childhood Experiences', *Applied Cognitive Psychology* 9(3).

5   Julia Shaw, *The Memory Illusion* (Random House Books, 2016), pp. 72–8.

6   Gillian Murphy et al., 'False Memories for Fake News During Ireland's Abortion Referendum', *Psychological Science*, 1(11).

7   Jon Stone, 'British public still believe Vote Leave "£350million a week to EU" myth from Brexit referendum', *Independent*, 28 October 2018.

8   'Eyewitness Identification Reform', Innocence Project, https://innocenceproject.org/eyewitness-identification-reform/.

9   Murphy et al., 'False Memories for Fake News'.

10 Justin Storbeck and Gerald L. Clore, 'With Sadness Comes Accuracy; With Happiness, False Memory: Mood and the False Memory Effect', *Psychological Science* 16(10).

4. Have your parents fucked you up?

1   MaTCH website, https://match.ctglab.nl/#/home.

2   These can be measured by, for example, the CANTAB IED task and the Halpern Critical Thinking Assessment, respectively: 'Intra-Extra Dimensional Set Shift', Cambridge Cognition, https://www.cambridgecognition.com/cantab/cognitive-tests/executive-function/intra-extra-dimensional-set-shift-ied/; Heather A. Butler, 'Halpern Critical Thinking Assessment Predicts Real-World Outcomes of Critical Thinking', *Applied Cognitive Psychology* 26(5).

3   Leor Zmigrod et al., 'The psychological roots of intellectual humility: The role of intelligence and cognitive flexibility', *Personality and Individual Differences* 141.

4   Heather A. Butler et al., 'Predicting real-world outcomes: Critical thinking ability is a better predictor of life decisions than intelligence', *Personality and Individual Differences* 25.

5   Dan M. Kahan et al., 'Motivated numeracy and enlightened self-government', *Behavioural Public Policy* 1(1).

6   David Robson, *The Intelligence Trap: Revolutionise Your Thinking and Make Wiser Decisions* (Hodder & Stoughton, 2019), pp. 45–54.

7   D. S. Janowsky, 'Introversion and extroversion: implications for depression and suicidality', *Current Psychiatry Reports* 3(6).

8   Martin C. Melchers et al, 'Similar Personality Patterns Are Associated with Empathy in Four Different Countries', *Frontiers in Psychiatry* 7(290).

9   Nicholas A. Turiano et al., 'Personality and Substance Use in Midlife: Conscientiousness as a Moderator and the Effects of Trait Change', *Journal of Research in Personality* 46(3).

10 Wenfu Li et al., 'Brain structure links trait creativity to openness to experience', *Social Cognitive and Affective Neuroscience* 10(2); Cyril J. Sadowski and

Helen E. Cogburn, 'Need for Cognition in the Big-Five Factor Structure', *The Journal of Psychology* 131(3).

11   Małgorzata A. Gocłowska et al. 'Novelty seeking is linked to openness and extraversion, and can lead to greater creative performance', *Journal of Personality* 87(2).

12   Sabrina Hoppe, 'Eye Movements During Everyday Behaviour Predict Personality Traits', *Frontiers in Human Neuroscience* 12.

13   Brent W. Roberts et al., 'Patterns of mean-level change in personality traits across the life course: a meta-analysis of longitudinal studies', *Psychological Bulletin* 132(1).

14   Mirjam Stieger et al., 'Changing personality traits with the help of a digital personality change intervention', *PNAS* 118(8).

15   Miriam Frankel, 'How to alter your personality: why your character isn't fixed in stone', *New Scientist*, 12 January 2022.

16   There is a long list of such tasks for each personality trait in the appendix of a recent paper on volitional personality change: Nathan W. Hudson et al., 'You have to follow through: Attaining behavioral change goals predicts volitional personality change', *Journal of Personality and Social Psychology* 117(4).

17   Ibid.

18   Christian N. Brinch and Taryn Ann Galloway, 'Schooling in adolescence raises IQ scores', *PNAS* 109(2).

19   Christopher R. Huber and Nathan R. Kuncel, 'Does College Teach Critical Thinking? A Meta-Analysis', *Review of Educational Research* 86(2); Daniel Willingham, 'Can I Learn to Think More Rationally?', *Scientific American* 2(74).

20   Jennifer M. Fletcher et al., 'Heritability of Preferred Thinking Styles and a Genetic Link to Working Memory Capacity', *Twin Research and Human Genetics* 17(6).

21   Cristina de Andrade Varanda and Fernanda Dreux Miranda Fernandes, 'Cognitive flexibility training intervention among children with autism: a longitudinal study', *Psicologia: Reflexão e Crítica* 30.

22   Jiangzhou Sun et al., 'Training Your Brain to Be More Creative: Brain Functional and Structural Changes Induced by Divergent Thinking Training', *Human Brain Mapping* 37.

23   Anne Corbett et al., 'The Effect of an Online Cognitive Training Package in Healthy Older Adults: An Online Randomized Controlled Trial', *Journal of Post-Acute and Long-Term Care Medicine* 16(11).

24   George Savulich et al., 'Improvements in Attention Following Cognitive Training With the Novel "Decoder" Game on an iPad', *Frontiers in Behavioural Neuroscience* 13.

25 Bruno Bonnechère et al., 'Brain training using cognitive apps can improve cognitive performance and processing speed in older adults', *Scientific Reports* 10.

5. Do your emotions rule your mind?

1   Jennifer S. Lerner et al., 'Heart Strings and Purse Strings: Carryover Effects of Emotions on Economic Decisions', *Psychological Science* 15(5); D. G. Dutton and A. P. Aron, 'Some evidence for heightened sexual attraction under conditions of high anxiety', *Journal of Personality and Social Psychology* 30(4); Norbert Schwarz and Gerald Clore, 'Mood, misattribution, and judgments of well-being: Informative and directive functions of affective states', Journal of Personality and Social Psychology 45(3).

2   Scott B. Patten, 'Major Depression Prevalence Is Very High, But the Syndrome Is a Poor Proxy for Community Populations' Clinical Treatment Needs', *The Canadian Journal of Psychiatry* 53(7); 'Mental health facts and statistics', Mind website: https://www.mind.org.uk/information-support/types-of-mental-health-problems/statistics-and-facts-about-mental-health/how-common-are-mental-health-problems/; Borwin Bandelow and Sophie Michaelis, 'Epidemiology of anxiety disorders in the 21st century', *Dialogues in Clinical Neuroscience* 17(3).

3   Cynthia Fu, 'People with depression can sometimes experience memory problems – here's why', The Conversation, 9 February 2021, https://theconversation.com/people-with-depression-can-sometimes-experience-memory-problems-heres-why-153392.

4   Cynthia Fu et al., 'Widespread Morphometric Abnormalities in Major Depression: Neuroplasticity and Potential for Biomarker Development', *Neuroimaging Clinics of North America* 30(1).

5   Johannes C. Eichstaedt et al., 'Facebook language predicts depression in medical records', PNAS 115(44); Mohammed Al-Mosaiwi and Tom Johnstone, 'In an Absolute State: Elevated Use of Absolutist Words Is a Marker Specific to Anxiety, Depression, and Suicidal Ideation', *Clinical Psychological Science* 6(4).

6   Mohammed Al-Mosaiwi, 'People with depression use language differently – here's how to spot it', The Conversation, 2 February 2018, https://theconversation.com/people-with-depression-use-language-differently-heres-how-to-spot-it-90877.

7   Jonathan P. Rosier et al., 'Cognitive mechanisms of treatment in depression', *Neuropsychopharmacology* 37(1).

8   Ruth I. Karpinski et al., 'High intelligence: A risk factor for psychological and physiological overexcitabilities', *Intelligence* 66.

9   Claire H. Salmond et al., 'Cognitive reserve as a resilience factor against depression after moderate/severe head injury', *Journal of Neurotrauma* 23(7).

10   Elizabeth A. Phelps, 'Emotion and Cognition: Insights from Studies of the Human Amygdala', *Annual Review of Psychology* 57.

11   Florian Ferreri et al., 'Current research on cognitive aspects of anxiety disorders', *Current Opinion in Psychiatry* 24(1).

12   Junchol Park and Bita Moghaddam, 'Impact of anxiety on prefrontal cortex encoding of cognitive flexibility', *Neuroscience* 345.

13   Francesca Starita et al., 'Threat Learning Promotes Generalization of Episodic Memory', *Journal of Experimental Psychology: General* 148(8).

14   Katharina Kircanski, 'Cognitive Aspects of Depression', *Wiley Interdisciplinary Reviews: Cognitive Science* 3(3).

15   Laura de Nooij et al., 'Cognitive functioning and lifetime major depressive disorder in UK Biobank', *European Psychiatry* 63(1).

16   P. L. Rock et al., 'Cognitive impairment in depression: a systematic review and meta-analysis', *Psychological Medicine* 44(10).

17   Colette R. Hirsch et al., 'The extent and nature of imagery during worry and positive thinking in generalized anxiety disorder', *Journal of Abnormal Psychology* 121(1).

18   Eleanor Leigh and Colette R. Hirsch, 'Worry in imagery and verbal form: Effect on residual working memory capacity', *Behaviour Research and Therapy* 49(2).

19   Jeremy A. Yip and Stéphane Côté, 'The Emotionally Intelligent Decision Maker: Emotion-Understanding Ability Reduces the Effect of Incidental Anxiety on Risk Taking', *Psychological Science* 24(1).

20   Mark Fenton-O'Creevy et al., 'Thinking, feeling and deciding: The influence of emotions on the decision making and performance of traders', *Journal of Organizational Behaviour* 32(8).

21   Suzanne Ross, 'Explainer: what is emotional intelligence and why do you need it?' The Conversation, 21 January 2015, https://theconversation.com/explainer-what-is-emotional-intelligence-and-why-do-you-need-it-36437.

22   Jonathan P. Roiser et al., 'Cognitive mechanisms of treatment in depression', *Neuropsychopharmacology* 37(1).

23   Dr Olivia Remes, *The Instant Mood Fix* (Ebury Press, 2021), p. 143.

24   David Robson, *The Expectation Effect: How Your Mindset Can Transform Your Life* (Canongate, 2022), p. 105.

25   Daniela Schiller et al., 'Preventing the return of fear in humans using reconsolidation update mechanisms', *Nature* 463(7277).

26   Elizabeth A. Phelps and Stefan G. Hofmann, 'Memory editing from science fiction to clinical practice', *Nature* 572(7767).

6. Are you an optimist?

1   Tali Sharot, 'The optimism bias', *Primer* 21(23).

2   Tali Sharot et al., 'How unrealistic optimism is maintained in the face of reality', *Nature Neuroscience* 14(11).

3   R. Chordhury et al., 'Optimistic update bias increases in older age', *Psychological Medicine* 44(9).

4   Neil Garrett et al., 'Updating Beliefs under Perceived Threat', *Journal of Neuroscience* 38(36).

5   Jerry M. Burger and Michele L. Palmer, 'Changes in and Generalization of Unrealistic Optimism Following Experiences with Stressful Events: Reactions to the 1989 California Earthquake', *Personality and Social Psychology Bulletin* 18(1).

6   Timothy C. Bates, 'The Glass is Half Full *and* Half Empty: A population-representative twin study testing if Optimism and Pessimism are distinct systems', *Journal of Positive Psychology* 10(6).

7   Ola Svenson, 'Are we all less risky and more skillful than our fellow drivers?' *Acta Psychologica* 47(2).

8   J. Kruger and D. Dunning, 'Unskilled and unaware of it: how difficulties in recognizing one's own incompetence lead to inflated self-assessments', *Journal of Personality and Social Psychology* 77(6).

9   Jan R. Magnus and Anatoly A. Peresetsky, 'Grade Expectations: Rationality and Overconfidence', *Frontiers in Psychology* 8(2346).

10 Kelly Kasulis, 'CEO hubris costs millions', *Boston Globe*, 13 October 2018.

11 Julie K. Norem, 'The right tool for the job: Functional analysis and evaluating positivity/negativity' in W. G. Parrott (ed.), *The Positive Side of Negative Emotions* (The Guilford Press, 2014).

12 Julie K. Norem, 'Defensive pessimism, anxiety, and the complexity of evaluating self-regulation', *Social and Personality Psychology Compass* 2(1).

13 Transport and Infrastructure Council, *Australian Transport Assessment and Planning Guidelines*, https://www.atap.gov.au/sites/default/files/02-optimsim-bias.pdf.

7. Are you really from Mars or Venus?

1   Jason Wilson, 'White nationalist hate groups have grown 55% in Trump era, report finds', *Guardian*, 18 March 2020.

2   Nancy S. Love, 'Shield Maidens, Fashy Femmes, and TradWives: Feminism, Patriarchy, and Right-Wing Populism', *Frontiers in Sociology* 5.

3   Alena Kate Pettit, 'Why Your Husband Should Always Come First', The Darling Academy, https://www.thedarlingacademy.com/articles/why-your-husband-should-always-come-first/.

4   '#TradWife: "Submitting to my husband like it's 1959"', BBC News, 17 January 2020, https://www.bbc.co.uk/news/av/stories-51113371.

5   Catherine Rottenberg and Shani Orgad, 'Tradwives: the women looking for a simpler past but grounded in the neoliberal present', The Conversation, 7 February 2020, https://theconversation.com/tradwives-the-women-looking-for-a-simpler-past-but-grounded-in-the-neoliberal-present-130968.

6   Genevieve Fox, 'Meet the neuroscientist shattering the myth of the gendered brain', *Guardian*, 24 February 2019.

7   Matthew Wills, 'Evolution: how Victorian sexism influenced Darwin's theories – new research', The Conversation, 20 January 2022, https://theconversation.com/evolution-how-victorian-sexism-influenced-darwins-theories-new-research-175261.

8   Gina Rippon, 'How "neurosexism" is holding back gender equality – and science itself', The Conversation, 27 October 2016, https://theconversation.com/how-neurosexism-is-holding-back-gender-equality-and-science-itself-67597.

9   Diane F. Halpern and Mary L. LaMay, 'The Smarter Sex: A Critical Review of Sex Differences in Intelligence', *Educational Psychology Review* 12.

10 Mo Costandi, 'Snapshots explore Einstein's unusual brain', Nature, 16 November 2012, https://www.nature.com/articles/nature.2012.11836.

11 Rippon, 'How "neurosexism" is holding back gender equality'.

12 Daphna Joel et al., 'Sex beyond the genitalia: The human brain mosaic', *PNAS* 112(50).

13 Yi Zhang et al., 'The Human Brain Is Best Described as Being on a Female/Male Continuum: Evidence from a Neuroimaging Connectivity Study', *Cerebral Cortex* 31(6).

14 Gina Rippon, 'Are male and female brains really different?' The Conversation, 9 February 2016, https://theconversation.com/are-male-and-female-brains-really-different-54092.

15 Theodore D. Satterthwaite et al., 'Linked Sex Differences in Cognition and Functional Connectivity in Youth', *Cerebral Cortex* 25(9).

16 Cindy M. de Frias et al., 'Sex Differences in Cognition are Stable Over a 10-Year Period in Adulthood and Old Age', *Aging, Neuropsychology and Cognition* 13(3–4).

17 Marja Leonhardt and Stian Overå, 'Are There Differences in Video Gaming and Use of Social Media among Boys and Girls? – A Mixed Methods Approach', *International Journal of Environmental Research and Public Health* 18(11).

18 E. Zell et al., 'Evaluating gender similarities and differences using metasynthesis', *American Psychologist* 70(1); Janet S. Hyde, 'Sex and cognition: gender and cognitive functions', *Current Opinion in Neurobiology* 38.

19 Tessie H. H. Herbst, 'Gender differences in self-perception accuracy : the confidence gap and women leaders' underrepresentation in academia', *SA Journal of Industrial Psychology* 46(1).

20 David M. Greenberg et al., 'Testing the Empathizing–Systemizing theory of sex differences and the Extreme Male Brain theory of autism in half a million people', *PNAS* 115(48).

21 Sheri A. Berenbaum and Melissa Hines, 'Early Androgens Are Related to Childhood Sex-Typed Toy Preferences', *Psychological Science* 3(3).

22 Melissa Hines et al., 'Prenatal androgen exposure alters girls' responses to information indicating gender-appropriate behaviour', *Philosophical Transactions of the Royal Society B* 371(1688).

23 Cordelia Fine, Daphna Joel and John Dupre, 'How we inherit masculine and feminine behaviours: a new idea about environment and genes', The Conversation, 18 August 2017, https://theconversation.com/how-we-inherit-masculine-and-feminine-behaviours-a-new-idea-about-environment-and-genes-82524.

24 Sonia Sodha, 'Male violence against women is about so much more than toxic masculinity', *Guardian*, 6 March 2022.

25 Thomas F. Denson et al., 'Aggression in Women: Behavior, Brain and Hormones', *Frontiers in Behavioral Neuroscience* 12.

26 Justin M. Carré et al., 'Testosterone Reactivity to Provocation Mediates the Effect of Early Intervention on Aggressive Behavior', *Psychological Science* 25(5).

27 Tom Stafford, 'When society isn't judging, women's sex drive rivals men's', The Conversation, 28 April 2015, https://theconversation.com/when-society-isnt-judging-womens-sex-drive-rivals-mens-40863.

28 Gijsbert Soet et al., 'The Gender-Equality Paradox in Science, Technology, Engineering, and Mathematics Education', *Psychological Science* 29(4).

29 Anne M. Koenig and Alice H. Eagly, 'Stereotype Threat in Men on a Test of Social Sensitivity', *Sex Roles* 52; P. G. Davies et al., 'Clearing the Air: Identity Safety Moderates the Effects of Stereotype Threat on Women's Leadership Aspirations', *Journal of Personality and Social Psychology* 88(2).

30 Maddy Savage, 'Why do women still change their names?' The Life Project, 24 September 2020, https://www.bbc.com/worklife/article/20200921-why-do-women-still-change-their-names#:~:text=In%20the%20US,%20most%20women,they%20still%20follow%20the%20practice.

31 Viren Swami, 'Is feminism killing romance?' The Conversation, 1 December 2016, https://theconversation.com/is-feminism-killing-romance-69676.

8. Are you paying attention?

1   Petter Johansson et al., 'Failure to Detect Mismatches Between Intention and Outcome in a Simple Decision Task', *Science* 310(5745).

2   Lars Hall et al., 'How the Polls Can Be Both Spot On and Dead Wrong: Using Choice Blindness to Shift Political Attitudes and Voter Intentions', *PLoS ONE* 8(4).

3   Thomas Strandberg et al., 'False beliefs and confabulation can lead to lasting changes in political attitudes', *Journal of Experimental Psychology: General* 147(9).

4   Anna Sagana et al., 'Warnings to Counter Choice Blindness for Identification Decisions: Warnings Offer an Advantage in Time but Not in Rate of Detection', *Frontiers in Psychology* 9(981).

5   Melanie Sauerland et al., '"Yes, I Have Sometimes Stolen Bikes": Blindness for Norm-Violating Behaviors and Implications for Suspect Interrogations', *Behavioral Sciences and the Law* 31(2).

6   Thomas Strandberg et al., 'False beliefs and confabulation can lead to lasting changes in political attitudes', *Journal of Experimental Psychology General* 147(9).

7   Shane Frederick, 'Cognitive Reflection and Decision Making', *Journal of Economic Perspectives* 19(4).

9. Can you change your mind?

1   Walter Kaufmann, *Nietzsche: Philosopher, Psychologist, Antichrist* (Princeton University Press, 1974), p. 42.

2   Timothy J. Madigan, 'Nietzsche & Schopenhauer On Compassion', *Philosophy Now* 29.

3   Grace Neal Dolson, 'The Influence of Schopenhauer upon Friedrich Nietzsche', *The Philosophical Review*, 10(3).

4   S. R. Mehrotra, 'Gandhi and the British Commonwealth', *India Quarterly* 17(1).

5   Michael Gilead et al., 'That's My Truth: Evidence for Involuntary Opinion Confirmation', *Social Psychological and Personality Science* 10(3).

6   Keith E. Stanovich and Richard F. West, 'On the Relative Independence of Thinking Biases and Cognitive Ability', *Journal of Personality and Social Psychology*, 94(4).

7   Martina Lind et al., 'Choice-Supportive Misremembering: A New Taxonomy and Review', *Frontiers in Psychology* 8(2062).

8   Heuristics are mental shortcuts, such as rules of thumb or generalisations.

9   For more on this subject, see Carol Tavris and Elliot Aronson, *Mistakes Were Made (but Not by Me)* (Houghton Mifflin Harcourt, 2007).

10 J. Kruger and D. Dunning, 'Unskilled and unaware of it: how difficulties in recognizing one's own incompetence lead to inflated self-assessments', *Journal of Personality and Social Psychology* 77(6).

11 Michael P. Hall and Kaitlin T. Raimi, 'Is belief superiority justified by superior knowledge?' *Journal of Experimental Social Psychology* 76.

12 Jamie Ducharme, 'The Sunk Cost Fallacy Is Ruining Your Decisions. Here's How', *Time*, 26 July 2018.

13 Giorgio Coricelli, 'Regret and its avoidance: a neuroimaging study of choice behavior', *Nature Neuroscience* 8(9).

14 'Mindware: Critical Thinking for the Information Age', Coursera, https://www.coursera.org/learn/mindware.

15 Charles G. Lord et al., 'Considering the Opposite: A Corrective Strategy for Social Judgment', *Journal of Personality and Social Psychology* 47(6).

16 Charlotte Olivia Brand and Tom Stafford, 'Covid-19 vaccine dialogues increase vaccination intentions and attitudes in a vaccine-hesitant UK population', PsyArXiv Preprints, https://psyarxiv.com/kz2yh.

17 Eyal Winter, 'A fear of regret can lock us into bad relationships, jobs and habits – here's how to break free', The Conversation, 13 February 2019, https://theconversation.com/a-fear-of-regret-can-lock-us-into-bad-relationships-jobs-and-habits-heres-how-to-break-free-111115.

18 George Bernard Shaw, *Everybody's Political What's What?* (Constable, 1944), p. 330.

10. Do you trust your gut?

1 Valerie van Mulukom, 'Is it rational to trust your gut feelings? A neuroscientist explains', The Conversation, 16 May 2018, https://theconversation.com/is-it-rational-to-trust-your-gut-feelings-a-neuroscientist-explains-95086.

2 Konstantinos V. Katsikopoulos et al., 'Transparent modeling of influenza incidence: Big data or a single data point from psychological theory?' *International Journal of Forecasting* 38(2).

3 Gerd Gigerenzer, *How to Stay Smart in a Sane World* (Allen Lane, 2022), pp. 2–3.

4 Yi Wang et al., 'Meta-analytic Investigations of the Relation Between Intuition and Analysis', *Journal of Behavioral Decision Making* 30(1).

5 Viktor Dörfler and Colin Eden, 'Understanding "expert" scientists: Implications for management and organization research', *Management Learning* 50(5).

6 Judit Pétervári et al., 'The Role of Intuition in the Generation and Evaluation Stages of Creativity', *Frontiers in Psychology* 7(1420).

7 Van Mulukom, 'Is it rational to trust your gut feelings?'

8 Erik Dane et al., 'When should I trust my gut? Linking domain expertise to intuitive decision-making effectiveness', *Decision Processes* 119(2).

9   David Robson, 'Intuition: when is it right to trust your gut instincts?' 4 April 2022, BBC Worklife, https://www.bbc.com/worklife/article/20220401-intuition-when-is-it-right-to-trust-your-gut-instincts.

10   Jeremy A. Yip et al., 'Follow your gut? Emotional intelligence moderates the association between physiologically measured somatic markers and risk-taking', *Emotion* 20(3).

11   Anna Alkozei et al., 'Increases in Emotional Intelligence After an Online Training Program Are Associated With Better Decision-Making on the Iowa Gambling Task', *Psychological Reports* 122(3).

11.   Are you good with numbers?

1   Joanna Berendt, 'With No Boys Born in Nearly 10 Years, a Polish Village Finds Fame in Its Missing Males', *New York Times*, 6 August 2019.

2   Craig Anderson, 'Polish village hasn't seen a boy born in nearly 10 years – here's how that computes', The Conversation, 21 August 2019, https://theconversation.com/polish-village-hasnt-seen-a-boy-born-in-nearly-10-years-heres-how-that-computes-122176.

3   Amos Tversky and Daniel Kahneman, 'Judgment under Uncertainty: Heuristics and Biases', *Science* 185(4157).

4   Charles T. Clotfelter and Philip J. Cook, 'The "Gambler's Fallacy" in Lottery Play', *NBER Working Papers Series*, no. 3769.

5   Cass R. Sunstein, 'Probability Neglect: Emotions, Worst Cases, and Law', *112 Yale Law Journal* 61.

6   Cass R. Sunstein and Richard Zeckhauser, 'Overreaction to Fearsome Risks', *Environmental and Resource Economics* 48.

7   Amos Tversky and Daniel Kahneman, 'Availability: A heuristic for judging frequency and probability', *Cognitive Psychology* 5(2).

8   Denis Campbell, 'Cervical cancer testing drive will aim to tackle huge surge in no-shows', *Guardian*, 20 July 2018.

9   Amos Tversky and Daniel Kahneman, 'Judgment under Uncertainty: Heuristics and Biases: Biases in judgments reveal some heuristics of thinking under uncertainty', *Science* 185(4157).

10   Rupert Croft, 'On the measurement of cosmological parameters', *Quarterly Physics Review* 1; Thomas Kitching, 'Cosmology is in crisis – but not for the reason you may think', The Conversation, 8 January 2016, https://theconversation.com/cosmology-is-in-crisis-but-not-for-the-reason-you-may-think-52349.

11   Jeffrey Gassen et al., 'Unrealistic Optimism and Risk for COVID-19 Disease', *Frontiers in Psychology* 12.

12. Are you a creature of habit?

1 Karen D. Ersche et al., 'Creature of Habit: A self-report measure of habitual routines and automatic tendencies in everyday life', *Personality and Individual Differences* 116.

2 Wendy Wood et al., 'Habits and Goals in Human Behavior: Separate but Interacting Systems', *Perspectives on Psychological Science* 17(2).

3 Nick Chater, 'Why Most People Follow Routines', The Conversation, 16 August 2018, https://theconversation.com/why-most-people-follow-routines-101630.

4 David M. Lipton, Ben J. Gonzales and Ami Citri, 'Dorsal Striatal Circuits for Habits, Compulsions and Addictions', *Frontiers in Systems Neuroscience* 13(28).

5 Theodore P. Zanto and Adam Gazzaley, 'Aging of the frontal lobe', *Handbook of Clinical Neurology* 163.

6 Rebecca Overmeyer et al., 'Self-regulation is negatively associated with habit tendencies: A validation of the German Creature of Habit Scale', *Personality and Individual Differences* 163.

7 Ben Eppinger et al., 'Of goals and habits: age-related and individual differences in goal-directed decision-making', *Frontiers in Neuroscience* 7(253).

8 Wolfram Schultz, 'Behavioral Theories and the Neurophysiology of Reward', *Annual Review of Psychology* 57.

13. Do you stereotype people?

1 Phillip Atiba Goff et al., 'The Essence of Innocence: Consequences of Dehumanizing Black Children', *Journal of Personality and Social Psychology* 106(4).

2 CSI Admin, 'New CSI research reveals high levels of job discrimination faced by ethnic minorities in Britain', Centre for Social Investigation, 18 January 2019, http://csi.nuff.ox.ac.uk/?p=1299.

3 Claude M. Steele and Joshua Aronson, 'Stereotype Threat and the Intellectual Test Performance of African Americans', *Journal of Personality and Social Psychology* 69(5).

4 Carolyn E. Gibson et al., 'A Replication Attempt of Stereotype Susceptibility (Shih, Pittinsky, & Ambady, 1999): Identity Salience and Shifts in Quantitative Performance', *Social Psychology* 45(3).

5 Baoshan Zhang et al., 'Effects of Aging Stereotype Threat on Working Self-Concepts: An Event-Related Potentials Approach', *Frontiers in Aging Neuroscience* 9(223).

6 Anne M. Koenig and Alice H. Eagly, 'Stereotype Threat in Men on a Test of Social Sensitivity', *Sex Roles* 52.

7 T. Rees and J. Salvatore, 'Questioning stereotypes disrupts the effects of stereotype threat', *Sport, Exercise, and Performance Psychology* 10(2).

8   Songqi Liu et al., 'Effectiveness of Stereotype Threat Interventions: A Meta-Analytic Review', *Journal of Applied Psychology* 106(6).

9   Thomas F. Pettigrew et al., 'Recent advances in intergroup contact theory', *International Journal of Intercultural Relations* 35(3).

10   Robson, *The Expectation Effect*, pp. 198–201.

11   Andy Martens et al., 'Combating stereotype threat: The effect of self-affirmation on women's intellectual performance', *Journal of Experimental Social Psychology* 42(2).

14. Are you in love?

1   Lockdown Love Stories, https://www.lockdownlovestories.com/.

2   Dan Jones, 'The love delusion', *New Scientist*, 28 March 2007.

3   Parashkev Nachev, 'Love: is it just a fleeting high fuelled by brain chemicals?' The Conversation, 13 February 2020, https://theconversation.com/love-is-it-just-a-fleeting-high-fuelled-by-brain-chemicals-129201.

4   A. de Boer et al., 'Love is more than just a kiss: a neurobiological perspective on love and affection', *Neuroscience* 10(201).

5   Ibid.

6   Miranda M. Lim et al., 'Enhanced partner preference in a promiscuous species by manipulating the expression of a single gene', *Nature* 429.

7   Andreas Bartels and Semir Zeki, 'The neural correlates of maternal and romantic love', *NeuroImage* 21(3).

8   Semir Zeki, 'The Neurobiology of Love', *FEBS Letters* 581(14).

9   De Boer et al., 'Love is more than just a kiss'.

10   Donatella Marazziti and Domenico Canale, 'Hormonal changes when falling in love', *Psychoneuroendocrinology* 29(7).

11   Zeki, 'The Neurobiology of Love'.

12   De Boer et al., 'Love is more than just a kiss'.

13   Ibid.

14   Ibid.

15   Daniel Kahneman, *Thinking, Fast and Slow* (Allen Lane, 2011), p. 4.

16   Arthur G. Miller, 'Role of physical attractiveness in impression formation', Psychonomic Science 19; Genevieve L. Lorenzo et al., 'What Is Beautiful Is Good and More Accurately Understood: Physical Attractiveness and Accuracy in First Impressions of Personality', Psychological Science 21(12).

17   Viren Swami and Adrian Furnham, 'Is love really so blind?' *The Psychologist* 21.

18   Viren Swami, Lauren Waters and Adrian Furnham, 'Perceptions and meta-perceptions of self and partner physical attractiveness', *Personality and Individual Differences* 49(7).

19 Paul J. E. Miller et al., 'Positive Illusions in Marital Relationships: A 13-Year Longitudinal Study', *Personality and Social Psychology Bulletin* 32(12).

20 Sandra L. Murray, John G. Holmes and Dale W. Griffin, 'The benefits of positive illusions: Idealization and the construction of satisfaction in close relationships', *Journal of Personality and Social Psychology* 70(1).

21 Susanne Vosmer, 'The myth of romantic love may be ruining your health', The Conversation, 4 January 2017, https://theconversation.com/the-myth-of-romantic-love-may-be-ruining-your-health-70803.

22 Victor Karandashev, 'A Cultural Perspective on Romantic Love', *Online Readings in Psychology and Culture* 5(4).

23 Jeremy L. McNeal, 'The Association of Idealization and Intimacy Factors with Condom Use in Gay Male Couples', *Journal of Clinical Psychology in Medical Settings* 4.

24 Jens Förster, Kai Epstude and Amina Özelsel, 'Why Love Has Wings and Sex Has Not: How Reminders of Love and Sex Influence Creative and Analytic Thinking', *Personality and Social Psychology Bulletin* 25(11).

25 Wu Youyou et al., 'Birds of a Feather Do Flock Together: Behavior-Based Personality-Assessment Method Reveals Personality Similarity Among Couples and Friends', *Psychological Science* 28(3); Viren Swami, 'Why opposites rarely attract', The Conversation, 24 March 2017, https://theconversation.com/why-opposites-rarely-attract-74873; Andrew T. Lehr and Glenn Geher, 'Differential Effects of Reciprocity and Attitude Similarity Across Long- Versus Short-Term Mating Contexts', *The Journal of Social Psychology* 146(4).

26 Arthur Aron, Meg Paris and Elaine N. Aron, 'Falling in love: Prospective studies of self-concept change', *Journal of Personality and Social Psychology* 69(6).

27 Theresa E. DiDonato, '7 Ways Your Relationship Can Change Who You Are', 25 February 2015, https://www.psychologytoday.com/gb/blog/meet-catch-and-keep/201502/7-ways-your-relationship-can-change-who-you-are; Kevin P. McIntyre et al., 'When "we" changes "me": The two-dimensional model of relational self-change and relationship outcomes', *Journal of Social and Personal Relationships* 32(7).

28 Viren Swami, 'How to turn your emotional baggage into dating success', The Conversation, 13 February 2017, https://theconversation.com/how-to-turn-your-emotional-baggage-into-dating-success-72696; Ty Tashiro and Patricia Frazier, '"I'll never be in a relationship like that again": Personal growth following romantic relationship breakups', *Personal Relationships* 10(1).

29   Kristin D. Neff and S. Natasha Beretvas, 'The Role of Self-compassion in Romantic Relationships', *Self and Identity* 12(1).

15.   What language(s) do you speak?

1   Hossein Kaviani, Olivia Sagan and Mehrangiz Pournaseh, '"Emotion-Related Words" in Persian Dictionaries: Culture, Meaning and Emotion Theory', *International Journal of Linguistics, Literature and Culture* 2(3).

2   Panos Athanasopoulos et al., 'The psychological reality of spatio-temporal metaphors' in Angeliki Athanasiadou (ed.), *Studies in Figurative Thought and Language* (John Benjamins, 2017).

3   Rafael E. Núñez and Eve Sweetser, 'With the Future Behind Them: Convergent Evidence From Aymara Language and Gesture in the Crosslinguistic Comparison of Spatial Construals of Time', *Cognitive Science* 30(3).

4   Lynden K. Miles et al., 'Can a mind have two time lines? Exploring space–time mapping in Mandarin and English speakers', *Psychonomic Bulletin & Review* 18.

5   Keith Chen, 'Could your language affect your ability to save money?' (TED Talk), June 2012, http://www.ted.com/talks/keith_chen_could_your_language_affect_your_ability_to_save_money.

6   Guillaume Thierry et al., 'Unconscious effects of language-specific terminology on preattentive color perception', *Psychological and Cognitive Sciences* 106(11).

7   Evelina Fedorenko and Rosemary Varley, 'Language and thought are not the same thing: evidence from neuroimaging and neurological patients', *Annals of the New York Academy of Sciences* 1369(1).

8   Caitlin M. Fausey and Lera Boroditsky, 'English and Spanish Speakers Remember Causal Agents Differently', *Proceedings of the Annual Meeting of the Cognitive Science Society* 30.

9   Panos Athanasopoulos et al., 'Two Languages, Two Minds: Flexible Cognitive Processing Driven by Language of Operation', *Psychological Science* 26(4).

10   Panos Athanasopoulos and Emanuel Bylund, 'Whorf in the Wild: Naturalistic Evidence from Human Interaction', *Applied Linguistics* 41(6).

11   Alice Gaby, 'The Thaayorre Think of Time Like They Talk of Space', *Frontiers in Psychology* 3(300).

12   Alican Mecit, L. J. Shrum and Tina M. Lowrey, 'COVID-19 is Feminine: Grammatical Gender Influences Future Danger Perceptions and Precautionary Behavior', *Journal of Consumer Psychology* 8.

13   Simon R. Cox et al., 'Bilingualism, social cognition and executive functions: A tale of chickens and eggs', *Neuropsychologia* 91.

14   Sayuri Hayakawa et al., 'Using a Foreign Language Changes Our Choices', *Trends in Cognitive Science* 20(11).

16. Do you believe in evil?

1 'Daniel Kahneman: Biographical', NobelPrize.org, https://www.nobelprize.org/prizes/economic-sciences/2002/kahneman/biographical/.

2 'The TED interview: Daniel Kahneman wants you to doubt yourself – here's why' (transcript), https://www.ted.com/talks/the_ted_interview_daniel_kahneman_wants_you_to_doubt_yourself_here_s_why/transcript?language=en.

3 Aliraza Javaid, 'The sociology and social science of "evil": is the conceptions of pedophilia "evil"?' *Philosophical Papers and Review* 6(1).

4 Stephen Reicher, S. Alexander Haslam and Rakshi Rath, 'Making a Virtue of Evil: A Five-Step Social Identity Model of the Development of Collective Hate', *Social and Personality Psychology Compass* 2(3).

5 Peter K. Jonason and Gregory D. Webster, 'The Dirty Dozen: A Concise Measure of the Dark Triad', *Psychological Assessment* 22(2).

6 Delroy L. Paulhus and Kevin M. Williams, 'The Dark Triad of personality: Narcissism, Machiavellianism and psychopathy', *Journal of Research in Personality* 36(6).

7 Ibid.

8 Adrian Furnham, Steven C. Richards and Delroy Paulhus, 'The Dark Triad: A 10-year review', *Social and Personality Psychology Compass* 7(3).

9 Jeremy Coid et al., 'Psychopathy among prisoners in England and Wales', *International Journal of Law and Psychiatry* 32(3).

10 Adrian Furnham, Yasmine Daoud and Viren Swami, '"How to spot a psychopath". Lay theories of psychopathy', *Social Psychiatry and Psychiatric Epidemiology* 44(6).

11 Peter Muris et al., 'The Malevolent Side of Human Nature: A Meta-Analysis and Critical Review of the Literature on the Dark Triad (Narcissism, Machiavellianism, and Psychopathy)', *Perspectives on Psychological Science* 12(2).

12 Furnham et al., 'The Dark Triad'.

13 Ibid.

14 Ibid.

15 Jack McCullough, 'The Psychopathic CEO', *Forbes*, 9 December 2019.

16 Adrian Furnham, 'Shining a light on the dark side', *The Psychologist* 32.

17 Ernest H. O'Boyle et al., 'A meta-analytic review of the Dark Triad–intelligence connection', *Journal of Research in Personality* 47(6).

18 Elliot Panek, 'Narcissism on social media tells us a lot about ourselves', The Conversation, 24 September 2013, https://theconversation.com/narcissism-on-social-media-tells-us-a-lot-about-ourselves-18308.

19 Muris et al., 'The Malevolent Side of Human Nature'.

20 Ibid.

21 Furnham et al., 'The Dark Triad'.

22 Muris et al., 'The Malevolent Side of Human Nature'.

23   Laura K. Johnson et al., 'Subclinical Sadism and the Dark Triad', *Individual Differences* 40(3).

24   Erin Evelyn Buckels, 'The psychology of everyday sadism' (PhD thesis), https://open.library.ubc.ca/soa/cIRcle/collections/ubctheses/24/items/1.0369056; Simon McCarthy-Jones, 'From psychopaths to "everyday sadists": why do humans harm the harmless?', The Conversation, 24 September 2020, https://theconversation.com/from-psychopaths-to-everyday-sadists-why-do-humans-harm-the-harmless-144017.

25   David Livingstone Smith, '"Less Than Human": The Psychology of Cruelty', NPR, 29 March 2011, https://www.npr.org/2011/03/29/134956180/criminals-see-their-victims-as-less-than-human?t=1635356481264&t=1648048648607; David Livingstone Smith, 'Dehumanisation paves the way for the very worst things…' *The Psychologist* 34.

26   Stanley Milgram, 'Behavioral study of obedience', *The Journal of Abnormal and Social Psychology* 67(4).

27   S. Alexander Haslam, 'Contesting the "Nature" Of Conformity: What Milgram and Zimbardo's Studies Really Show', *PLoS Biology* 10(11).

28   Stephen Reicher, S. Alexander Haslam and Rakshi Rath, 'Making a Virtue of Evil: A Five-Step Social Identity Model of the Development of Collective Hate', *Social and Personality Psychology Compass* 2(3).

29   Alex Haslam and Stephen Reicher, 'Rethinking long-held beliefs about the psychology of evil', The Conversation, 20 November 2012, https://theconversation.com/rethinking-long-held-beliefs-about-the-psychology-of-evil-10830.

30   Roy F. Baumeister, *Evil: Inside Human Violence and Cruelty* (W. H. Freeman, 1999), pp. 35, 48.

31   Ibid., p. 34.

32   The University of Sheffield Department of Social Studies, 'The Sociology of Evil', https://www.sheffield.ac.uk/socstudies/research/sociology-evil.

33   Michael Hand, 'A world of heroes and villains: why we should challenge children's simplistic moral beliefs', The Conversation, 31 January 2020, https://theconversation.com/a-world-of-heroes-and-villains-why-we-should-challenge-childrens-simplistic-moral-beliefs-130561.

17.   Are you happy?

1   Jimmy Stamp, 'Who Really Invented the Smiley Face?' *Smithsonian*, 13 March 2013; Harvey Ball World Smile Foundation, 'About Smiley', https://www.worldsmile.org/about/about-smiley.

2   Smiley, 'Our Story', https://smiley.com/our-story.

3   Lowri Dowthwaite, 'Striving for happiness could be making you unhappy – here's how to find your own path', The Conversation, 24 April 2019, https://

theconversation.com/striving-for-happiness-could-be-making-you-unhappy-heres-how-to-find-your-own-path-115104.

4 Ibid.

5 June Gruber, Iris B. Mauss and Maya Tamir, 'A Dark Side of Happiness? How, When, and Why Happiness Is Not Always Good', *Perspectives on Psychological Science* 6(3).

6 Yukiko Uchida and Shinobu Kitayama, 'Happiness and unhappiness in east and west: Themes and variations', *Emotion* 9(4).

7 Kahneman, *Thinking, Fast and Slow*, p. 407.

8 Amir Mandel, 'Why Nobel Prize Winner Daniel Kahneman Gave Up on Happiness', *Haaretz*, 7 October 2018.

9 Ibid.

10 Ibid.; Mercatus Center, 'Daniel Kahneman on Cutting Through the Noise (Ep. 56 – Live at Mason), Medium, 19 December 2018, https://medium.com/conversations-with-tyler/tyler-cowen-daniel-kahneman-economics-bias-noise-167275de691f.

11 Gruber et al., 'A Dark Side of Happiness'.

12 Rafa Euba, *You Are Not Meant to Be Happy: So Stop Trying!* (Crux Publishing, 2021), p. 47.

13 Ed Diener et al., 'Why People Are in a Generally Good Mood', *Personality and Social Psychology Review* 19(3).

14 Gruber et al., 'A Dark Side of Happiness'; Karuna Subramaniam and Sophia Vinogradov, 'Improving the neural mechanisms of cognition through the pursuit of happiness', *Frontiers in Human Neuroscience*, 7(452).

15 Shigehiro Oishi, Ed Diener and Richard E. Lucas, 'The Optimum Level of Well-Being: Can People Be Too Happy?' in Ed Diener (ed.), *The Science of Well-Being: Social Indicators Research Series, vol. 37* (Springer, 2009).

16 Euba, *You Are Not Meant to Be Happy*, p. 10.

17 Nicholas B. Allen and Paul B. T. Badcock, 'Darwinian models of depression: A review of evolutionary accounts of mood and mood disorders', *Progress in Neuro-Psychopharmacology and Biological Psychiatry* 30(5); Paul W. Andrews and J. Anderson Thomson, Jr, 'The bright side of being blue: Depression as an adaptation for analyzing complex problems', *Psychological Review* 116(3)

18 Lowri Dowthwaite, 'Happiness, Personality & Metacognition' (research project), https://www.researchgate.net/project/Happiness-Personality-Metacognition.

19 Iris B. Mauss et al., 'Can Seeking Happiness Make People Happy? Paradoxical Effects of Valuing Happiness', *Emotion* 11(4).

20 Gruber et al., 'A Dark Side of Happiness'.

21 Oishi et al., 'The Optimum Level of Well-Being'.

22   June Gruber, 'Four Ways Happiness Can Hurt You', Greater Good, 3 May 2012, https://greatergood.berkeley.edu/article/item/four_ways_happiness_can_hurt_you.

23   Galen V. Bodenhausen et al., 'Happiness and stereotypic thinking in social judgment', *Journal of Personality and Social Psychology* 66(4).

24   Alixandra Barasch, Emma Levine and Maurice E. Schweitzer, 'Bliss is Ignorance: The Interpersonal Costs of Being Very Happy', SSRN, 20 September 2013, https://papers.ssrn.com/sol3/papers.cfm?abstract_id=2328358.

25   Rafael Euba, 'Humans aren't designed to be happy – so stop trying', The Conversation, 19 July 2019, https://theconversation.com/humans-arent-de-signed-to-be-happy-so-stop-trying-119262.

18. Should you see a doctor?

1   Rachel Cooke, 'Revealed: the real Mo Mowlam', *Guardian*, 17 January 2010.

2   Toby Helm, 'How Mo Mowlam misled Tony Blair for nine years about her killer cancer', *Guardian*, 17 January 2010.

3   BTRC, 'Professor Mark Glaser', https://btrc-charity.org/about-us/who/trustees/professor-mark-glaser/.

4   'Political tributes to Mo Mowlam', BBC News, 19 August 2005, http://news.bbc.co.uk/1/hi/northern_ireland/4165230.stm.

5   Alis Heshmatollah et al., 'Long-term trajectories of decline in cognition and daily functioning before and after stroke', *Journal of Neurology, Neurosurgery & Psychiatry* 92.

6   'Tell-tale signs of heightened stroke risk may appear up to 10 years earlier', BMJ, 6 July 2021, https://www.bmj.com/company/newsroom/tell-tale-signs-of-heightened-stroke-risk-may-appear-up-to-10-years-earlier/.

19. Is your gut thinking for you?

1   Catherine Price, 'Probing the Mysteries of Human Digestion', *Distillations*, 13 August 2018.

2   John F. Cryan, 'More than a gut feeling', *The Psychologist* 32.

3   John F. Cryan et al., 'The Microbiota-Gut-Brain Axis', *Physiological Reviews* 99(4).

4   John Cryan, 'Feed Your Microbes – Nurture Your Mind' (TED talk), https://www.youtube.com/watch?v=vKxomLM7SVc.

5   Ibid.

6   Cryan et al., 'The Microbiota-Gut-Brain Axis'.

7   E. Hoban et al., 'Regulation of prefrontal cortex myelination by the microbiota', *Translational Psychiatry* 6(4); Christine Fülling, Timothy G. Dinan and John F. Cryan, 'Gut Microbe to Brain Signaling: What Happens in Vagus . . .' *Neuroview* 101(6).

8   Fülling et al., 'Gut Microbe to Brain Signaling'.

9   Caitlin Cowan et al., 'Gutsy Moves: The Amygdala as a Critical Node in Microbiota to Brain Signaling', *BioEssays* 40(1).

10 Fülling et al., 'Gut Microbe to Brain Signaling'.

11 Javier A. Bravo et al., 'Ingestion of *Lactobacillus* strain regulates emotional behavior and central GABA receptor expression in a mouse via the vagus nerve', *PNAS* 108(38).

12 Cowan et al., 'Gutsy Moves'.

13 Michele Crumeyrolle-arias et al., 'Absence of the gut microbiota enhances anxiety-like behavior and neuroendocrine response to acute stress in rats', *Psychoneuroendocrinology* 42.

14 P. Zheng et al., 'Gut microbiome remodeling induces depressive-like behaviors through a pathway mediated by the host's metabolism', *Molecular Psychiatry* 21(6).

15 Kirsten Tillisch, 'Brain Structure and Response to Emotional Stimuli as Related to Gut Microbial Profiles in Healthy Women', *Psychosomatic Medicine* 79(8).

16 Cryan, 'Feed Your Microbes' (TED talk).

17 Eoin Sherwin et al., 'Microbiota and the social brain', *Science* 366(6465).

18 Cowan et al., 'Gutsy Moves'.

19 Noah Snyder-Mackler, 'Socially structured gut microbiomes in wild baboons', The Molecular Ecologist, 17 March 2015, https://www.molecularecologist. com/2015/03/17/socially-structured-gut-microbiomes-in-wild-baboons/.

20 Sherwin et al., 'Microbiota and the social brain'.

21 Ibid.

22 Ibid.

23 Marcus Boehme et al., 'Microbiota from young mice counteracts selective age-associated behavioral deficits', *Nature Aging* 1; John Cryan, 'Gut bacteria rewind ageing brain in mice', The Conversation, 9 August 2021, https://the-conversation.com/gut-bacteria-rewind-ageing-brain-in-mice-165831.

24 Cryan, 'Gut bacteria rewind ageing'; Hyun Ho Choi and Young-Seok Cho, 'Fecal Microbiota Transplantation: Current Applications, Effectiveness, and Future Perspectives', *Clinical Endoscopy* 49(3).

20. Are you hangry?

1   Amanda N. Hudson, Hans P. A. Van Dongen and Kimberly A. Honn, 'Sleep deprivation, vigilant attention, and brain function: a review', *Neuropsychopharmacology* 45.

2   Hannah T. Neprash and Michael L. Barnett, 'Association of Primary Care Clinic Appointment Time With Opioid Prescribing', *JAMA Network Open* 2(8).

3   K. A. Honn et al., 'Cognitive flexibility: A distinct element of performance impairment due to sleep deprivation', *Accident Analysis & Prevention* 126.

4   Paula Alhola and Päivi Polo-Kantola, 'Sleep deprivation: Impact on cognitive performance', *Neuropsychiatric Disease and Treatment* 3(5).

5   Sophie E. Williams and Jessica S. Horst, 'Goodnight book: sleep consolidation improves word learning via storybooks', *Frontiers in Psychology* 5(184).

6   Sonia Ghumman and Christopher M. Barnes, 'Sleep and prejudice: a resource recovery approach', *Journal of Applied Social Psychology* 43.

7   Debbie S. Ma et al., 'When Fatigue Turns Deadly: The Association Between Fatigue and Racial Bias in the Decision to Shoot', *Basic and Applied Social Psychology* 35(6).

8   Martin Hagger et al., 'A Multilab Preregistered Replication of the Ego-Depletion Effect', *Perspectives on Psychological Science* 11(4).

9   Maria L. Thomas et al., 'Neural basis of alertness and cognitive performance impairments during sleepiness. I. Effects of 24 h of sleep deprivation on waking human regional brain activity', *Journal of Sleep Research* 9.

10   Williamson and A. Feyer, 'Moderate sleep deprivation produces impairments in cognitive and motor performance equivalent to legally prescribed levels of alcohol intoxication', *Occupational and Environmental Medicine* 57(10).

11   Alhola and Polo-Kantola, 'Sleep deprivation'.

12   Paul M. Litvak et al., 'Fuel in the Fire: How Anger Impacts Judgment and Decision-Making' in M. Potegal et al. (eds), *International Handbook of Anger* (Springer, 2010).

13   Shai Danziger et al., 'Extraneous factors in judicial decisions', *PNAS* 108(17).

14   Jordan Skrynka and Benjamin T. Vincent, 'Hunger increases delay discounting of food and non-food rewards', *Psychonomic Bulletin & Review* 26.

15   Julia C. Basso and Wendy A. Suzuki, 'The Effects of Acute Exercise on Mood, Cognition, Neurophysiology, and Neurochemical Pathways: A Review', *Brain Plasticity* 2(2).

16   Lisa C. Silbert et al., 'Trajectory of white matter hyperintensity burden preceding mild cognitive impairment', *Neurology* 79(8).

17   Nils Opel et al., 'White matter microstructure mediates the association between physical fitness and cognition in healthy, young adults', *Scientific Reports* 9.

18   Basso and Suzuki, 'The Effects of Acute Exercise'.

19   John Axelsson and Tina Sundelin, 'Napping in the afternoon can improve memory and alertness – here's why', The Conversation, 26 February 2021, https://theconversation.com/napping-in-the-afternoon-can-improve-memory-and-alertness-heres-why-154423.

20   Caroline Davies, 'From Aristotle to Einstein: a brief history of power nappers', *Guardian*, 27 August 2021.

21   Martin Dresler et al., 'Non-pharmacological cognitive enhancement', *Neuropharmacology* 64.

22   Martin Dresler et al., 'Hacking the Brain: Dimensions of Cognitive Enhancement', *ACS Chemical Neuroscience* 10(3).

23   U. Müller et al., 'Effects of modafinil on non-verbal cognition, task enjoyment and creative thinking in healthy volunteers', *Neuropharmacology* 64(5).

24   Colin Sugden et al., 'Effect of pharmacological enhancement on the cognitive and clinical psychomotor performance of sleep-deprived doctors: a randomized controlled trial', *Annals of Surgery* 255(2).

25   Andreas G. Franke et al., 'Methylphenidate, modafinil, and caffeine for cognitive enhancement in chess: A double-blind, randomised controlled trial', *European Neuropsychopharmacology* 27(3).

26   Ibid.

21. Are you high?

1   Susan Greenfield, *The Private Life of the Brain* (Allen Lane, 2000), p. 91.

2   'What are some ways that cocaine changes the brain?' National Institute on Drug Abuse, https://nida.nih.gov/publications/research-reports/cocaine/what-are-some-ways-cocaine-changes-brain.

3   Martin Dresler et al., 'Hacking the Brain: Dimensions of Cognitive Enhancement', *ACS Chemical Neuroscience* 10(3).

4   Neil Vickers, 'Opium as a Literary Stimulant: The Case of Samuel Taylor Coleridge', *International Review of Neurobiology* 120.

5   'What is fentanyl?' National Institute on Drug Abuse, https://www.drugabuse.gov/publications/drugfacts/fentanyl; Emily B. Campbell, 'OxyContin created the opioid crisis, but stigma and prohibition have fueled it', The Conversation, 16 September 2021, https://theconversation.com/oxycontin-created-the-opioid-crisis-but-stigma-and-prohibition-have-fueled-it-167100.

6   'Opioid Overdose Crisis', National Institute on Drug Abuse, https://www.drugabuse.gov/drug-topics/opioids/opioid-overdose-crisis.

7   David J. Nutt and Harriet de Wit, 'Putting the MD back into MDMA', *Nature Medicine* 27.

8   David Nutt, David Erritzoe and Robin Carhart-Harris, 'Psychedelic Psychiatry's Brave New World', *Cell* 181(1).

9   Ben Marcus, 'LSD and the Elephant', Science Unsealed Blog, 27 June 2016, https://www.illinoisscience.org/2016/06/lsd-and-the-elephant/.

10 James J. H. Rucker et al., 'Psychedelics in the treatment of unipolar mood disorders: a systematic review', *Journal of Psychopharmacology* 30(12); Robin

L. Carhart-Harris and Guy M. Goodwin, 'The Therapeutic Potential of Psychedelic Drugs: Past, Present, and Future', *Neuropsychopharmacology* 42(11).

11 Nutt et al., 'Psychedelic Psychiatry's Brave New World'.

12 Ibid.

13 R. L. Carhart-Harris et al., 'Psilocybin with psychological support for treatment-resistant depression: six-month follow-up', *Psychopharmacology* 235; Nutt et al., 'Psychedelic Psychiatry's Brave New World'; Clare Tweedy, 'Psychedelics: how they act on the brain to relieve depression', The Conversation, 19 May 2022, https://theconversation.com/psychedelics-how-they-act-on-the-brain-to-relieve-depression-183320.

14 Rosalind Watts et al., 'Patients' Accounts of Increased "Connectedness" and "Acceptance" After Psilocybin for Treatment-Resistant Depression', *Journal of Humanistic Psychology* 57(5).

15 James J. H. Rucker, Jonathan Iliff and David J. Nutt, 'Psychiatry & the psychedelic drugs. Past, present & future', *Neuropharmacology* 142.

16 Nutt et al., 'Psychedelic Psychiatry's Brave New World'.

17 S. Parker Singleton et al., 'LSD flattens the brain's energy landscape: evidence from receptor-informed network control theory', bioRxiv, 17 May 2021, https://doi.org/10.1101/2021.05.14.444193; Ian Sample, 'Acid test: scientists show how LSD opens doors of perception', *Guardian*, 19 May 2021.

18 Nutt et al., 'Psychedelic Psychiatry's Brave New World'.

22. Are you an addict?

1 Duncan Campbell, 'The cop and the robber – a unique friendship', *Guardian*, 22 January 2012.

2 Harry Howard, '"I was vilified for doing the right thing": Scotland Yard DCI who inspired *Prime Suspect* fights the tears as she recalls moment she entered the canteen and 'everybody' walked out because she had suspended a bent police officer', MailOnline, 28 April 2021, https://www.dailymail.co.uk/news/article-9520313/Scotland-Yard-DCI-inspired-Prime-Suspect-cries-recalls-abuse-fighting-corruption.html.

3 Campbell, 'The cop and the robber'.

4 Doug Sellman, 'The 10 most important things known about addiction', *Addiction* 105(1).

5 Ibid.

6 Ibid.

7 W. Hall and M. Weier, 'Lee Robins' studies of heroin use among US Vietnam veterans', *Addiction* 112(1).

8 Lee N. Robins, Darlene H. Davis and David N. Nurco, 'How Permanent Was Vietnam Drug Addiction?' *American Journal of Public Health* 64(12).

9 Sellman, 'The 10 most important things known about addiction'.

10 Salvatore Campanella et al., 'Increased Cortical Activity in Binge Drinkers during Working Memory Task: A Preliminary Assessment through a Functional Magnetic Resonance Imaging Study', *PLoS ONE* 8(4).

11 Sellman, 'The 10 most important things known about addiction'.

12 Steve Connor, 'White people become less racist just by moving to more diverse areas, study finds', *Independent*, 3 March 2014.

23. Are you getting old?

1 Bruno Bernardes de Jesus, 'Telomerase gene therapy in adult and old mice delays aging and increases longevity without increasing cancer', *EMBO Molecular Medicine* 4(8).

2 Dara Mohammadi and Nicola Davis, 'Can this woman cure ageing with gene therapy?' *Observer*, 24 July 2016.

3 Ronald S. Petralia, Mark P. Mattson and Pamela J. Yao, 'Communication Breakdown: The Impact of Ageing on Synapse Structure', *Ageing Research Reviews* 14.

4 Mischa von Krause et al., 'Mental speed is high until age 60 as revealed by analysis of over a million participants', *Nature Human Behaviour* 6.

5 Cristina G. Wilson et al., 'Age-differences in cognitive flexibility when overcoming a preexisting bias through feedback', *Journal of Clinical and Experimental Neuropsychology* 40(6); Robert T. Kurlychek and Terry Steven Trepper, 'Accuracy of Perception of Attitude: An Intergenerational Investigation', *Perceptual and Motor Skills* 54(1).

6 J. D. Henry, W. von Hippel and K. Baynes, 'Social inappropriateness, executive control, and aging', *Psychology and Aging* 24(1); Gabriel A. Radvansky, David E. Copeland and William von Hippel, 'Stereotype activation, inhibition, and aging', Journal of *Experimental Social Psychology* 46(1).

7 'Do people become more prejudiced as they grow older?' BBC News, 17 July 2015, https://www.bbc.co.uk/news/magazine-33523313.

8 Abram Rosenblatt et al., 'Evidence for terror management theory: I. The effects of mortality salience on reactions to those who violate or uphold cultural values', *Journal of Personality and Social Psychology* 57(4).

9 Lori J. Nelson et al., 'General and Personal Mortality Salience and Nationalistic Bias', *Personality and Social Psychology Bulletin* 23(8).

10 Jeff Greenberg et al., 'Evidence for terror management theory II: The effects of mortality salience on reactions to those who threaten or bolster the cultural worldview', *Journal of Personality and Social Psychology* 58(2).

11 Jeff Schimel et al., 'Stereotypes and terror management: Evidence that mortality salience enhances stereotypic thinking and preferences', *Journal of Personality and Social Psychology* 77(5).

12 R. J. Russac et al., 'Death anxiety across the adult years: an examination of age and gender effects', *Death Studies* 31(6); Richard A. Klein et al., 'Many Labs 4: Failure to Replicate Mortality Salience Effect With and Without Original Author Involvement', *Collabra: Psychology* 8(1).

13 'The Gothenburg H70 Birth cohort study' (research project), University of Gothenburg, https://www.gu.se/en/research/the-gothenburg-h70-birth-cohort-study.

14 'Väljargrupper' ('Voter groups'), SVT, https://www.svt.se/special/valu2018-valjargrupper/.

15 Ingmar Skoog, '70 är det nya 50 ('70 is the new 50')', Delegationen för senior arbetskraft, https://seniorarbetskraft.se/wp-content/uploads/2020/06/Rapport-21_70-%C3%A4r-det-nya-50_webb.pdf.

16 Wändi Bruine de Bruin, JoNell Strough and Andrew M. Parker, 'Getting older isn't all that bad: Better decisions and coping when facing "sunk costs"', *Psychology and Aging* 29(3).

17 Hal R. Arkes and Catherine Blumer, 'The psychology of sunk cost', *Organizational Behavior and Human Decision Processes* 35(1).

18 'How and why your thinking skills change', Age UK, https://www.ageuk.org.uk/information-advice/health-wellbeing/mind-body/staying-sharp/thinking-skills-change-with-age/.

19 Daniel Barulli and Yaakov Stern, 'Efficiency, capacity, compensation, maintenance, plasticity: emerging concepts in cognitive reserve', *Trends in Cognitive Science* 17(10); 'Cognitive Reserve', Age UK, https://www.ageuk.org.uk/information-advice/health-wellbeing/mind-body/staying-sharp/thinking-skills-change-withage/cognitive-reserve/.

20 E. S. Sharp et al., 'Cognitive engagement and cognitive aging: is openness protective?' *Psychology and Aging* 25(1).

21 'A quarter of millennials believe depression is "normal" in older age', RSPH, 8 June 2018, https://www.rsph.org.uk/about-us/news/a-quarter-of-millennials-believe-depression-normal-in-older-age.html.

22 Robin J. Brunton and Greg Scott, 'Do We Fear Ageing? A Multidimensional Approach to Ageing Anxiety', *Educational Gerontology* 41(11).

24. Are you scared of being different?

1 'Percentage of the U.S. population who have completed four years of college or more from 1940 to 2020, by gender', Statista, https://www.statista.com/statistics/184272/educational-attainment-of-college-diploma-or-higher-by-gender/.

2 Pascal Molenberghs, 'The Neuroscience of In-group Bias', *Neuroscience & Behavioral Reviews* 37(8).

3   Ibid.

4   Naomi I. Eisenberger et al., 'Does Rejection Hurt? An fMRI Study of Social Exclusion', *Science* 302.

5   Solomon E. Asch, 'Opinions and Social Pressure', *Scientific American* 193(5).

6   Payel Kundu and Denise Dellarosa Cummins, 'Morality and conformity: The Asch paradigm applied to moral decisions', *Social Influence* 8(4); Rod Bond, 'Group Size and Conformity', *Group Processes & Intergroup Relations* 8(4).

7   Mirre Stallen and Alan G. Sanfrey, 'The neuroscience of social conformity: implications for fundamental and applied research', *Frontiers in Neuroscience* 9(337).

8   Campbell Pryor and Piers Howe, 'Conform to the social norm: why people follow what other people do', The Conversation, 17 December 2018, https://theconversation.com/conform-to-the-social-norm-why-people-follow-what-other-people-do-107446.

9   Juan M. Falomir-Pichastor, Fabrice Gabarrot and Mugny Gabriel, 'Conformity and Identity Threat: The Role of Ingroup Identification', *Swiss Journal of Psychology* 68(2).

10   Richard E. Nisbett and Timothy D. Wilson, 'The halo effect: Evidence for unconscious alteration of judgments', *Journal of Personality and Social Psychology* 35(4).

11   Harold Sigall and Nancy Ostrove, 'Beautiful but Dangerous: Effects of Offender Attractiveness and Nature of the Crime on Juridic Judgment', *Journal of Personality and Social Psychology* 31(3).

12   Leon Festinger, 'A Theory of Social Comparison Processes', *Human Relations* 7(2).

13   Sarah E. Hill and David M. Buss, 'Envy and Positional Bias in the Evolutionary Psychology of Management', *Managerial and Decision Economics* 27.

14   Tyler J. Burleigh and Daniel V. Meegan, 'Keeping Up with the Joneses Affects Perceptions of Distributive Justice', *Social Justice Research* 26.

15   Thomas F. Pettigrew et al., 'Recent advances in intergroup contact theory', *International Journal of Intercultural Relations* 35(3).

16   Damon Centola et al., 'Experimental evidence for tipping points in social convention', *Science* 360(6393).

17   Gregory J. Feist and Tara R. Brady, 'Openness To Experience, Non-Conformity, And The Preference For Abstract Art', *Empirical Studies of the Arts* 22(1); Hermann Brandstätter and Karl-Dieter Opp, 'Personality Traits ("Big Five") and the Propensity to Political Protest: Alternative Models', *Political Psychology* 35(4).

25. Where are you from?

1   Nicolas Geeraert, 'How knowledge about different cultures is shaking the foundations of psychology', The Conversation, 9 March 2018, https://

theconversation.com/how-knowledge-about-different-cultures-is-shaking-the-foundations-of-psychology-92696.

2   L.-J. Ji, Z. Zhang and R. E. Nisbett, 'Is It Culture or Is It Language? Examination of Language Effects in Cross-Cultural Research on Categorization', *Journal of Personality and Social Psychology* 87(1).

3   Geeraert, 'How knowledge about different cultures is shaking the foundations of psychology'.

4   Trish Greenhalgh, 'COVID: seven reasons mask wearing in the west was unnecessarily delayed', The Conversation, 13 July 2021, https://theconversation.com/covid-seven-reasons-mask-wearing-in-the-west-was-unnecessarily-delayed-164308; Christopher T. Leffler et al., 'Association of Country-wide Coronavirus Mortality with Demographics, Testing, Lockdowns, and Public Wearing of Masks', *The American Journal of Tropical Medicine and Hygiene* 103(6).

5   Jackson G. Lu, Peter Jin and Alexander S. English, 'Collectivism predicts mask use during COVID-19', *PNAS* 118(23).

6   Edward D. Vargas and Gabriel R. Sanchez, 'American individualism is an obstacle to wider mask wearing in the US', Brookings, 31 August 2020, https://www.brookings.edu/blog/up-front/2020/08/31/american-individualism-is-an-obstacle-to-wider-mask-wearing-in-the-us/.

7   Joseph Henrich, Steven J. Heine and Ara Norenzayan, 'The weirdest people in the world?' *Behavioral and Brain Sciences* 33(2–3); Geeraert, 'How knowledge about different cultures is shaking the foundations of psychology'.

8   Hazel R. Markus and Shinobu Kitayama, 'Culture and the Self: Implications for Cognition, Emotion, and Motivation', *Psychological Review* 98(2).

9   'Our Models', Hofstede Insights, https://hi.hofstede-insights.com/models.

10 'Compare Countries', Hofstede Insights, https://www.hofstede-insights.com/product/compare-countries/.

11 'Country Comparison: China, United Kingdom and the United States', Hofstede Insights, https://www.hofstede-insights.com/country-comparison/china,the-uk,the-usa/.

12 Markus and Kitayama, 'Culture and the Self'; Geeraert, 'How knowledge about different cultures is shaking the foundations of psychology'.

13 Steven D. Cousins, 'Culture and self-perception in Japan and the United States', *Journal of Personality and Social Psychology* 56(1).

14 Markus and Kitayama, 'Culture and the Self'.

15 Ching-Yu Huang and Michael E. Lamb, 'Are Chinese Children More Compliant? Examination of the Cultural Difference in Observed Maternal Control and Child Compliance', *Journal of Cross-Cultural Psychology* 45(4).

16   Ying Zhu et al., 'Neural Basis of Cultural Influence on Self-Representation',
      NeuroImage 34(3).

17   Takahiko Masuda and Richard Nisbett, 'Attending holistically vs. analytically:
      Comparing the context sensitivity of Japanese and Americans', *Journal of Per-
      sonality and Social Psychology* 81(5).

18   Takahiko Masuda et al., 'Culture and Aesthetic Preference: Comparing the
      Attention to Context of East Asians and Americans', *Personality and Social
      Psychology Bulletin* 34(9).

19   Tanya Marie Luhrmann et al., 'Sensing the presence of gods and spirits across
      cultures and faiths', *Proceedings of the National Academy of Sciences* 118(5).

20   T. M. Luhrmann, 'Thinking about thinking: the mind's porosity and the pres-
      ence of the gods', *Journal of the Royal Anthropological Institute* 26(S10).

21   T. M. Luhrmann, Padmavati Ramachandran and Hema Tharoor, 'Differences
      in voice-hearing experiences of people with psychosis in the USA, India and
      Ghana: Interview-based study', *The British Journal of Psychiatry: The Journal
      of Mental Science* 206(1).

22   Renee A. Holloway, Amy M. Waldrip and William Ickes, 'Evidence That a
      Simpatico Self-Schema Accounts for Differences in the Self-Concepts and
      Social Behavior of Latinos Versus Whites (and Blacks)', *Journal of Personality
      and Social Psychology* 96(5).

23   Ching-Yu Huang, 'How culture influences children's development', The
      Conversation, 19 July 2018, https://theconversation.com/how-culture-influ-
      ences-childrens-development-99791.

26. Do you lose your mind in a 'mob'?

1   S. D. Reicher, 'The St. Pauls' riot: An explanation of the limits of crowd action
      in terms of a social identity model', *European Journal of Social Psychology* 14(1).

2   Ibid.

3   Steve Mellen, 'St Pauls riots in Bristol remembered forty years on', BBC News,
      https://www.bbc.co.uk/news/uk-england-bristol-52105853.

4   Ibid.

5   Stephen Reicher et al., 'Capitol assault: the real reason Trump and the crowd
      almost killed US democracy', The Conversation, 5 January 2022, https://
      theconversation.com/capitol-assault-the-real-reason trump-and-the-
      crowd-almost-killed-us-democracy-174353.

6   David J. Bailey, 'Hard Evidence: this is the Age of Dissent – and there's much
      more to come', The Conversation, 11 January 2016, https://theconversation.
      com/hard-evidence-this-is-the-age-of-dissent-and-theres-much-more-to-
      come-52871.

7   Reuters Staff, '*Time* names "The Protester" 2011 Person of the Year', Reuters, 14 December 2011, https://www.reuters.com/article/us-time-person-idUS-TRE7BD0ZB20111214.

8   Matthew Radburn and Clifford Stott, 'The psychology of riots – and why it's never just mindless violence', The Conversation, 15 November 2019, https://theconversation.com/the-psychology-of-riots-and-why-its-never-just-mindless-violence-125676.

9   Clifford Stott and John Drury, 'Contemporary understanding of riots: Classical crowd psychology, ideology and the social identity approach', *Public Understanding of Science* 26(1).

10 Ibid.

11 Ibid.; Clifford Stott and John Drury, 'Crowds, context and identity: Dynamic categorization processes in the "poll tax riot"', *Human Relations* 53(2).

12 S. D. Reicher, 'The St. Pauls' riot'.

13 Stott and Drury, 'Contemporary understanding of riots'.

14 Mellen, 'St Pauls riots in Bristol'.

15 Stott and Drury, 'Crowds, context and identity'.

16 Jack Grey, 'Bristol George Floyd protest: Colston statue toppled', BBC News, 7 June 2020, https://www.bbc.co.uk/news/uk-england-bristol-52955868.

17 'Edward Colston statue: Four cleared of criminal damage', BBC News, 5 January 2022, https://www.bbc.co.uk/news/uk-england-bristol-59727161.

18 Reicher et al., 'Capitol assault'.

19 Clifford Stott et al., 'The evolving normative dimensions of "riot": Towards an elaborated social identity explanation', *European Journal of Social Psychology* 48(6).

20 Ibid.

21 Ibid.

22 Canadian Institute for Advanced Research, 'Group memberships boost self-esteem more than friends alone', Science News, 15 June 2015, https://www.sciencedaily.com/releases/2015/06/150615162617.htm#:~:text=The%20authors%20argue%20that%20groups,alone%2C%20new%20research%20has%20found.

23 Alex Haslam and Stephen Reicher, 'Rethinking long-held beliefs about the psychology of evil', The Conversation, 20 November 2012, https://theconversation.com/rethinking-long-held-beliefs-about-the-psychology-of-evil-10830.

27. Are you a sucker for advertising?

1   'Edward Bernays, "Father of Public Relations" And Leader in Opinion Making, Dies at 103', *New York Times*, 10 March 1995; Richard Gunderman, 'The

manipulation of the American mind: Edward Bernays and the birth of public relations', The Conversation, 9 July 2015, https://theconversation.com/
the-manipulation-of-the-american-mind-edward-bernays-and-the-birth-
of-public-relations-44393.

2   Sander L. Gilman and Zhou Xun (eds), *Smoke: A Global History of Smoking*
    (Reaktion Books, 2004), p. 340.

3   Anne Marie O'Keefe and Richard W. Pollay, 'Deadly Targeting of Women in
    Promoting Cigarettes', *Journal of the American Medical Women's Association*
    51(1–2).

4   Tom Stafford, 'Free thought: can you ever be a truly independent thinker?'
    The Conversation, 12 March 2020, https://theconversation.com/free-thought-
    can-you-ever-be-a-truly-independent-thinker-129033.

5   Derek Thompson, 'A Dangerous Question: Does Internet Advertising Work
    at All?' *The Atlantic*, 13 June 2014.

6   Gerard J. Tellis, *Effective Advertising* (Sage Publications, 2003).

7   Bradley T. Shapiro and Günter J. Hitsch, 'TV Advertising Effectiveness and
    Profitability: Generalizable Results from 288 Brands', *Econometrica* 89(4).

8   Ibid.

9   Demetrios Vakratsas and Tim Ambler, 'How Advertising Works: What Do
    We Really Know?' *Journal of Marketing* 63(1).

10 Agnes Nairn and Cordelia Fine, 'Who's messing with my mind? The impli-
    cations of dual-process models for the ethics of advertising to children',
    International Journal of Advertising 27(3).

11 Ibid.; Vakratsas and Ambler, 'How Advertising Works'.

12 Raffaello Rossi and Agnes Nairn, 'How children are being targeted with
    hidden ads on social media', The Conversation, 3 November 2021, https://
    theconversation.com/how-children-are-being-targeted-with-hidden-ads-
    on-social-media-170502.

13 'Biddable Youth' (report), University of Bristol, https://www.bristol.ac.uk/
    media-library/sites/news/2019/aug/D1261_Horne_DEMOS_Manage-
    ment%20report_2019_web.pdf; Nairn and Fine, 'Who's messing with my
    mind?'; Rossi and Nairn, 'How children are being targeted with hidden ads'.

14 Ibraheem Rehman et al., 'Classical Conditioning', StatPearls, https://www.
    ncbi.nlm.nih.gov/books/NBK470326/

15 'Is it true that Santa traditionally wears red because of Coca-Cola?' Coca-Cola
    Australia, https://www.coca-colacompany.com/au/faqs/is-it-true-that-santa-
    traditionally-wears-red-because-of-coca-cola.

16 'The Definitive History of Santa Clause', Coca-Cola Australia, https://www.
    coca-colacompany.com/au/news/definitive-history-of-santa-claus; 'Did

Coke really turn Santa red and white?' BBC News, 24 December 2007, http://news.bbc.co.uk/1/hi/magazine/7152054.stm.

17 Raffaello Rossi et al., '"Get a £10 Free Bet Every Week!" – Gambling Advertising on Twitter: Volume, Content, Followers, Engagement, and Regulatory Compliance', *Journal of Public Policy & Marketing* 40(4).

18 B. Zafer Erdogan, 'Celebrity Endorsement: A Literature Review', *Journal of Marketing Management* 15(4).

19 Ibid.

20 Nairn and Fine, 'Who's messing with my mind?'

21 Baba Shiv and Alexander Fedorikhin, 'Heart and Mind in Conflict: the Interplay of Affect and Cognition in Consumer Decision Making', *Journal of Consumer Research* 26(3).

22 Robert George Heath, 'How advertisers seduce our subconscious', The Conversation, 23 August 2016, https://theconversation.com/how-advertisers-seduce-our-subconscious-60578.

28. Is digital technology rewiring your mind?

1 'Announcing AI21 Studio and Jurassic-1 Language Models', AI21 Labs (blog), https://www.ai21.com/blog/announcing-ai21-studio-and-jurassic-1.

2 Alex Connock and Professor Andrew Stephen, 'We invited an AI to debate its own ethics in the Oxford Union – what it said was startling', The Conversation, 10 December 2021, https://theconversation.com/we-invited-an-ai-to-debate-its-own-ethics-in-the-oxford-union-what-it-said-was-startling-173607.

3 Garfield Benjamin, 'Silicon Valley wants to read your mind – here's why you should be worried', The Conversation, 16 August 2019, https://theconversation.com/silicon-valley-wants-to-read-your-mind-heres-why-you-should-be-worried-121707; Simon McCarthy-Jones, 'Freedom of thought is under attack – here's how to save your mind', The Conversation, 21 October 2019, https://theconversation.com/freedom-of-thought-is-under-attack-heres-how-to-save-your-mind-124379.

4 Angela Giuffrida, 'The Italian hamlet that gives a glimpse of life before the web', *Guardian*, 2 January 2022.

5 Gary W. Small et al., 'Brain health consequences of digital technology use', *Dialogues in Clinical Neuroscience* 22(2).

6 Erica Pandey, 'Sean Parker: Facebook was designed to exploit human "vulnerability"', Axios, 9 November 2017, https://www.axios.com/sean-parker-facebook-was-designed-to-exploit-human-vulnerability-1513306782-6d18fa32-5438-4e60-af71-13d126b58e41.html.

7 Olivia Solon, 'Ex-Facebook president Sean Parker: site made to exploit human "vulnerability"', *Guardian*, 9 November 2017.

8   Simon McCarthy-Jones, 'Social networking sites may be controlling your mind – here's how to take charge', The Conversation, 5 December 2017, https://theconversation.com/social-networking-sites-may-be-controlling-your-mind-heres-how-to-take-charge-88516.

9   Daria J. Kuss and Mark D. Griffiths, 'Social Networking Sites and Addiction: Ten Lessons Learned', International Journal of Environmental Research and Public Health 14(3).

10 Small et al., 'Brain health consequences'.

11 Brian A. Primack et al., 'Social Media Use and Perceived Social Isolation Among Young Adults in the U.S.', American Journal of Preventive Medicine 53(1).

12 Michele Traviso, 'Measuring magnetism: how social media creates echo chambers', Nature Italy, 23 February 2021, https://www.nature.com/articles/d43978-021-00019-4.

13 Giuliana Mazzoni, 'Our obsession with taking photos is changing how we remember the past', The Conversation, 4 January 2019, https://theconversation.com/our-obsession-with-taking-photos-is-changing-how-we-remember-the-past-109285.

14 Marianne Etherson and Thomas Curran, 'Social media: teenage girls with perfectionist tendencies need to take extra care – here's how', The Conversation, 3 November 2021, https://theconversation.com/social-media-teenage-girls-with-perfectionist-tendencies-need-to-take-extra-care-heres-how-95479.

15 Mazzoni, 'Our obsession with taking photos'.

16 Michal Kosinski, David Stillwell and Thore Graepel, 'Private traits and attributes are predictable from digital records of human behavior', PNAS 110(15); Harry Davies, 'Ted Cruz using firm that harvested data on millions of unwitting Facebook users', Guardian, 11 December 2015; S. C. Matz et al., 'Psychological targeting as an effective approach to digital mass persuasion', PNAS 114(48).

17 Wu Youyou, Michal Kosinski and David Stillwell, 'Computer-based personality judgments are more accurate than those made by humans', PNAS 112(4).

18 Clifton B. Parker, 'Michal Kosinski: Computers Are Better Judges of Your Personality Than Friends', Stanford Graduate School of Business, 23 January 2015, https://www.gsb.stanford.edu/insights/michal-kosinski-computers-are-better-judges-your-personality-friends.

19 Michal Kosinski, 'Facial recognition technology can expose political orientation from naturalistic facial images', Scientific Reports 11.

20 'Why Facebook knows you better than your mum', Cambridge Judge Business School, 15 December 2015, https://www.jbs.cam.ac.uk/insight/2015/why-facebook-knows-you-better-than-your-mum/.

21 Ibid.

22   Matz et al., 'Psychological targeting'.
23   Ibid.
24   Agata Błachnio et al., 'Self-presentation styles, privacy, and loneliness as predictors of Facebook use in young people', *Personality and Individual Differences* 94.
25   McCarthy-Jones, 'Social networking sites may be controlling your mind'.
26   Stephen Buranyi, 'Rise of the racist robots – how AI is learning all our worst impulses', *Guardian*, 8 August 2017; Jeffrey Dastin, 'Amazon scraps secret AI recruiting tool that showed bias against women', Reuters, 11 October 2018, https://www.reuters.com/article/us-amazon-com-jobs-automation-in-sight-idUSKCN1MK08G.
27   McCarthy-Jones, 'Freedom of thought is under attack'.

29. How powerful is your 'sixth sense'?
1   Sarah Garfinkel, 'How the body and mind talk to one another to understand the world', Aeon, 15 February 2019, https://aeon.co/ideas/how-the-body-and-mind-talk-to-one-another-to-understand-the-world.
2   Sahib S. Khalsa and Rachel C. Lapidus, 'Can Interoception Improve the Pragmatic Search for Biomarkers in Psychiatry?' *Frontiers in Psychiatry* 25(7).
3   Gary G. Berntson and Sahib S. Khalsa, 'Neural Circuits of Interoception', *Trends in Neurosciences* 44(1); David Robson, 'Interoception: the hidden sense that shapes wellbeing', *Guardian*, 15 August 2021.
4   Caroline Williams, 'Interoception: This "sixth sense" could be key to better mental health', *New Scientist*, 2 February 2022.
5   Sarah Garfinkel, 'The science inside our hearts and minds' (video), October 2017,   https://www.ted.com/talks/dr_sarah_garfinkel_the_science_inside_our_hearts_and_minds.
6   Sahib S. Khalsa et al., 'Interoception and Mental Health: A Roadmap', *Biological Psychiatry: Cognitive Neuroscience and Neuroimaging* 3(6); Lisa Quadt et al., 'Interoceptive training to target anxiety in autistic adults (ADIE): A single-center, superiority randomized controlled trial', *EClinicalMedicine* 39.
7   William James, 'What is an Emotion?' *Mind* 9(34).
8   Garfinkel, 'How the body and mind talk to one another'.
9   Berntson and Khalsa, 'Neural Circuits of Interoception'.
10   Khalsa et al., 'Interoception and Mental Health: A Roadmap'.
11   Ibid.
12   Sarah Garfinkel et al., 'Interoceptive dimensions across cardiac and respiratory axes', *Philosopical Transactions of the Royal Society B* 371(1708).
13   Garfinkel, 'The science inside our hearts and minds'.
14   Sarah Garfinkel et al., 'Fear from the Heart: Sensitivity to Fear Stimuli Depends on Individual Heartbeats', *Journal of Neuroscience* 34(19).

15 Ivana Konvalinka et al., 'Synchronized arousal between performers and related spectators in a fire-walking ritual', *Proceedings of the National Academy of Sciences* 108(20).

16 Chatrin Suksasilp and Sarah Garfinkel, 'Towards a comprehensive assessment of interoception in a multi-dimensional framework', *Biological Psychology* 168.

17 Garfinkel, 'How the body and mind talk to one another'.

18 Berntson and Khalsa, 'Neural Circuits of Interoception'.

19 Louise Connell, Dermot Lynott and Briony Banks, 'Interoception: The forgotten modality in perceptual grounding of abstract and concrete concepts', *Philosophical Transactions of the Royal Society B* 373(1752); Briony Banks and Louise Connell, 'Multidimensional Sensorimotor Grounding of Concrete and Abstract Categories', *PsyArXiv Preprints*.

20 Giorgia Zamariola et al., 'Relationship between interoception and emotion regulation: New evidence from mixed methods', *Journal of Affective Disorders* 246.

21 Sahib S. Khalsa and Rachel Lapidus, 'Can Interoception Improve the Pragmatic Search for Biomarkers in Psychiatry?' *Frontiers in Psychiatry* 7.

22 Barnaby D. Dunn et al., 'Listening to Your Heart: How Interoception Shapes Emotion Experience and Intuitive Decision Making', *Psychological Science* 21(12).

23 Narayanan Kandasamy et al., 'Interoceptive Ability Predicts Survival on a London Trading Floor', *Scientific Reports* 6(1).

24 Justin S. Feinstein et al., 'The Elicitation of Relaxation and Interoceptive Awareness Using Floatation Therapy in Individuals With High Anxiety Sensitivity', *Biological Psychiatry: Cognitive Neuroscience and Neuroimaging* 3(6).

25 Sahib S. Khalsa et al., 'Reduced Environmental Stimulation in Anorexia Nervosa: An Early-Phase Clinical Trial', *Frontiers in Psychology* 11.

26 Quadt et al., 'Interoceptive training to target anxiety'.

27 Sarah Garfinkel et al., 'Discrepancies between dimensions of interoception in autism: Implications for emotion and anxiety', *Biological Psychology* 114.

28 Williams, 'Interoception'.

29 Robson, 'Interoception: the hidden sense'.

30 Williams, 'Interoception'.

Epilogue: Do you know yourself?

1 Miriam Frankel, 'How to alter your personality: why your character isn't fixed in stone', *New Scientist*, 12 January 2022.